DATE			

ROD STEWART

Vagabond Heart

ROD STEWART

Vagabond Heart

Geoffrey Giuliano

Carroll & Graf Publishers, Inc.
New York

For twenty-two years' hazardous duty this book is dedicated with love to Brenda Giuliano. A beautiful soul and a gentle lady.

You wear it well.

Originally published by New English Library, London

First Carroll & Graf edition 1994

Carroll & Graf Publishers, Inc.
260 Fifth Avenue
New York, NY 10001

Library of Congress Cataloging-in-Publication Data

Giuliano, Geoffrey.
    Rod Stewart : vagabond heart / Geoffrey Giuliano.
        p.   cm.
    Originally published: London : New English Library, c1993.
    ISBN 0-7867-0163-3 : $12.95
    1. Stewart, Rod.   2. Rock musicians--England--Biography.
  I. Title.
  ML420.S843G58   1994
  782.42166'092--dc20
    [B]   94-27597
                                                                    CIP
                                                                    MN

Manufactured in the United States of America

Contents

"Some accounts can never be settled.
Life itself extracts full payment."

Charles Dickens, *Great Expectations*

Foreword

You Wear It Well

After nearly a lifetime in music it's difficult to know what to say about someone like Rod the Mod. I could fill a book with the interesting people I've hung out with over the years – Keith Moon, Jimi Hendrix, Steve Winwood, Brian Jones, Sly Stone, Germaine Greer, and on and on. But Mr Stewart is a different kettle of fish altogether. For a start, no one I know in showbiz can lay into a soccer ball quite like the old boy. A talent, I'm convinced, could have made the sod quite a reasonable living had he not chosen to climb up on stage way back when to try his luck. That he is a very decent singer is by now, I suppose, fairly well established, but back in his Hoochie Coochie days playing second fiddle to the unforgettable Long John Baldry, he might have ended up just another passing face in the long line of undistinguished hopefuls that turned to music for a future when the itchy prospect of getting an "honest" job loomed high on the horizon. Once again Mr Stewart was a definite cut above.

Now that he's become the mega force he has, with women worldwide swooning at the very thought of this lanky, spiky-headed get, I can't help but think back to the days when Rod was just a nipper strutting across the bar-room, dressed to the nines, simply begging for attention from the opposite sex (and getting it!). Of course, being such a colorful character hasn't hurt him one bit. Personally, my hat's off to anyone who can ultimately upstage the likes of a geezer like Long John. But that's another tale . . .

Suffice it to say that Ginger Baker remembers Rod Stewart as quite a good lad who has managed to hold his own (and indeed prosper) in a business that has claimed many stout hearts. A distinction not to be lightly dismissed in the tragic wake of the rise and fall of icons like poor Jimi and Beatle John (to name but two of the stoutest). The rest of the story, fortunately, is inside.

Read on . . .

Ginger Baker June 1992

Introduction

The First Cut Is The Deepest

It is with pleasure that I offer up the salty tale of one Roderick David Stewart, Esq., adventurer, athlete, womaniser, composer and, oh yes . . . stout-hearted crooner. Mr Stewart endures like the stoic mountains of the Scottish Highlands or the wispy echo of faraway pipes. That he has taken up residence in our personal history is now beyond question. A sexy scoundrel, naughty beyond all reason, wildly unrepentant, insatiable and, impossibly, eternally in love with himself. All requisite qualities of our most cherished public figures.

His photo gracing more secretaries' bulletin boards than perhaps any living soul since Ol' Blue Eyes first mesmerised a generation of willing females a grandmother ago, Stewart continues to exude the sort of age-less appeal that forever guarantees the fluttering hearts of the devoted.

The men, I think, admire him more for the sheer force of his jagged, razor's-edge vocals and stirring lyrical ability than his famous S-bend and spiky electric coif, but who knows? That he has led a remarkably charmed life is to understate. Making love to perhaps more beautiful women than even Guinness would care to count, he prefers liaisons with long-legged, blonde model types because, as his manager so rightly states, "he can".

A poor boy from London's outskirts, Stewart brings to his art both the quiet desperation and musical recklessness common to people dragged up from nowhere and suddenly presented with the unguarded adulation that pop fame inevitably brings. Never really wanting to hurt, he has nonetheless broken, or at least severely damaged, more than a common man's quota of hearts. What makes Stewart's emotional impact so impossible is the charming, seamless way in which he perpetually gets what he wants and the matey, good-natured way in which he does it.

Geoffrey Giuliano
"Skyfield"
Lockport, New York

1

Second Coming

"Whoa, Stewart! She's on again!"

Mal's voice echoed through the corridors of the house, and from somewhere down the hall Rod's floated back. "Hold on! Here I come!"

"You can move up to *my* workout video in just two weeks and have a body like mine!" proclaimed the sexy young girl on the television. "I'd love to have a body like yours!" Stewart bellowed back.

Several months later, Rod Stewart looked fondly at his new young bride, supermodel Rachel Hunter, a quarter of a century his junior, and freely admitted, "I was a bit of a fan. She was on CNN all the time, every ten minutes, advertising that *Sports Illustrated* body-building video. Me and Malcolm, my personal assistant, out in Los Angeles, would sit around and wait for her to appear."

Six months later, Stewart was at Roxbury's, a club on Sunset Boulevard, and there she was. The happy couple remembers. "He was making these funny faces at me," the new Mrs Stewart recalls. "Then he imitated me from the commercial. I was very surprised that he even knew who I was!"

"I pumped my muscles and repeated her line, 'You can move up to my workout video . . .'"

"And I said, 'Would you please stop doing that, because you're really bugging me.' Then I walked off."

It was apparently love at first sight.

When Rachel Hunter, the second Mrs Rod Stewart, was born in New Zealand in 1968, halfway around the world her future husband had already made his first album, *Truth*, with the Jeff Beck Group. By the time she was nine, dancing around her family's lounge while "Maggie May" blasted out of the radio, he was a full-blown superstar.

When Hunter left school at sixteen, determined to forge a career in modelling, Stewart was already separated from his first wife, and well on his way to becoming a father for the third time. When they finally met, Rachel was twenty and Rod a well-preserved forty-five. "He likes them young alright, does Rodders," his mates would laugh. "But he'll be back with the missus by morning."

"The Missus," of course, was Kelly Emberg, the lanky Swedish model who had been Stewart's constant companion ever since his turbulent first marriage, to Alana Hamilton, was dissolved some eight years earlier. The unwed mother of Rod's youngest child, Ruby, she was still only twenty-six years old, beautiful, and very, very determined.

"Rod and I will be marrying soon," she would say, "just as soon as he's got things settled with his ex." For seven long years, he had been trying to get things settled with Alana, but Kelly tried not to think about that. These things had to be done right.

Alana had willingly signed a pre-nuptial agreement, but now her lawyer was calling it unfair and coercive. Her husband, it was charged, had had a string of mistresses during the union, and no court in the land would ever find in his favor. Stewart was already paying her $300,000 a year to keep the house and bring up the kids; though according to the tabloid press she was looking for a cool million.

Now there was a third woman in the picture, a reserved New Zealander scarcely out of her teens. She was young enough to be Rod's daughter, which meant she was definitely old enough to be his wife. "I knew within a week I wanted to marry her," laughs Stewart upon reflection. *Really* marry her, not just say he would, not do it for the sake of an unborn child, nor to keep up appearances. "She's got a teasing way about her, and an intelligence I've not found in most models – and I've known quite a few in my day."

Stewart, however, resolved to be patient, launching himself on a solid week of romantic dinners and pricey floral reminders, followed by over a month of phone calls and impromptu journeys to see her at work. One afternoon in late summer 1990, just after Rachel's twenty-first birthday, they went to the beach for a picnic. Rachel packed tuna-fish sandwiches; Rod, though, brought a ring.

On bended knee, Stewart wondered if she might consent to become his wife, and on 15 December, in a Presbyterian church in Beverly Hills, she did. The élite congregation of 250 included Stewart's two eldest children – Kimberley, aged eleven, and Sean, ten. But not, sadly, his parents, his long time partner-in-crime Ronnie Wood, who was recovering from a car accident, or his close friend and sparring partner, Elton John. Elton's wedding gift to the couple, though, epitomises the relationship he and Stewart have enjoyed for more than two decades. It was a ten-pound gift certificate from the British pharmaceutical chain, Boots the Chemists. Robert Stewart had passed away that September, eighty-six years old and as devoted to his youngest son as ever. Elsie Stewart, herself now almost totally wheelchair-bound, had been stricken with multiple sclerosis, and was unable to undertake the long haul to LA.

Elsie missed both a moving ceremony and an uproarious finale. In full view of the entire congregation, Rachel grabbed her husband's famous bum. "I couldn't resist a little squeeze," she later quipped.

Rod retaliated at the reception when Rachel, in a fit of high-spirited mischievousness, hoisted her ivory wedding dress up around her hips, tipped back into her chair, and thrust a long leg out at her husband. Stewart fell to his knees and, seizing Rachel's frilly garter in his teeth, hauled it down her leg, over her foot and finally, with the garter still gripped firmly between his teeth, pulled his bride to her feet and waltzed her around the crowded room.

"I was always the one who was never going to get married again," Stewart admits. "But deep down in my soul, I wanted to be. It's sort of a sissy thing to admit, though, so I never did." There is, however, the thorny question of the Grand Canyon gulf in age between the two.

"Sometimes I wish Rachel was thirty, just to keep people off my back," says Rod. "Mind you, she's got the brain of a thirty-year-old, though. She looks like a thirty-year-old and the next minute she can look like a twelve-year-old schoolgirl. I didn't marry her because she's twenty-one or twenty-two. That's ridiculous. Besides," he added, "I don't really notice the age difference. We're both like a couple of kids."

Stewart revealed that he had even given Rachel a personally guided tour of his tempestuous past. "I've told her all about my old relationships, but it's impossible for me to remember everybody I've made love to. I try and point them out if Rachel and I are out together and we bump into someone I've dated before."

The near-inevitable fall-out swiftly followed. Kelly Emberg, infuriated at losing her man, furious, too, at the speed with which Stewart had finally settled everything with Alana Hamilton, immediately filed suit.

Bang! – $40,000 a month in child support. Bang! – $10 million for emotional distress. Bang! – $25 million in lost earnings. The first suit was delivered to Rod just two days before his wedding, while he was attending a function at Ruby's school.

Any compassion Rachel may have had for the embittered Swedish model went straight out the window right then and there. "She's the sort of woman who gives blondes a bad name," Rachel has said, and warned that if Kelly ever dared turn up at the house, she would set the Great Dane on her. "I had a great deal of sympathy for her in the beginning, but what she wants simply isn't right. Kelly is obviously a money-hungry cow."

Stewart, too, shot her down himself a little later. "What nobody understands is that Kelly left me. It's the truth. She decided to leave –

3

she had another geezer, she bought herself a house, and I was left high and dry. That's when I met Rachel."

Next in line was provocative Regan Newman, the minor model whom Stewart reportedly dated once or twice. Just weeks before his wedding, she squealed to the world's media that "[Rod and I] did it in an elevator!"

Stewart, however, pleaded not guilty. "Absolute fucking bullshit. Made love in an elevator! I'm very shy. I do not get my block and tackle out just anywhere. I'm not like that. What did I ever do to this girl? That smelly, shitbag, fucking, bastard bitch! I've never made love in an elevator in my life. The back of a limousine is about the most unconventional I've ever been." And that, he hastened to add, was with Rachel, thank you very much.

Oh, but what tales he could tell, if he was of a mind to. Or maybe he already has . . . the big-bosomed girl with the Dutch accent, who changes his point of view in one song, the Oriental lady who does it in another, the insatiable older woman who stole him away from school in a third, and the unnamed beauties who flocked to his side when he wondered if they thought he was sexy. When Rod Stewart celebrated twenty-five years in rock'n'roll in 1989 and brought together five dozen songs in a lavish boxed set, he could have called it anything. But he chose to call it *Storyteller* because, minus all the non-stop razzle-dazzle of his career, that is essentially what he is.

"Warners are printing 200,000 boxes," Rod's manager Arnold Stiefel complained. "I keep telling them it's not enough." Based on the success of Stewart's last album, *Out of Order*, which contained a colossal four hit singles, and the extraordinary business he did on his fourteen-month tour, it didn't take a nuclear scientist to see that the raspy crooner was more popular than ever.

"We thought it was the right time to introduce his older material to the generations of new fans who don't know songs like 'Handbags and Gladrags' or 'Cut Across Shorty'."

The elegant collection opens with Stewart's first ever single, recorded in London in 1964, and doomed to almost immediate obscurity – "Good Morning Little Schoolgirl". From thereon in, it skips through the 1960s with his solo version of Sam Cooke's "Shake", a solitary extract from the collection of tapes made by Steampacket, the unwieldy would-be supergroup he joined in 1965, and finally touches down with his stint with Jeff Beck, and thereafter scarcely misses a beat – or a hit. The lavish package closes with three new songs – two popular re-recordings and one brand-new performance.

Compiling it, says Greg Geller, who was assigned the task by Warners, was like putting together a giant jigsaw puzzle. Material had to be licensed from eight different record companies, but they all came through "like champs".

Then there was Stewart himself. He was closely involved with the compilation, and although he made his feelings known about the merits of the various tunes, "He never stood in the way of any key songs we wanted.

"I know he didn't like his version of 'Shake'. I heard from him several times about all the bum notes in his performance. But he never said we couldn't use it."

Stewart reserved criticism of his own past performances for the liner notes. Setting himself the task of chronicling "my illustrious, albeit chequered musical past", he contributed a line or two about each song on the album. Not every one, however, was truthful, nor even correct. But many were witty, and a few even quite revealing.

"Shake" he described as "an obscure recording brought down from the attic." He had "no opinion at all" of his version of "Pinball Wizard"; he called "Love Touch" "silly"; and as for "So Much to Say", an obscure 1968 b-side, he admitted he had "nothing at all to say", beyond the fact that the song itself was "a humble 12-bar shambles" and that he didn't personally want it included in the collection.

Storyteller was every bit the huge success Arnold Stiefel predicted, paving the way for two further, similarly far-reaching retrospective collections. Unreleased at the time of writing, one focuses upon Rod's old mucker in the Faces, bassist Ronnie Lane, the other on the Faces themselves, and according to Ronnie Wood's brother Art will include the band's first recordings backing Art under the unlikely name of Quiet Melon.

Not all that Stewart had been involved in of late was so furiously nostalgic, however. The two hit singles which Warners released from *Storyteller* were both brand-new recordings, one a specially re-recorded version of "This Old Heart of Mine", which paired Rod with the song's original vocalist, Ron Isley of the Isley Brothers, and "Downtown Train", a Tom Waits song that was swiftly to embroil Stewart in a very public slanging match.

According to Detroit rocker Bob Seger, he recorded the song for his own use, and just happened to mention the fact to Rod. The next thing he knew, Stewart had done his own version, and as he tore up the charts with the song, Seger commented bitterly, "He's a non-person to me now. You find out what you find out about people, unfortunately. I just don't think about Rod any more."

Stewart, however, countered angrily, "It's most disappointing to hear something like this, since the geezer very well knows the truth. It just sounds like sour grapes to me." Stewart had been intending to record

5

the song since 1985, when Rob Dickens, at Warners' London office, introduced it to him.

Interestingly, "Downtown Train" eventually became the first Rod Stewart single since "Do Ya Think I'm Sexy" to make the Top Ten on both sides of the Atlantic. It earned Stewart a Grammy nomination, and also gave its name to a second compilation, creaming off the best of *Storyteller*.

While "Downtown Train – Selections From *Storyteller*" still hovered in the charts, Stewart scored another hit when his version of Elton John's plaintive "Your Song" was included on an album dedicated to the music of John and lyricist Bernie Taupin. It was Stewart's way of saying thank you to a fellow musician whose friendship had remained uncompromised through almost two decades of travails. "I've always felt as if that was my song," Rod confesses. "I thought I could do it better than Elton as well."

With that impassioned performance still finding its way into the hearts of the public, Stewart topped everything with the release of a brand-new album. The sensational *Vagabond Heart* promptly outsold every Rod Stewart record of the past ten years, produced another three hit singles, and even drummed up a little controversy when Rod unveiled his video for "The Motown Song".

The song itself was an affectionate tribute to the sixties Tamla hits Stewart had been listening to while growing up. The video, however, posed the question: who are tomorrow's would-be pop stars listening to? Sinead O'Connor, Michael Jackson, Madonna and Vanilla Ice were all featured in the animated short, and Ice, at least, was outraged. "It's a cheap shot!" he retorted. "How many records has Rod Stewart sold lately?"

Another video from the album, *Broken Arrow*, formally introduced the new Mrs Stewart to her husband's record-buying public, although Rod complains, "We hate that fucking video." He later admitted that he and Rachel tried to stop its release, "but they said they'd spent $200,000 on it and if I wanted to make another one I have to pay half the costs. So I thought 'fuck that'!" The video was eventually a deserving nominee at the American Music Awards ceremony.

Then there was the accompanying tour, the sort of mammoth exercise that would exhaust a performer half Stewart's age, but which he threw himself into with heart-jolting regularity – and that despite almost continual problems with the abnormally high pollen count which plagued western Europe during the summer of 1990.

"I've never had that problem before," Stewart recalled. "It made my throat swell up. I had to have fucking cortisone, which is like a steroid, to take it all down again."

What he didn't know was that he was supposed to take the pills on a full belly with a glass of milk. "I'd been taking them on an empty stomach." And by the time he arrived in Sheffield: "I was bleeding internally for an hour and a half whilst I was on the stage. I shouldn't have gone on. Every time I closed my eyes I had to hold on to the mike stand, because if I'd let go I would have fallen arse over tit. I was singing away and kept thinking I was in my mum's kitchen. I was hallucinating, which is apparently what you do when you bleed internally."

The damage, fortunately, was neither serious nor lasting, and the tour continued virtually unabated. By the time the show had lumbered on to America, both Stewart and his audience were at their very best. "If the country's in recession, there's a lot of people out there who just don't seem to have noticed," remarked one journalist, and at a time when cancelled shows had become part and parcel of the 1991–92 rock'n'roll season, there was no doubting he was correct.

When Stewart took his final bows after the Valentine's Day 1991 Los Angeles show, the last date of his American tour, he had achieved one of the most spectacularly successful, profitable outings in recent showbiz memory. Audience figures stretched into the hundreds of thousands; millions more tuned into the LA show when it was broadcast live on pay-per-view television and nationwide radio.

To his credit, though, Stewart takes the adulation in his stride. "We've been through a lot together," he will say of his die-hard fans, "I'm glad we're still together." Stewart speaks of his audience as one might speak of an old lover – sometimes with affection, sometimes, as when they sent "Love Touch" soaring toward the top of the charts, with incredulity. But never with disdain. "What amazes me is that the public will allow me to make such humungous fucking mistakes and still come back. They let me get away with it! I'm proud of them, especially when I do 'Reason to Believe' and tell them the album is now twenty years old. I can hear there's people out there who bought the album and know the song. It's a wonderful feeling of satisfaction. I have people come backstage every night saying, 'Can I have your autograph for my mum?'

"I'd be nowhere without them," he admits, and while many rockers certainly say that, Stewart is one of the few who truly believes it, particularly when he himself looks back on some of the excesses he has submitted them to.

"Isn't it a wonder I've survived some of my fucking terrible career moves?" he laughs. "Sometimes I worry about me! 'Do Ya Think I'm Sexy?' If I was a male fan, I'd think 'Up yours, Jack!'"

Arnold Stiefel, Stewart's manager since the acrimonious departure of Rod's long-term co-conspirator Billy Gaff in 1983, agrees. That song, he says, "offended and eroded Rod's core male audience." He admits that

7

much of the subsequent decade was spent trying to rebuild the respect that Stewart had lost among his more macho contingent.

The reward for all that work, insists Stewart, comes two or three times a week when letters arrive from school groups asking to use "Forever Young" – the second single from 1989's *Out of Order* – at some charitable event or other. It is, he says, "very satisfying" – so much so that he can even forgive the handful of reviewers who, with a better memory for titles than actual songs, described the tune as a Bob Dylan cover. The worst thing about that, he continues, was that "'Forever Young' was one of my hardest songs to compose, because I was trying to write it about kids without being sappy." He regards the confusion as a compliment, nevertheless.

Rod Stewart has earned his headlines for trashing hotels and escorting leggy young blondes, for drinking like a fish and fucking like a rabbit. At times the music scarcely even entered into it. Even Dee Harrington, Rod's constant companion before she was edged aside by Britt Ekland in 1975, admits that Rod's continued success owes as much to him changing girlfriends as anything he might achieve on stage. "But those are not the things I want to be remembered for," Stewart complains. "I want to be remembered as a songwriter – a bloody good songwriter." To be compared to the immortal Bob Dylan, a performer whose songs Stewart has frequently and reverently recorded, was certainly a massive step forward in that direction.

If Rod Stewart can hold his own with the giants of rock, however, he can also blend in with the crowd. It is a talent of which he is justifiably proud, and which even his detractors cannot help but admire. "He's very real and down to earth," Alana Hamilton enthuses. "He likes to go down to the pub and drink with the boys and just be a regular guy, which used to drive me crazy. He wants to be a regular person." And he wants to keep his regular friends. With the exception of Elton John, Rolling Stone Ronnie Wood, and "a handful of others", he nurses a healthy disrespect for his fellow pop stars.

"I don't mean to sound cynical, but I just don't find them particularly interesting," Rod admits, adding that he would rather be out on a field playing soccer with his mates, "regular carpenters and working-class blokes", than living it up with the rich and famous.

When he goes home to England – since 1987 he has maintained a sixteenth-century country estate, Copped Hall, in Epping Forest – he enjoys nothing more than to take in a soccer match, then amble down to the pub.

The Theydon Oak, in the picturesquely named London suburb of Theydon Bois, is his regular, and in all the years he's been going there, it is said he has never paid for a drink. When he first started visiting, of course, he created something of a stir. They'd read the papers, they'd heard the scandals, and when word first got around he was moving into the neighborhood they'd even grumbled quietly about loud parties, limos and naked girls in the woods.

But Rod Stewart wasn't like that any more. Maybe he never really was. Now, when he walks into the Oak, the locals scarcely even notice he's there. To some of them he's "Rod", to others "Mr Stewart". But to all of them he's just one of the regulars, and woe betide the pressman who drops by on the make for a saucy story. He's as likely to be shown the door as he is to be pointedly ignored.

"Not everything you read about Rod Stewart is true," the singer himself warns. "You don't know what's been written about me, just unbelievable, foul stuff. Not from the rock press, I can take that. But the tabs, the British tabs. They're wicked . . . They're the only thing I don't like about Britain, the dread of the Sunday papers." Shortly after his return to England with his new bride Rachel, one paper ran a picture of the pair sunbathing in their underwear. The headline read "YOU BARE IT WELL!"

Only rarely will he truly let on how he feels about his treatment in the press: when a particularly spiteful lie gets reported as gospel, or a baleful acquaintance spills his or her guts. The rest of the time, "living well," he laughs, "is still the best revenge!"

But when *Vagabond Heart*, his heralded 1991 album, made it on to the street, he couldn't resist letting his feelings be known. Doodling away the sleeve notes, he wrote, "Many foolish and hurtful things have been written about myself in the press over the years, most of which have been severely embroidered half truths."

He wasn't complaining, he noted, just stating a fact. Because Rod knows, as he hopes do the guilty, "that those who scribbled with crooked nib will one day have to answer to the great Editor in the sky."

Point taken.

2

Spoil The Child

The youngest of five children, Rod led an uneventful – if pampered – childhood. Both his parents and older siblings kept a watchful eye on all he did, encouraging him in his dreams, supporting him in his disappointments. But the familial Stewart has paid them all back handsomely, with houses, holidays and extravagant gifts galore.

Several years ago, when his sister Peggy was stricken with multiple sclerosis, his family had to beg him *not* to keep offering them money. Rod's brother Don has likewise traveled the world alongside him, attending soccer matches. To his friends and family he can be the most generous man alive. But to his enemies, Stewart can be moody, greedy, ruthless and often embarrassingly rude.

Throughout his rickety, extended rise to fame, every facet of his nature – generous and giving, guarded and grasping – has served him well. There are few people whose life and times seem at first so open to scrutiny, yet somehow remain so consistently shrouded in secrecy and innuendo.

Of his later career, the years since Rod Stewart has become a household name throughout the English-speaking world, it seems that the only people who speak out publicly are those with a grudge to bear, or a tale to tell. His friends, family and closest associates have unilaterally maintained a tight-lipped silence; while Stewart himself has gone out of his way to weave a personal mythology from which even he must have difficulty separating fact from fable.

Of his formative years in rock'n'roll, spent with a succession of poorly paid nowhere bands, much has been written, but even today, in conversation with the people around him, little of import has been revealed.

Of his childhood, the only thing that can be known for certain is that when Stewart tells the world he came in with a bang, he means it!

The explosion may not have inspired Elsie Stewart's labor pains on 10 January, 1945, but it certainly reminded her where she was. Less than thirty minutes after a dreaded Nazi flying bomb reduced nearby Highbury police station to a smoking heap of rubble, Elsie gave birth to her third son. "I've always thought I was very lucky because that bomb fell just a stone's throw from where I lived," Rod later remarked. "I've sort of had the feeling that I nearly didn't make it."

Roderick David was the first of the Stewart clan to be born in England. Eight years younger than brother Bob Junior, Rod jokes that he was conceived in an air-raid shelter. It is probably the only thing about his remarkably charmed life he would change. All four of his brothers and sisters – Don, Mary, Peggy and Bobby – were born in their father's native Glasgow, where Robert Stewart worked as a builder. Even today, when Stewart talks of home – which he seems to do an awful lot – you have to ask him *which* home. The place he was born? Or the place he wishes he was?

The Stewarts moved to London shortly before the Second World War broke out in 1939. Elsie was an affable North Londoner, who met Edinburgh-born Robert in 1928. A former navy man – he had run away to sea when he was just fourteen in 1917 – Robert now worked as a master builder. With his meager savings, they purchased a small newsagent's shop at 507 Archway Road, in Highgate, North London. The family resided in a cramped, dreary flat directly above the shop.

Archway is by no means one of London's most salubrious areas. Wedged between fashionable Hampstead and trendy Islington, it presents the visitor with an unending vista of terraced homes, winding their way up the hill toward the Heath. Railroad lines, spreading out from King's Cross and the City, run like iron arteries beneath the stony streets. Only on Saturday afternoons does the neighborhood come to life, when a short walk takes the population to Highbury Stadium, home of Arsenal Football Club.

The Stewart family blended in well with the area's cosmopolitan face, their deep Scots accents no more noticeable than the thick Irish brogue spilling over from nearby Kilburn, the infectiously vulgar Cockney trickling up from the East End or the haughty, clipped tones of the privileged Hampstead set.

Sadly, the family newsagent is a dying breed in the England of today, overtaken by chipper convenience stores and faceless nationwide chains that have sprung up on every high-street corner. But back then, such stores were a focal point of the immediate community, the first port of call for commuters on their way to the bus stop and train station. Besides newspapers and magazines, they also traded in cigarettes, tobacco, and confectionery, plus a whole range of other essentials such as bread, milk and tea.

Every morning, Mr and Mrs Stewart would rise at dawn to haul in the bundles of newspapers that had been delivered to the front of their shop, preparing themselves for the long day ahead.

11

For a family of four children, such a steady business seemed heaven-sent. The Stewarts may have been strict about their brood helping themselves to sweets, but when the weekly comics were delivered, their kids would inevitably be the first in the shop, each making a beeline for his or her favorite title.

Many of those that Rod remembers so fondly today are still with us – *Beano* and *Dandy* have both celebrated fifty years of regular publication, and look set for fifty more. Still others have long since faded into memory. There was *Ace Malloy*, the action-packed adventures of a modern-day jet-fighter pilot; there was *Comet*, with the gripping exploits of "Dick Barton – Special Agent"; and, of course, *Tip Top*, featuring "Artie the Autograph Hunter". One day, the Stewart boys dreamed, perhaps Artie would be asking them for their autographs. Because one day they would all be world-famous footballers, they were convinced of that. And their sports-crazed dad would have liked nothing more.

Football is more a religion in Scotland than a mere mortal pastime. Other nations may have more successful teams – Brazil, for instance, or Germany – but none support their players with more passion than the Scots. On a good night, the Tartan Army is worth a one-goal start to its eleven blue-shirted heroes, and there have been many good nights, particularly when the opposition is "The Auld Enemy", England. For 120 years now the two rivals, England and Scotland, have met almost annually, their bitter enmity now legendary.

It was a Scot – the late Bill Shankly, manager of the all-conquering Liverpool club – who made the off-hand remark now enshrined in Scottish sporting lore. Asked if he thought the game was a matter of life and death, Shanks growled, "It's far more important than that!" To Rod Stewart, who will travel halfway around the world to catch the Scottish team in action, Shankly's words have become something of a code of life. "As much as I love women and music," Stewart once said, "my first love will always remain football."

The young Stewart caught the footballing bug from his father, who had been a keen player himself. Even into his late forties, he played regularly for a local team, the Highgate Redwings – and while he never moved beyond a strictly amateur grade, Robert Stewart was determined his sons one day would. Just before the war, three other Scottish brothers – David, Jim and Bob Corbett – had turned out for the East London team West Ham United. Robert's greatest dream was that his brood might one day emulate them.

At the dog track with his friends, in the pub or down at the betting shop, this normally dour, introverted man would burst into life with his dreams. "They've all got what it takes, all three of them," he would brag to his mates. "Mark my words, my lads are going to be famous."

Inevitably, the boys' bedroom walls were plastered with pictures of their favorite players, painstakingly cut from newspapers and books. Years later, Stewart was to remember, "One of my earliest memories is of the pictures my brothers had on their bedroom walls." They were, of course, all Scottish footballers. He grew up with the names of Scotland's greatest players on his lips – Tommy Docherty, Jimmy Scoular, Billy Liddell, and the toughest and most universally admired of them all, Denis Law.

Law made his debut for Scotland in 1959, when Rod was just fourteen. Fifteen years later, Stewart was invited to Manchester United's ground to meet his boyhood hero. "You'll never believe it!" he couldn't help spouting to everyone when he returned that evening. "I saw Denis Law's cock in the locker-room!" Dreams, apparently, still do come true.

Growing up, Stewart gravitated with his family into supporting Arsenal. Throughout the English football season, Robert and his three sons would join 50,000 other spectators every second Saturday, to cheer the mighty Reds on their way.

Oftentimes the Stewarts' Scots idols also appeared at the ground, seriously dividing the family's loyalties. Should they take their accustomed places on the North Bank terrace, to roar the Reds on to victory? Or defect for the day and support their stout-hearted countrymen?

More often than not, they stuck with Arsenal, and were rewarded with one of the most successful chapters in the team's history. Twice, in 1950 and 1952, the Stewart clan supported Arsenal through to the final of England's premier football tournament, the FA Cup. Twice more they saw them take the Football League Championship, a forty-two match competition that ranks among the most gruelling in the world.

With a father who encouraged him to kick at every stone, can or ball he found, it is hardly surprising that Stewart had already mapped out his future. He was going to play football for Scotland.

Robert and Elsie, it seems, had all the time in the world for their youngest child, so much so that to this day he still looks back on his boyhood and winces, "I was a spoiled brat." Of course, they could come down like a ton of bricks on him when he deserved it. In later years, Robert tore his superstar son off a strip for being photographed in public wearing a T-shirt with FUCK on the back; he berated him further for telling the press that he liked taking dirty pictures, and laid into him once more for refusing to perform "Sailing" at a show attended by royalty. During Rod's highly publicised dalliance with actress Britt Ekland, it was Robert who told him to stop acting the poofter when he

13

appeared on TV. "You're a man, for Christ's sake, you should bloody well behave like one."

In later years Rod was to admit that the only thing he worried about was what his dad would think of his behavior. "If I upset my dad, then I'm really in trouble. He is nearer to me than anything."

But at the same time the Stewarts were adamant that nothing was too good for their little Rod. He only had to mention a whim and it would soon be realised. Even though money was often tight, his parents indulged his passion for model railways, setting Stewart off on a lifelong hobby. Later, when they noticed him taking an interest in their Al Jolson records, they encouraged him to start collecting those as well.

This unabashed love of Jolson was another great Stewart family tradition. Both Stewart's grandfather and his brothers did "fantastic Jolson impersonations", and Rod followed in their footsteps. Christmases in the Stewart household were never complete until the entire family gathered around the piano in the living-room to sing old Jolson songs.

Al Jolson passed away in 1950. The following year, Rod saw the movie *The Jolson Story* for the first time. Since then, he has seen both it, and its sequel, *Jolson Sings Again*, dozens of times. "I got so bowled over by him," Stewart remembers. "The more I read about him, and I've read several books, I flatter myself and try to compare myself to him. It was the attitude to his audience that influenced me and the way he sold a number I thought was just magnificent."

Still, young Master Stewart had no intention of making a career in music. Despite having been born with a pronounced curvature of the spine (which was never corrected and actually left him with a slight hump), he appeared to be a born footballer.

Turning out every weekend for the local Finchley youth team was his greatest weapon against those cruel schoolmates who mocked his stooped stance, and ridiculed the domineering nose which highlighted his unnaturally thin ant-eater face. Ignoring their barbs, he would wait until sports class, then reveal them for the fools they were with his skill on the ball. Of course, if they persisted with their taunts, there were always Rod's big brothers to help sort them out.

Stewart played soccer throughout his elementary-school days, at Highgate Primary, and when, in 1956, he moved on to the William Grimshaw Secondary Modern School in nearby Hornsey, he swiftly graduated to their school team as well.

The English education system of the 1950s divided its inmates into separate streams very early on. At the age of eleven, pupils would take their first "serious" examination, a rigorous general-knowledge test called the Eleven Plus.

Those who passed would move on to highly prized Grammar School educations; those who failed – and Stewart was always far too busy with football to pay much attention to his lessons – were packed off to Secondary Moderns, with further academic advancement a very dim prospect. Teaching standards were lower, discipline slacker, and when it came time for the all-important finals, few "Modern" scholars were ever considered up to scratch.

Still, Stewart prospered in that grim red-brick slice of Victorian England. Polite to his elders, always nicely dressed and well spoken, he became first a staff favorite, and later a school prefect.

This was, of course, a position of considerable authority among the school heirarchy, and one that had to be managed with care by its favored inductees. Charged with such iron-clad duties as ensuring classrooms and hallways were empty at break time, reporting illicit smokers and alerting the staff to playground fights, the prefect can very easily find himself a figure of some resentment, particularly if he has already won a reputation as a goody-goody.

The untouchable Stewart, though, was all but immune from such negative distinctions. To make the school football team – indeed, to star on it week after week – gave him an advantage that left him all but impervious to such juvenile assaults. He may have been a good boy, but he was also a super footballer, and that was a hell of a lot more important.

One young man who consistently crossed Stewart's path was a lad by the name of Dave Davies. Two years younger than Rod and fresh out of junior school, he was as rough and rude as Stewart was polished, and as explosive a mischief-maker as any. Davies joyously bullied boys smaller than himself, and casually fired off stink bombs at his elders as if he were passing a cup of tea.

But he also had a rather well-defined footballing ability, as did his elder brother Ray, which in later years would prompt people to wonder at the fact that no less than *three* future rock'n'roll stars were among the ranks of the William Grimshaw XI. Ray and Dave Davies, of course, went on to form the Kinks, one of the most successful, innovative bands of the sixties and seventies.

Stewart's heady career as a prefect ended shortly before his schooldays themselves, when he let off a fire extinguisher without first finding a fire to point it at. That, however, was just the most public of a series of increasingly regular transgressions – as Rod grew older, he became significantly bolder. Suddenly authority didn't seem so great an asset to a young man just beginning to discover his sexuality. Besides, the petty restrictions he was led to uphold seemed irrelevant to the intriguing world waiting just beyond the Grimshaw gates. He was soon unceremoniously stripped of his prefect's badge.

Stewart bowed out of school forever in 1960. A vapid succession of odd jobs floated past afterwards. His first position was at Sam Kid's Wallpapers in Kentish Town, and he had a short-lived stint at the Framery, in nearby Muswell Hill. Stewart also helped out in the family shop, and even attempted delivering newspapers, a job that finally collapsed when the long-suffering Elsie had to admit there was no way she could rouse him in time to make his appointed rounds.

For a time Stewart helped out in brother Bobby's sign-painting business, had another job erecting fences, and even tried his hand at digging graves, working within the spectacular gloom of Highgate Cemetery, a somber plot universally known for the grave of Karl Marx.

His initiation into the trade was suitably morbid. The other cemetery workers bundled him into a coffin, then closed the lid. Such a stunt was traditional rather than personal, but Stewart still remembers it as "a very, very frightening experience. It doesn't sound like it, but once you get in there and they close the lid on you, you wonder if they'll just leave you there."

One thing such treatment did succeed in doing was to cure Stewart of what had been a recurring fear of death. Indeed, he reckons that was why he took the job in the first place: "I thought the best way of beating my fear of death was to confront it, to get as close to it as possible. And I've never had any problems with it since."

Strangely, Stewart remembers his time digging graves as being a lot more fun than it sounds. "We only spent two days a week actually digging holes," he later mused. The rest of the time would be spent doing gardening work, and during the balmy summer months, it often seemed quite idyllic. But who wants to dig holes and weed graves for the rest of their life?

Only one of Stewart's many transient occupations appealed to him, and even this he threw up after less than a month. Just before he left school, Stewart was picked to play for the Middlesex Schoolboys football team, an honor which truly set him far above the garden-variety juvenile footballer. He was also offered a trial with England's national schoolboy team, and while he didn't make the grade, one team showed a very genuine interest in advancing his football career.

Brentford FC is certainly not one of English football's greatest names. Based in the south-western fringe of London – a hefty commute from Stewart's Highgate home – the club was founded in 1889, and in 1920 they were admitted to the Football League.

Since then, they had hovered at the lowest level of competition. But still, a trial with *any* Football League club was not something to be sniffed at. With his thoroughly delighted father egging him on, Stewart signed on as a professional footballer just in time for the 1961–62 season. His salary was to be a princely eight pounds a week.

Footballers in the early 1960s may not have been the highest-paid entertainers in the country, but they were certainly the most adored. The life of an apprentice professional footballer, however, was significantly less romantic. Getting up at eight in the morning, Stewart would traipse across London on the rush-hour underground trains, then spend his day doing almost anything but playing football. There were boots to clean, lockers to empty, floors to mop, with the undisputed highlight of the week watching the first team train.

Years later, Ginger Baker – who played alongside Rod in a showbiz team at the end of the sixties – extolled Stewart's soccer-playing abilities. "Rod has always been a very good player. He could easily have made it as a professional. The team we were in was put together by Cream's manager, Robert Stigwood, and it was bloody good. It was serious stuff as well, none of these drunken pop stars falling over everywhere – Stigwood had a full-size football pitch in the grounds of his house, and we had a lot of professional players of considerable standing in the side. Rod could always hold his own with any of them."

Stewart's first adventure in football, however, was doomed to failure. After three weeks, he quit. "I never even kicked a ball," he later mused.

Rock'n'roll meant little to Stewart at the time. True he had been reasonably keen on Eddie Cochran for a while, even teaching himself to play "C'mon Everybody" on the shoddy acoustic guitar his parents bought him. But most everything else passed him by, even the Beatles, who first broke through in 1962, when Stewart was seventeen.

Instead, Rod followed his art-school friends into the so-called Protest scene, a grass-roots movement born of folk music and surcharged with the spirit of youthful rebellion. He didn't particularly hold with it philosophically, however; it was really more just something to do. But as with so many other things that he was to drift into, Stewart threw himself into the life with a vengeance.

Some of his new mates had recently formed their own band, the Raiders, and one day they invited Rod along to the studio to help out on some vocals. What followed might well have put the sixteen-year-old Stewart off rock'n'roll forever; after just ten minutes, the producer, Joe Meek, walked into the studio, looked in Rod's direction, and blew a giant raspberry. Stewart quietly left shortly afterwards.

Constantly borrowing cash off his parents, Stewart generally spent his nights out with friends, and his days sleeping off the evening's excesses. Sometimes he would bring his new mates round to the flat – bewilderingly unkempt beings who spoke in a strange hip slang and appeared to be nothing more or less than vagabonds.

But Robert and Elsie never objected. If their Rod was happy, that was enough. When he arrived home one night and announced that he intended hitchhiking to Paris, they scarcely batted an eyelid, knowing he would be back within a few days – and indeed he was. The rigors of sleeping rough on the Left Bank apparently were more than enough to send the always comfort-conscious Stewart scurrying home again.

But Stewart wasn't quite cured of his wanderlust. Shortly after the aborted French adventure, Rod announced he intended spending Easter on the Aldermaston March in the company of Bobby and his wife, and the Raiders. "Not that there'll be much marching done," he laughed. "We're traveling by Land Rover."

The march, the first of many over the next few years, was bound for Aldermaston, a small village in Berkshire which had been selected as the headquarters of Britain's Atomic Weapons Research Establishment. It was a magnet for every Ban the Bomb activist in the country, and the Easter marches brought thousands of them down upon the sleepy little village.

Rod's first Aldermaston March took place in that spring of 1961, shortly before he joined Brentford Football Club. In his donkey jacket and roll-neck sweater he didn't particularly stand out from the crowd; he was just another part-time beatnik faking his way through a few choruses of "We Shall Overcome".

Stewart himself admits that he was not overly committed to the cause: "I believed in it, of course, but I couldn't really get that involved. I mean, you'd never own up at the time that you were just going along for a giggle, but probably thousands of kids went along to get screwed. There used to be terrible orgies!" He later bragged that he lost his virginity on one of the marches. His partner, a seventeen-year-old from Bristol, was to remain an occasional companion for some months longer, right up until the day, says Stewart, when she announced she was pregnant.

After weeks of dropping hints about her condition, and Stewart's far-ranging responsibilities to her, she finally confronted him on Brighton beach one evening that summer. The way Rod remembers it, he was sitting on some rocks strumming his guitar, while the poor girl ranted and raved about marriage, babies and a hundred other things that simply didn't matter to him.

Suddenly, she snatched his guitar away and in a move which Pete Townshend, the trowel-nosed master of auto-destruction, would have admired, smashed the hapless instrument to pieces against a rock. Stewart walked out of her life almost immediately thereafter, but the saga of the forgotten love-child was one which has haunted him ever since. Beginning with "Jo's Lament", a song on his second album,

Gasoline Alley, Stewart has delighted in dropping obtuse hints about an illegitimate child – and then frequently denying them in the next breath.

Aldermaston, 1961, was virtually Stewart's social "coming out" party. It inspired him, for a few weeks at least, to leave home once again, moving into a derelict houseboat in Shoreham, near Brighton, with twenty or so like-minded beatniks.

Although the commune did its best to make the dreary houseboat look presentable, it was continually running up against local objections: the "greybeards", as Stewart insisted on calling his elders, "didn't like the idea of us not working, so they got the police to drive us out with hoses of cold water. Then they towed the boat away and sank it."

The beatniks did not give up without a fight, however. Led by a fierce, bearded gentleman named John the Road, they gathered together a motley arsenal of weapons, including a musket, which John fired off at the police. According to newspaper reports it was that, rather than any local objections, which prompted the police to bring out the water cannon, but the end result was the same. The beatniks were defeated, and Stewart reluctantly returned home.

Back in London, Stewart's favorite haunt was Finch's, a pub-come-folk club on Goodge Street. But he was no stranger to the many other dives which were springing up across the city – Under the Olive Tree in Croydon, and the Porcupine in Leicester Square.

Most of the so-called clubs were set in a room or two somehow attached to a pub. Even the legendary Les Cousins, in Soho's Greek Street, was nothing more than a hot, smelly basement, whose sweat-soaked denizens were more likely to be found sinking pints in the Pillars of Hercules across the street than discussing Bertrand Russell in the smoky, crowded club. Stewart apparently wasn't the only guy on the circuit more concerned with getting laid than the Cuban Missile Crisis.

Stewart remembers how surprised he was when he stumbled on to the scene. His musical tastes were already drifting in the direction of the great American folk balladeers, but for a long time he was sure he was the only one. "Then you'd read interviews and find there were like 3000 others at art school, all into the same thing."

More than anything, it was the prospect of meeting women which drew Stewart toward the stage – an ambition which over the years has, of course, been more than aptly fulfiiled. He already stood out in the crowd. Every penny he earned (or was given to him by his parents) would be spent on clothes. At a time when a nondescript bagginess was still the very height of fashion, the elegantly attired Stewart, with his ready wit and easy smile, quickly became the focus of attention. After a while, though, even that wasn't enough. Now he wanted applause.

Putting aside his natural reserve, Stewart started dragging his tatty guitar along to the clubs. At first he would simply sit at a table, strumming for friends and any young women who passed by. He remembers, "I was still learning how to play, struggling through the three-chord thing." His party piece remained "a very, very good 'C'mon Everybody', and if I were asked politely, I would do that, then fall down in the gutter outside the pub."

As his confidence grew, however, so too did his audience. Finally, he made the jump from the floor to the stage – and was never to look back.

Stewart's repertoire evolved slowly, and seldom strayed from the same well-plodded paths that every other aspiring young folkie trod. It revolved around Ramblin' Jack Elliott and Woody Guthrie, the Kingston Trio and Joan Baez. Every so often he would swing into hearty staples such as "Cocaine", "San Francisco Bay" and "Salty Dog", and considered himself well ahead of the pack when he discovered banjo virtuoso Derroll Adams. Within days of hearing him for the first time, Stewart abandoned his guitar and took up the banjo himself.

He was also busy absorbing the collective music of Topic, a small folk-oriented label whose artists aggressively plumbed new depths of mediocrity in the race to stay ahead of the crowd. Finally, there was Hamilton Camp, whose first album, released in 1964, was littered with obscure Bob Dylan songs. In later years, Stewart was to credit Camp with turning him on to many of the Dylan compositions he was later to record himself.

"After Dylan brought out that first album, we had thousands of Bob Dylans running about in their Bob Dylan caps," remembers Rod. "Everybody was doing a Dylan – it was a big scene. There was a close circle of folkie-types. Donovan was into that routine as well, limping about on one leg . . ." With his knowledge of Camp's work, Stewart was able to approach the Great Master from a different angle, but still admits, "I was doing the whole bit with the banjo and harmonica and hat, washed-out denims . . ."

Stewart would rehearse for his off-the-cuff performances by heading out on equally impromptu busking expeditions, just Stewart and his beat-up old banjo, scratching out the standards of the day outside underground stations and pubs. On the pavement at his feet a battered hat waited for passers-by to fling in a few coins. Rod would stop only when it got too dark, or when the humorless bobbies arrived to move him along.

Perhaps the brightest light on the scene at that time was Raymond "Wizz" Jones, a brilliant young guitarist who was shocked in later years to discover just how many future rock and folk luminaries were regularly sitting in his audience. Jones later opened his own club in Leicester Square, the Porcupine, which swiftly became a home away from home for the capital's army of buskers.

"We were part of a crowd that people these days would call hippies," says Jones. "In those days, though, they were 'Bohemians'." Clientele included "people like Jimmy Page, Long John Baldry and Davy Graham. Eric Clapton was one of those hanging out there at the time as well."

Stewart made no greater impression on Wizz than these others, but that was not the story Rod himself told. In later years, he would credit Wizz Jones as his creative guru – an honor which Jones is quick to shrug off. "In the days when I remember him, his voice was pretty nondescript, though he wouldn't sing that much in public – and I didn't even know he played guitar."

That wasn't how Stewart told the story, though. In the summer of 1962, fresh from the latest Aldermaston March, he packed up his banjo and made his way over the Channel to Europe. It was a trail beaten out by hundreds, maybe even thousands, of Stewart's fellow beatniks, as venerable a pilgrimage as the mystic East would become to people his age five years later.

Stewart says he was simply "wandering around, mostly Spain and Italy, trying to get myself together." But he loved the experience, and once remarked, "I think that's something everybody should get out of them; when my kids grow up, I'm going to say, 'Alright, out you bastards, get out on the road and live.'"

Spain, he claimed, was the easiest to work in, and had he stayed there, all may have been well. But he soon crossed over to the South of France, working his way up and down the beaches with one eye on his banjo and the other on the horizon – not only for potential conquests, but for the long arm of the law as well.

The French gendarmerie were notoriously hard on the legions of rootless, lusty Englishmen who were descending in ever-increasing numbers upon their sun-soaked beaches, often turning the Mediterranean coast into a battleground as they pursued these hapless guitar-slingers with threats of jail and deportation.

Stewart was to be no exception. Arrested for common vagrancy, he was delivered, penniless, to the British Consul in St Tropez – an institution which was by now thoroughly sick of having young English wastrels dumped on its doorstep. Stewart was subsequently issued a third-class air ticket back to London and to this day probably owes the money for his fare.

When Stewart returned home, his mother burned his jeans because they smelt so bad. "I had this beautiful pair of Levis that had taken me all these months to fade, and she burnt them. It was like losing a leg!" His girlfriend Sarah, the beautiful blonde who was to accompany Stewart throughout most of the 1960s, but whose surname history fails to record, agrees with Rod's mother, "They smelt to high heaven."

In later years, Stewart was to build an entire personal mythology around this little jaunt, turning a few weeks spent busking into a veritable European tour, undertaken with Wizz Jones forever by his side – an adventure which Jones vehemently denies. Indeed, many of the Stewart/Wizz tales which have surfaced over the years, Jones insists, are nothing more than pure fabrication.

"It's true we used to hang around Eel Pie Island [a club in Twickenham]," says Wizz. "We shared some girlfriends – that was around 1959/ 60. [And] we jammed in London, but we never *ever* played together in France. You often used to meet people on the road you'd met in London, [but] I can't remember meeting him there at all."

The truth of his tales notwithstanding – and Stewart certainly wasn't the only teenager to embroider his adventures before returning home – Rod was now deeply embroiled in the culture of beatnik disrespectability.

In many ways, though, Stewart was still very much a stay-at-home lad, dividing his time between his brother Bob's sign-painting business and part-time employment making picture frames for various London dealers. He still played with his model railroads, still went to Arsenal games with his dad, and had the music scene not suddenly slammed his life into a whole new gear, he might have maintained his strange double life right up until adulthood finally jolted him into some semblance of lower-middle-class respectability.

By early 1963, it was becoming clear that the Beatles' breakthrough was not an isolated phenomenon. Bands were springing up everywhere, and with them a whole new phase of teenage awareness. The old adage of sex, drugs and rock'n'roll may seem a cliché today, but in Beat Boom Britain it was an irresistible alternative culture, and one in which the adventurous Stewart wholeheartedly immersed himself.

The city was burning with rhythm and blues, a peculiar electric hybrid of lost American Negro spirituals and the fiery snottiness of rebellious youth. Throwing aside the standards even of rock's first wave of rebels, the new generation of Teddy Boys, with their immaculately manicured quiffs and painstakingly ornamented jackets and drainpipes, sported hair down to the collar, trousers which flared, and shirts which could not be any tighter.

At the forefront of this explosion – musically, if not sartorially – was Cyril Davies, a blues harmonica player who gravitated into the harsher

R & B after linking up with Alexis Korner in the new legendary Blues Incorporated.

Decrying the Beatles' poppy influence over the nascent British music scene, Davies and Korner opted for the grittier sounds of the American South – not only the raucous rock of Chuck Berry and Bo Diddley, but also the darker, earlier songs of Robert Johnson, Elmore James and Willie Dixon.

In London and the south, the blues was primarily a suburban occupation. Like the Punk rockers of fifteen years later, the Rolling Stones, the Yardbirds, the Artwoods and the Action all erupted out of London's dormitory suburbs. Even further afield, groups like the Zombies and the Silence flourished, dreaming of the day when they, too, could take the train to the big city, and add their voices to the roar of electricity being generated there nightly.

Stewart was an early apostle of the Stones. "I remember Jagger's old lady taking me over to see them – Chrissie Shrimpton, Jean Shrimpton's sister, the model. She took me over, saying it was this 'unbelievable' band. There were only about fifteen people there. They were incredible . . . they'd sit there on these stools and play, and that was their big thing. It was really weird."

Stewart started attending Stones gigs on a regular basis, but it wasn't Jagger and company who most caught his eye, but rather the Dimensions, an enthusiastic, if unadventurous, four-piece who were regulars at Ken Colyer's Studio 51 jazz club in London's Oxford Street, and who frequently appeared during the interval.

Disorganised, ramshackle, sometimes painfully out of tune, the Dimensions made it all look so easy. One night, Stewart decided to find out once and for all if it actually was. "At that time it was very popular to walk around with a harmonica in your pocket, pretending to be Cyril Davies," says Chris Townson, a member of the Leatherhead-based Silence. "Everybody was doing it, and it didn't matter whether or not you could play the thing, it was just the done thing to have one."

Stewart was one of the fad's greatest adherents, and true to fashion didn't have a clue how to play. But when he jumped up on the Dimensions' stage and started wailing away, it didn't seem to matter. He was enthusiastic, he was loud, and the Dimensions were impressed. They invited him to join the band soon afterwards.

Stewart agreed, but set himself an immediate goal – to learn how to play that blasted harp. "I used to wonder why I kept running out of breath." He says it wasn't until he started watching Mick Jagger closely that he finally figured out what he was doing wrong.

Ironically, the Dimensions wouldn't let him sing. In fact, he barely even played harp. "I did two numbers a night and then I went home."

Stewart was happy regardless. "To me, it was great just being up there on stage."

Stewart definitely cut a dashing figure, out-dressing the rest of the group with a vengeance, even putting his previously embarrassing S-bend back to good use. As future lover Britt Ekland once remarked, "the one advantage of the curvature was that his rear end protruded, and no one wiggled it quite like Rod."

Today the Dimensions are remembered wholly for Rod's fleeting involvement. Stewart, however, has less than satisfying memories of the group. "We had two guys who wanted to do all the Beatles' hits, there was me who was into the blues, and the other guy wanted to imitate Ray Charles, so the combination never quite hit it off. The fellas who wanted to do the Beatle thing went back to being bricklayers."

London at this time was a magnet, not only for would-be R & B bands, but to a host of other performers, too. One such hopeful was Jimmy Powell, an unsuccessful pop singer from Birmingham.

One night, Powell recalls, his agent, Malcolm Nixon, told him to go along to the Marquee Club in London, to see the Cyril Davies All Stars – at that time, still the most important band on the R & B circuit.

Powell, history recalls, was duly impressed, so the next day Nixon gave him a pile of R & B records and that evening introduced him to Rod and the Dimensions, whose bookings Nixon also arranged. Powell was offered fifty pounds a week to "knock the band into shape". Shortly thereafter, he appointed himself their lead singer.

"I went out and got it together," says Powell. "I rigged up a show and he [Nixon] put us in supporting Cyril. We went down a fucking storm! All of a sudden there were two R & B bands on the circuit, us and Cyril, but we were the band to go out into the provinces because we were young, we'd all got hair and teeth. We were doing places like Mecca [a chain of ballrooms which dominated the UK concert circuit at this time] and dying a death, but in one or two places we went down stupendous, so we kept going, built up a reputation and ended up doing eight or nine gigs a week."

As for Powell leading the band into true R & B, Stewart reckons it was actually he who got Powell "to start playing the blues, because I was a blues singer, and that's what we were doing, playing the twelve-bars, we knew three chords and we used all of them." Today Stewart looks back on Powell as a man whose career was a non-starter until he jumped on the R & B bandwagon and rapidly continued going nowhere thereafter.

Before Powell joined, Stewart had been considering moving into the spotlight, taking over on vocals for one or two songs. When he suggested it to Powell, however, he was quickly shouted down.

"I think Powell was just a little bit jealous," says Stewart. "He knew I could sing. Occasionally I joined in a few backing vocals and tended to blow him off stage, because I really overdid it. You know, shouting as loud as I could on the backing vocals, whenever I got the chance."

Powell would complain bitterly afterwards, but the self-possessed Stewart was typically unrepentant. So was the band's management. One evening, as the Dimensions headed up the motorway to a show in Birmingham, a new plan was announced.

The old van was rattling along, the band members lounging in the back with their instruments, choking on exhaust fumes. Suddenly the silence that falls like a shroud over such long, boring journeys was broken.

"We think Rod should be allowed to sing a few numbers," someone erupted.

Powell was horrified. "But I'm the vocalist. He's just the harp player for Christ's sake."

"Yeah, and you'll still be a fuckin' vocalist. But Rod looks great, you've seen the birds eyeing him. It won't hurt you to give him a go. Maybe he'll share his birds out with you afterwards!"

Powell argued the point all the way into Birmingham, but to no avail. That night Stewart was to make his in-concert debut as the Dimensions' lead singer.

No one remembers now what he sang, or even how well he sang it. They were all too busy watching as Powell, relegated to the sidelines for the first time ever, threw down his own microphone and stormed off stage.

Powell himself denies the story, claiming instead that Stewart had long since established himself as the band's second singer. He says he merely got pissed off because Rod never knew when to stop singing. "He would stick two or three more numbers on to the end of his spot and I would be stuck there waiting like a lemon to come on and he wouldn't come off!

"We would have rows, but he didn't change. Rod was a very demanding person. He wanted everything he wanted when he wanted it. And when he didn't get it he was so fucking disruptive! He just wanted to be the star, all the time."

The Dimensions' big break came in September 1963, when the Stones were asked to open Bo Diddley's British tour. Their weekly spot at Ken Colyer's went immediately to the Dimensions, and Stewart remembers they were emptying the room almost as quickly as the Stones used to fill it. He quit, he says, about two weeks later.

"I never used to get any money," Stewart complains. "I think they thought, 'Oh, he's a silly bastard, just likes being on the stage, don't give him any bread.' I never got a decent deal out of that group."

Another squabble between Stewart and Powell, and one which persists to this very day, concerns the harp-playing on "My Boy Lollipop", a hit for Jamaican singer Millie Small. According to both Rod and Small's producer Chris Blackwell, it was Stewart who played the familiar riff – his unofficial recording debut. Powell, however, insists that it was he and that Blackwell simply remembers Stewart "because he went on to become the known name."

On 7 January, 1964, Cyril Davies died of leukemia. To the still-burgeoning British blues boom, it was a devastating blow, like the loss of a father. To the members of Davies' band, the R & B All Stars, it was almost the end. Only the persistence of their vocalist, "Long" (as in tall, rather than the penile dimensions as rumor once claimed) John Baldry, kept them going. "Cyril," he would say, "would have wanted us to."

Stewart had often stopped by to see the All Stars play. He liked Baldry best – a laconic Adonis who projected an aura of untouchable beauty and spoke in the sharp, measured tones of an aristocrat. Baldry had a devastating sense of humor, and was all the funnier because you never knew when he was being serious.

One bitterly cold Sunday night in early January, after an evening at Eel Pie, Stewart was at Twickenham rail station, waiting for the train home. It was late, and he was pacing up and down the long, open-air platform, singing to himself and wailing away on his harmonica. He was playing "Smokestack Lightning" when suddenly someone tapped him on the shoulder.

It was Baldry. "Young man, it sounds like you've got a good voice there for singing R & B."

At first, Stewart thought he was having him on, but Baldry was deeply serious.

Long John explains, "I asked him if he would care to come down and have a play the following Tuesday at the Marquee. Cyril was still alive at the time, but was very unwell and wasn't doing any of the gigs. He died on Wednesday of that week, the evening after the gig Rod sat in on. The day after, I called him up and asked, 'How would you like to do the gig permanently?'"

When the All Stars got together that evening, Baldry announced his decision to continue the band. He would be keeping the group together, but added, "I'm going to change the name. We'll be Long John Baldry and the Hoochie Coochie Men now."

"What about Cyril?" asked Rod. "No one can ever replace him." Baldry looked at him intently and said, "Perhaps you could."

Stewart was promised thirty-five pounds a week. Baldry would continue to sing lead, of course, but Rod was to be second singer. "And when you're not singing, you'll be blowing harp."

Stewart quit Bob's sign-writing business the next day, much to the astonishment of his parents. They were aware of his flirtation with the Dimensions, of course, and sat patiently by while he spent hours wailing away on his harmonica. But surely that had all been just a fad? Something to do while he decided what he really wanted to make of his life. They had no idea at all that he could sing, let alone that he even wanted to. Now here was someone offering him thirty-five quid a week to do exactly that. But they weren't going to stand in his way. "Go for it, boy," said Robert. There was still more than enough time for a real career later on.

Rod Stewart made his professional debut on 6 January, 1964 and was as nervous as hell. Even though Baldry had given him only one number to sing, "Night Time Is the Right Time", as show-time approached Stewart's nerve gave out. He knew the song, he knew how he wanted to sing it, he just didn't think he would be able to go through with it.

In the dressing-room he sat silently, immaculate in his muffler, his pleated trousers suspended just above his winkle-picker shoes, and his hair painstakingly flattened against the top of his head.

"Here, mate, have one of these."

Cliff Barton, the Hoochie Coochie Men's bass player, handed Stewart a tablet of speed. "It'll calm you down." Rod gratefully swallowed the tiny pill, and when he took the stage: "I didn't half sing that number. I was up for three days after, of course."

That first ordeal over, Stewart's courage – and Baldry's enthusiasm – was bolstered significantly. While Baldry was adamant about keeping the slower numbers to himself, he willingly allowed Stewart the faster crowd-pleasers. Soon Rod was taking the spotlight for two songs – "Tiger in Your Tank" and "Dimple in Your Jaw" – and even the remaining band members, who had originally resented this flashy little git with the stuck-out arse, slowly began coming around.

"When I first joined," remembers Stewart, "no one wanted to know. John was the only one who believed in me. They were a horrible load of bastards in that band, but they all changed their mind in the end."

Baldry agrees. "In the beginning, people were saying 'Ooh good God, he's awful', and they couldn't believe his shyness! He stood with his back to the audience, he just couldn't handle looking at the audience at all! Of course now he's probably the most confident person in the world."

Stewart, it seems, made an immediate impression, both on the Hoochie Coochie Men and their fans. No longer hump-backed Roderick

Stewart, he was now forever Rod the Mod. While the rest of the group turned up in the same shoddy togs they'd worn all week, Stewart would invariably arrive resplendent in a new outfit.

Rod's favored look at this stage included his perennial muffler, a pair of gloves, a smartly tailored jacket, trousers tight around the bum, and his long hair hanging down to his collar. Friends of the time, like Ian Whitcomb, admit that they often felt embarrassed being out with him "because everyone would turn around and look. If you wore your hair like Stewart in 1964 people would wonder whether you were homosexual."

Whitcomb was one of the suburban would-be bluesmen who caught Stewart during his earliest days of elegance. "Rod was a sight for eyes used to the monochrome drabness of male fashions of the fifties. Men were in color again for the first time since Queen Victoria! The peacock struts, the backcombed hair teased into an electric shock, the leer from a fully painted, slightly skeletal face, the swag from a tight satin ass . . ."

"I used to have my hair like Dusty Springfield," Rod confesses. "It stood six inches above my head. I used bottles of hair lacquer; it was like a rock when you touched it. We used to hold our hair on the Underground platform so the bouffant wouldn't get blown down when the trains came through!"

Whitcomb continued, "Your regular bricklayer would have pronounced Rod and his ilk queers. But Stewart was not gay; rather his style was the start of an androgynous strain in pop which was to remain puzzling to outsiders."

Tony Secunda, who in later years would achieve notoriety as the quick-witted manager of pop vandals the Move, says, "Rod didn't mix very well with people; he didn't hang out much and was fairly disliked. We considered him to be a poser with a rough voice." But even he concedes women found him irresistible. "Rod was always with chicks, he was never with any guys."

Ex-Cream drummer Ginger Baker remembers Rod's early appeal. "We all used to pull Rod's leg mercilessly while he was with Baldry, because John was so very camp. Rod himself wasn't, but we always teased him about spending so much time with John." It was Baker, incidentally, who created the nicknames which have dogged Rod and John ever since. "He renamed me Ada," Baldry laughs, "and he started calling Rod Phyllis."

He also remembers walking into the men's room at Eel Pie Island one night and finding that someone – again Baker is generally regarded as the culprit – had daubed a trailer for the band's next show on the wall: "Ada Baldry and her Hoochie Coochie Ladies, featuring Phyllis Stewart." Baldry thought it was hilarious. Rod, on the other hand, was more than a little put out. He'd been doing his best to keep his nom-de-Baker secret, and here it was sprayed around for all the world to see.

Notices of forthcoming Hoochie Coochie Men gigs now included a brief postscript: "Featuring Rod the Mod, or 'The Mod's Delight'." "I used to be more worried about what I looked like than the music," Stewart later confessed.

Among Stewart's growing coterie of admirers was a pair of would-be pop managers named John Rowlands and Geoff Wright, who had been introduced to him by a young film-maker, Francis Megahy.

Megahy, with his partner Fred Burnley, was planning to make a television film about Stewart, to be called, of course, "Rod the Mod". Rowlands, who was a member of the audience, was invited along to one of the shoots, at the City Road College in London.

Already a well-established press agent, as well as an occasional actor and, in Germany, a popular comedian, Rowlands went to the show with a recent conversation still fresh in his mind.

He and Geoff Wright, another PR man, had been discussing how best to break into pop management.

"The whole secret of that field is to find the artiste first," Wright told him. "You go away and find someone, and maybe we could go into it together."

Three days later, Rowlands was back on the phone.

"I've found him."

Stewart had invited Rowlands down to the Hoochie Coochie Men's next show, at the Marquee Club on Oxford Street. Wright tagged along, and was duly mesmerised. "Rod was producing an electric atmosphere. There was no doubt in my mind he was a potential recording star.

"His act with Baldry was tremendous, and there was always a large number of girls who had come along specially to hear him. He was perpetually surrounded by beautiful birds, even in those days. Yet when he was on stage he used to handle the microphone without even looking at the audience, and then after he'd finished his spot he'd walk off to the bar and have a few beers."

Immediately following the show, the two raced backstage to speak to Stewart. The singer was enthusiastic, but typically non-committal.

"What about the band? I'm earning good money here and I don't want to jeopardise that."

Rowlands assured him they would sort something out with Baldry, who promptly agreed, "I'd never stand in Rod's way." He knew as well as anybody that once Stewart's mind was made up, only a fool would try and thwart him. Rod always got his own way in the end.

"There's another thing, though," said Stewart. "You'll have to talk

29

to me mum and dad. I have to have their consent before I can sign anything." Still only nineteen, the law considered him a minor. Rowlands and Wright agreed, and having thought the whole business over thoroughly, arranged to visit Stewart's parents.

Robert and Elsie couldn't believe what they were hearing. They knew Rod was messing about with some pop group and making a bit of money at it as well, but they *still* hadn't heard him sing. As a matter of fact, he hadn't even asked them down to one of his shows.

Rowlands and Wright, though, couldn't blame him. Stewart's act was certainly risqué for those days. Shaking his bum like a pair of maracas, always on the look-out for a grope behind the amplifiers, moving like a lord through a crowd that lived on uppers and downers washed down with booze, the unbuttoned life Stewart led on the road was a long, long way from his parents' modest flat on seedy Archway Road.

His would-be managers, of course, mentioned none of this. Instead they simply told Stewart's parents, "Rod has fantastic potential. We have no doubt we can get him a major recording contract."

Rowlands remembers, "What surprised them was that Rod was so keen to do it. To them it seemed almost a miracle that he had made up his mind because he'd always been so uncertain about everything before."

With barely a nudge from either Rowlands or Wright, the Stewarts agreed to sign the contract. If it was what Rod wanted, they were happy to go along with it. Now there was only Stewart himself left to convince.

Wright later remembered, "Rod had the contract for about two weeks before he signed it, and during that time he discussed it with his brother, Don, who was an accountant. I think that's why Rod was so shrewd with his money. He always had his brother to turn to for advice. He had long been handling Rod's financial affairs, and even in those days he was picking up about seventy pounds a week."

The pair swiftly learned just how tough a team Stewart and his brother made. The management agreement they had drawn up took a percentage off the top of all Stewart's earnings, not only as a solo artist but also as a member of the Hoochie Coochie Men.

"But I was doing that long before you guys came along," Stewart complained. "I don't think it's right that you should be collecting from that as well."

The pair reluctantly had to agree. It was either that or lose the deal.

Stewart finally signed the contract in June 1964, and with the deal done, Rowlands and Wright took him out for a meal to celebrate. They ordered champagne, but when they turned to toast this future pop potentate, he was fast asleep. The excitement of the past few weeks had apparently finally caught up with him.

That same month, Long John invited Stewart to join him in the studio to record a single. Baldry would handle the a-side, "You'll Be Mine", but the b-side, the gospel-inspired "Up Above My Head", was a song Baldry specifically selected for Stewart. It was to be a duet.

"You'll Be Mine" was Baldry's first solo single, and clearly presaged the end of the Hoochie Coochie Men. Certainly Stewart thought so, and thus threw himself into various projects which his managers were now cooking up for him.

The first of these was a recording session at a tiny studio in Poland Street, just round the corner from the Marquee. The expenses were paid by Wright's own publishing company, Independent Music, and just to keep things in the family, Rowlands and Wright brought in musicians Stewart was already accustomed to working with – Ian Armitt, Micky Waller and Cliff Barton from the Hoochie Coochie Men.

Stewart had a free hand at the session, choosing the material he most enjoyed singing – "Work Song", "Moppers Blues", "She's a Heavy Heavy Momma", "Ain't That Loving You Baby", "Just Like I Treat You", "Don't You Tell Nobody", and the ubiquitous "Bright Lights, Big City", a staple of just about every R & B band in the country. His taste in music didn't set him apart from any one of a thousand other would-be singers. His voice, however, certainly did.

Stewart had still to develop the full-throated gravel roar of later days, but he used his natural huskiness to full advantage, teasing his tonsils into sounds which may not have been completely in tune, but certainly packed an emotional punch. He also possessed boundless energy and enthusiasm, so much so that in just one afternoon all seven songs were completed. Wright immediately set about finding Stewart a record contract.

He had already made up his mind that he wanted to take Stewart to Decca first. Some seven years earlier, Wright introduced Tommy Steele to the label, and had seen the young Cockney go on to become one of the venerable old company's finest successes. Now, with the Rolling Stones only the greatest of many R & B bands on the company's books, Decca seemed the ideal home for the raunchy Stewart.

Mike Vernon, Decca's in-house R & B expert and producer at their West Hampstead studios, agreed. Vernon already knew of Stewart. Earlier that year, he and his brother Richard had begun publishing R & B Monthly, an enthusiastic amateur magazine which meticulously charted the blossoming London scene. Night after night they would hang around the clubs, selling copies and generally making themselves known. Stewart was an avid fan of the magazine, scouring it first for any reference to himself and then reading it from cover to cover.

"I was particularly good friends with Eric Clapton," Vernon remembers, "and quite often when Keith Relf [the Yardbirds' singer] was unable to play both sets – he suffered terribly from laryngitis – I would sit in with the band and play harp and sing. There were a lot of people who used to do that – Gary Farr, Ronnie Jones, Mick Jagger, another guy who had the most ridiculous name of Hogsnort Rupert, and, of course, Rod. So when his management contacted me and asked me to take a look at Stewart at the Marquee one night, I already had some idea of what to expect, although I was amazed at just how good he had become."

Vernon suggested that Stewart make another set of demos, this time under his supervision at the West Hampstead studios. Once again, the Hoochie Coochie Men would be backing him up.

Fortunately Decca liked what they heard and, at the end of August, Rod the Mod was signed to a standard five-year contract with annual options and a guaranteed minimum of two singles per year.

The next job was to choose a producer to work with Stewart on his first record. Mike Vernon, of course, was interested. So was Andrew Loog Oldham, the Rolling Stones' young manager. He had handled production duties on almost all of the Stones' discs thus far, and often telephoned Rowlands' and Wright's offices to offer his services.

In the end, however, they opted for the less dynamic Ken Horrock, and went ahead and booked the session – 11 a.m. on 10 September, 1964, at Decca's Number Two Studio. They also pulled in a who's who of available session men – drummer Bobby Graham, guitarist Brian Daly, pianist Reg Guest, and future Led Zeppelin bassist John Paul Jones. Including refreshments, they expected to bring in the entire session for under forty pounds. Unfortunately, that was the only objective they actually realised – the total cost for the afternoon was thirty-five pounds, ten shillings. Nothing else went at all according to plan.

Stewart himself remembers that he arrived at the studio right on time and introduced himself to the secretary – a woman "with a face like a bag of chisels, [who] looked up in dismay and replied, 'Rod *who*?' "

Stewart repeated his name.

"Ah yes," the secretary replied. "Well, I'm sorry, Mr Stewart, but I'm afraid you're exactly one week early for your recording appointment."

The following week, the studio was packed. Ken Horrock and his engineer, the musicians, Rowlands and Wright, a few well-wishers . . . the only person missing was Rod.

"Give him five minutes, he's probably been held up on the train," someone said. Five minutes later, "just another five. He'll be along soon." And five minutes after that . . .

By noon, the musicians were getting understandably restless, but

Rowlands and Wright were out of their minds. Finally Wright picked up the phone and called Stewart's house.

Elsie answered the phone. "Hello?"

"Is Rod there, please?"

"Yes. But he's fast asleep, I'm afraid."

Wright bit his tongue. He wanted to shout, "Well get him up, you silly cow", but instead, he calmly continued, "He's supposed to be making his record today. All the musicians are waiting in the studio . . . we're all down here waiting for him."

"Well, I'd better get him out of bed, then." Elsie then lay the phone down carefully, and padded away.

A few minutes later, Stewart appeared on the phone still sounding half-asleep. "Oh Christ, I forgot, man. I'm sorry."

He'd been down to Eel Pie Island the previous night, he explained, and hadn't arrived home until four in the morning. "I'm sorry, I over-slept, mate."

'Well, you're up now, so jump in a taxi and get the hell over here as fast as you can. We'll be waiting for you.'

"Er . . . Well, I can't really afford a taxi," Rod replied as Wright fought back another burst of anger. Stewart was earning more than a lot of people his age. Was he really that broke? "You just get the taxi and I'll pay when you get here," Wright snarled. An hour later, Stewart rolled up at the studio.

By now, of course, there was no point yelling at him. The musicians were still waiting, and valuable time was rolling on. Wright remembers, "We didn't want to upset him, late though we were. We wanted to get a good session done. Everyone was relatively calm after Rod arrived and repeated his apologies." Then Stewart dropped his second bombshell, perhaps letting slip the real reason for his late arrival.

In the weeks preceding the session, Stewart, Rowlands and Wright had thrashed out which songs Rod would be recording, and having worked out the musical arrangements, they sent the boy home to memorise the lyrics. Stewart waited until the session was due to begin and then casually announced, "I haven't learned them. I decided I didn't really like them much."

Rowlands and Wright both spun around. "What's wrong with them?"

"I don't know, they're just a bit too commercial," Stewart coolly replied.

By now, everyone was back at breaking point. "So what do *you* want to record, then? Do you want to record anything? Or should we just pack up and go home now?"

"I've heard a couple of good songs on a new LP by Sonny Boy Williamson. I'd like to have a go at them."

"Have you brought them along?"

"No." Stewart was silent for a moment, while he thought. "But there's a record shop down the road with a copy of the album in the window. I could go down and buy it, we can run through the songs a couple of times, and the band can just busk it. Shall I go and fetch it?"

"Anything, *anything*. Go and get it, we'll be waiting."

As unflustered as ever, Stewart smiled slyly and carried on. "Okay, but I'll be needing some money to pay for it. Two pounds should do." At least the boy was consistent!

The two songs Stewart was so enamored of were "Good Morning Little Schoolgirl" and "I Am Gonna Move to the Outskirts of Town", and as he had predicted, once the band heard the songs, they soon had them down pat. He laid down his vocals, and after all the dramas of the first couple of hours, even Ken Horrock agreed that the job was well done.

Stewart himself was most impressed by the end result. "A white person can sing the blues with just as much conviction as a Negro," he said at the time. "All these colored singers singing about 'walking down the railroad' . . . they've never walked down a railroad track in their lives. Nor have I. You've got more to sing the blues about in the Archway Road than on any railroad track I know." It was a suitably arrogant response to the host of critics who greeted Stewart – and the thousand other blueswailin' young Stewarts out there – with doubts about either their sincerity or authenticity.

But the misfortune which was dogging Rowlands and Wright still had one final, cruel trick to play. Just weeks before Stewart recorded his "Good Morning Little Schoolgirl", the Yardbirds had taped their own rocking version, completely re-arranging the song, even slipping a veiled obscenity into one of the verses. And while their cover was only a minor hit, reaching number forty-four on the UK chart, even Stewart knew that in terms of presentation his version lagged far, far behind. "It was a good enough record, it was like a white attempt . . . before its time. But I thought it was good, anyway."

The record's failure, and the awful timing which added insult to injury, turned Decca right off. They simply neglected to ask Stewart for a second single, and by the end of the first year allowed his contract to lapse.

Nevertheless, some good did come of the exercise. To promote the record, Rowlands and Wright succeeded in booking Stewart on a succession of TV shows, beginning with the BBC's "Beat Room", on 6 August, 1964, and culminating in October with "Ready Steady Go", still the most important, and influential, pop television program Britain has ever produced – and that despite it vanishing from TV screens nearly a quarter of a century ago.

Stewart sang his song, then made his way backstage. He knew many of the artists appearing on the show that week, but one, standing by the bar with a beer, caught his eye. Stewart wandered over and introduced himself.

"Hi, I'm Rod."

"Yeah, Rod the Mod. Great song, mate."

Ronnie Wood was the guitarist with the Birds, a west London R & B band whose greatest claim to fame thus far had been an on-going battle with the American group, the Byrds, over who had the right to so distinctive a name. The two eventually agreed that the two bands could never be confused with one another, either visually or on record, but the publicity generated by the fracas was enough to win the Birds a recording deal with Decca almost immediately afterwards. Their first single, "You're On My Mind", was released on almost exactly the same day as Stewart's.

After the show, Stewart and Woody drifted away from the RSG studios in London's Kingsway, and found themselves a comfortable pub in Soho. Stewart already knew Woody's brother, Art – leader of another London band, the Artwoods. Soon they discovered they had a lot more in common, too.

They liked the same music, fancied the same type of girls, yet still Woody later admitted, "I'd always dug Rod when he was Rod the Mod. But I never thought anything would come of it. In fact, Stewart was one of the last people I would have imagined I'd end up spending my career with. You see, it's funny because we're totally different guys. We lead completely different lives . . . [but] there's a close tie in there somewhere. I mean, we often socialise together, which is pretty amazing in this day and age."

Woody was to remain a constant factor in Stewart's life for the next decade, something for which the singer was grateful. He would become a sounding-board for Stewart's ideas, a shoulder to cry on, and a buddy to loon about with. They drank together, bought their first cars together . . . and when they had tired of them, bought their second cars together as well. They even picked up girls together, Woody joining the slowly growing band of Rod's mates who, as Baldry remembers, were turning his newly purchased house in Reece Mews into a knocking shop.

Conveniently located, says Baldry, between the Cromwellian Club and South Kensington tube station, with its endless parade of high-stepping "dolly birds", Rod and his mates would frequently crash there for a night, usually with a new young lady in tow. Baldry himself would graciously leave, either for the pub or the cinema, and try not to imagine just what was taking place in his tastefully appointed home.

Slowly, Rod the Mod, with his expensive tastes and flashy demeanor, and Ron "Woody" Wood, with his cackling laugh and down-to-earth manner, worked their way through an apprenticeship which, when completed, would establish them among the most potent double acts in rock'n'roll.

3

Trial By Fire

Out on the town one night, Long John ran into TV producer Jack Good, then casting a Beatles television special, the ninety-minute "Around The Beatles".

It was a variety show with several different artists appearing, and Good thought the suave, sophisticated Baldry would be a natural. But there was one proviso. Music for the various performers was being supplied by one band, Sound Spectrum. The Hoochie Coochie Men were not invited.

The exposure the show offered was phenomenal. Shot in May 1964, by the middle of the following year it had been seen all over the world. To Baldry's manager, Martin Davies, it was a life-saver.

Long John, it seems, was going through severe financial difficulties at the time. "We had two saxophone players, there was Rod, a piano, guitar, bass and drums, plus numerous road staff, and it was a lot of financial upkeep," he recalls.

"I was entirely broke and thousands in debt. I've always believed in paying musicians good money, but I came unstuck with the Hoochie Coochie Men. There just wasn't the work and I was still paying out vast amounts – vans, clothes, instruments, wages, the whole bit. It simply left me broke." For a time, Baldry even considered declaring bankruptcy.

Stewart, though, was not unduly perturbed by the band's demise. He, too, was under pressure to strike out on his own, and shortly after "Good Morning Little Schoolgirl" was released, he agreed to give it a go, playing a solo concert with another of Rowlands' and Wright's clients, the Ad Libs, backing him up.

The show was not, at least from Stewart's perspective, a great success. But with managers insisting that it was just a matter of getting the right line-up behind him, Rod agreed to try again.

This time he linked up with a Southampton R & B band, the Soul Agents – a group whose greatest claim to fame thus far was playing their shows in bare feet.

With Stewart on vocals (and, of course, shoes – he was far too fashion-conscious ever to stoop to his bandmates' seamy level), the Soul Agents played a handful of shows throughout the winter of 1964–65, usually at the Marquee, but also at the Bromley Court Hotel.

But Stewart was still unhappy. The Soul Agents were strangers to him. They lived different lives, they ran with a different crowd. Stewart persevered simply because his managers told him to, and because he couldn't think of anything else to do.

Long John Baldry, too, was having second thoughts about a solo career – little more than one month after he had begun it. He was already considering putting together a new group when he ran into Giorgio Gomelski one night at the Crawdaddy.

Gomelski was one of the greatest things ever to happen to British R & B. Half-French, half-Russian, Gomelski's life was dominated by his undaunted passion for rhythm and blues, and he had traveled the world in search of it.

In London, Gomelski had established a jazz club, the Crawdaddy, where he highlighted a band whose potential he, almost alone in pre-Beatles London, recognised – the Dave Hunt Band, featuring guitarist Ray Davies, Stewart's old team-mate from the William Grimshaw XI.

Later, the embryonic Rolling Stones became the house band, and when they moved on, Gomelski brought in the Yardbirds. By 1963, the Crawdaddy was probably the best-known hang-out in London. Almost every night they weren't playing elsewhere, Stewart and Long John would be there, mixing with friends and musicians, and getting to know the likeable, charismatic European who loved them all so dearly.

Gomelski's favorite pastime was spotting new talent and nurturing it. In many ways it was a self-defeating exercise; had he maintained his early interest in the Rolling Stones, it would have been Giorgio Gomelski and not Andrew Oldham who oversaw the band's drive to stardom. But he had moved on, to discover the Yardbirds, and now, just one year later, they were being relegated to second place by another new project – Steampacket.

Amongst the many bands whose careers Gomelski was then handling was the Brian Auger Trinity, a funky R & B trio which featured Auger on keyboards, bassist Rick Brown, and old Hoochie Coochie drummer Mickey Waller.

Auger was a relatively recent convert to rhythm and blues; only two years earlier, he had won a jazz poll in the weekly *Melody Maker* magazine. But having recently replaced his piano with a Hammond organ, and with both Waller and Brown former members of Cyril Davies' All Stars, he was beginning to win a reputation on this new circuit, too.

"In May or June 1965, I got a call from John Baldry's managers, asking if I would be interested in meeting with them," remembers Auger.

"John had seen me play at the Twisted Wheel in Manchester, and was very interested in working with the Trinity.

"This was great news to me, because John was a fantastic draw, one of the biggest going at that point. He was also probably the best blues singer in Europe at the time.

"So I said I thought it was a great idea, because it would help pull me even further away from my own jazz roots.

"We talked about that for a while, and then John said, 'I have this sort of protégé I'd like to include in the band', and that was Rod."

Auger already knew Stewart. "I'd seen him with the Soul Agents a few times, and I knew he was a pretty good singer – he even sat in with the early Trinity a couple of times, at the Marquee. We jammed together and things like that, so I said I don't see any problem with that. I thought it was strange that there would be two singers in the band, but it could work.

"Then I thought why not extend it even further? I had recently done a couple of sessions with Julie Driscoll, who Giorgio was also managing at the time, so I suggested we include her as well. The idea was that I would come on and play a couple of instrumentals, then Julie could do her numbers, then Rod, then John. It would give a unique look to the band, and of course it would be completely different to anything else that was happening."

Predictably, the only objections came from Stewart. In all seriousness, he turned round and said, "Wait a minute! We're not going to be able to swear if we have a chick in the band! Why don't we get a tenor sax player instead?"

Two years younger than Stewart, Julie was best known as the vivacious secretary of the Yardbirds' fan club. Gomelski, however, was determined to introduce her to a wider audience – and with good reason. Not only did she have a fabulous voice, she was also a stunning beauty, "the best and sexiest thing in Europe" according to writer Nik Cohn. The idea of Julie and Stewart together on one stage would be enough to send every red-blooded libido in London into salivating overdrive. Guitarist Vic Briggs completed the line-up, and the dream was complete.

Auger remembers, "It was like a package thing. There was me playing more or less jazz stuff; Julie doing rhythm and blues things from Wilson Pickett through Aretha Franklin to Nina Simone and Oscar Brown, which was quite a variety of material; there was Rod, who was singing Tamla things and straight Chicago blues; and then there was John, who I thought was the best white blues singer of the period. It was quite good really."

Stewart's repertoire included several of the same grizzled old standards as he performed during his days with the Hoochie Coochie Men, plus the occasional Sam Cooke number – "Shake" and "Another Saturday Night", and the Drifters' "On Broadway". The greatest thrill, however, was when he performed "I Just Got Some", a blatantly sexual song which, although nobody could have known it back then, was to set the tone for the next two decades of Rod's life. "You can't hide it 'cos I know where it's at," he would leer at the girls clustered around the front of the stage; "my pockets are as heavy as a chunk of lead" – a reference, of course, to a sizeable erection; "I just got a taste of her meat and veg."

Musical ambitions aside, Steampacket was also something of a fashion show. "It was a very good visual band," Stewart later recalled, "with everybody trying to outdo each other with their clothes."

Photographs of the band bear him out. Center stage would be Julie, her eyes ringed with cobra-like eye-liner, dressed in the latest Swinging London chic. To her right was Rod, resplendent in white jacket and Beau Brummel shirt, his hair teased to perfection, the epitome of Moddom. And to her left, Baldry in a tight black sweater and trousers topped by his dazzling blond hair – the darling of the sexually adventurous. Rumor had it he was homosexual, a charge Baldry never denied. Rather, he would play on it, never missing an opportunity to throw a bit of tease into the set, letting loose a barrage of sexy non-sequiturs from his arsenal of camp one-liners.

Simon Napier Bell, who would one day replace Gomelski as manager of the Yardbirds, remembers "his incessant camp banter", and Stewart still recalls the words with which Baldry would introduce him: "And here he is, ladies – and whatever you've got with you – Rod 'The Mod' Stewart!"

"It was a very powerhouse band," recalls Tony Secunda. "They could go into a club and do the whole evening, each member performing their own specialty piece. It was very exciting." And Driscoll continues of the moments when she and Rod performed together, "Our voices went well together. We duetted on things like 'My Guy'." But she adds, although with scarcely a hint of the animosity which used to go down between the two performers, "I enjoyed working with Rod, except that we used to like the same kind of songs, and he always got the first pickings." Many a time, Julie would have quietly to acquiesce while Rod got the chance to perform a song she'd had her own heart set upon.

Steampacket had been together for less than three months when they got their big break. They were invited to tour Britain with the Rolling Stones and the Walker Brothers.

The Stones were now arguably as big as the Beatles. Their last three singles had topped the UK charts, and the unholy trinity of Jagger, Richard and Jones were no less household names than the lovable John, Paul, Ringo and George.

The Walker Brothers, on the other hand, were still relatively new to British audiences, but were destined for stardom regardless. Fronted by the almost supernaturally beautiful Scott Walker, the three Americans had two chart-toppers to their credit, and were just as capable as the Stones of whipping their predominantly adolescent female audience into a fit of ritual knicker-wetting.

The Stones/Walkers tour opened in Exeter, on 16 July, 1965, passed through Portsmouth, Bournemouth and Great Yarmouth, then climaxed on 1 August at the London Palladium.

Every night Steampacket would stand at the side of the stage, marvelling at the intensity of the hysteria which true pop superstardom could bring. "It was," Auger later remarked, "quite an eye-opener." Particularly so to Stewart, who vowed there and then that one day he too would be so screamed for.

But he doubted that it would happen with Steampacket, that unwieldy behemoth of a band. Club audiences loved them, and obviously appreciated what they were doing. When they played the National Jazz and Blues Festival in Richmond, they were one of the stars of the show. But on the wider circuit of ballrooms and theaters, the kids would rather scream for the poppy headliners than the progressive Steampacket. Not even Rod the Mod could charm his way through the chaos. There were times when he wondered what he was even doing in the band.

"Julie was always in love with somebody," he remembers. "Mickey Waller was in love with her, and Brian always wanted more money. Ricky Brown didn't want to leave home 'cause he'd just got married, so we couldn't go any further than Manchester," Stewart later recalled. He forgets to add that he was often very much in the thick of it himself.

For a short time, Stewart and Julie had themselves been lovers, and Auger recalls the night it ended. "Julie had all sorts of complexes about her appearance at that point. She was a very good-looking lady, but she had a bit of puppy fat on her, as a lot of teenagers do, and she was extremely sensitive about this.

"One night we were in the band room at Klooks Kleek in West Hampstead, and Rod and Julie had obviously had a bit of a spat. Suddenly, Rod made an extremely unkind reference to Julie's legs, which he knew she was very sensitive about, something along the lines of, 'Well the hell with you, Fat Legs.'

"Of course, this triggered a whole fucking screaming match which went on for about half an hour. Julie threw a glass of beer at Rod's feet, then hit him in the face and blacked his eye, and the rest of us were just sitting there with our mouths open, wondering how he could have said something that cruel.

"So this was going on, and it was really uncomfortable for the rest of us. Now, in films, when a lady is screaming, if you slap her round the face, it brings her to her senses. It works all the time in Hollywood, so our agent, George, whacked Julie one, only it made things worse."

The whole affair, he says, did little for his love of Stewart, while Baldry remembers that the incident permanently soured Rod and Julie's relationship. "Rod being Rod, he never got over it."

Driscoll was one of several girlfriends whose company Stewart enjoyed at this time – Jenny Ryland, one of Julie's best friends, was another – but according to Auger he was still spending most of his time with Sarah.

The mysterious Sarah was living with her mother in Wilton Crescent, London when she and Rod first met. Later, the pair of them set up house together, and Auger laughs as he remembers the countless phone calls he has received over the years from journalists wanting the scoop on the teenaged Stewart's sex life.

"Basically, we were all raving steamers at that time, and there were a lot of ladies about. But I don't remember Rod being particularly worse than anyone else – he had that one girlfriend, and pretty much stuck to her the whole time."

The biggest problem he had with Stewart, he remembers, was money. "He was a very happy-go-lucky kind of guy, but very close-fisted with money. We'd go out on a ten-day tour, and he would turn up with one pound in his pocket, then spend the rest of the time trying to get an advance on his next pay packet. One day I asked him why he didn't bring more money with him. He said, 'Well, I have to put it in my Post Office savings account. I've got to save it. That's what my mum tells me.' And then he turned round and said, 'Buy us a drink, someone?'"

It was on one such outing that Steampacket were booked to appear at a coming-out party for the privileged heirs to the Guinness brewing fortune. It was staged at the family estate in the north of England, and Auger remembers, "It turned out to be completely crazy; a typical Steampacket disaster."

The band arrived on time, and immediately found themselves in a scene straight out of an Evelyn Waugh novel. Everyone was walking around in gowns – dowagers, duchesses, with all the guys decked out in smoking-jackets.

Steampacket ran straight for the bar, lining up the double port and brandies. As Auger remembers, "By the time we were ready to play, a lot of drink had been imbibed."

Auger began the evening with a few short instrumental numbers, before Julie joined him for her showcase. So far, so good. Taking the microphone, Auger introduced Rod. There was a polite smattering of applause, but no Mr Stewart.

Brian tried again, just a little louder. Still nothing. Apologising profusely, Auger returned to his Hammond and played yet another song. Then he called over the band's roadie, Eric Brookes. "Where the hell is Rod?"

"I don't know. Last I saw of him he was knocking around with this red-headed bit with enormous tits. I'll go and look in a few bedrooms, shall I?" When the roadie returned, however, he was on his own. "Where is he?" Auger hissed impatiently. "Didn't you find him?"

"Oh, I found him alright, upstairs giving that redhead a bloody good rogering."

"Well, didn't you tell him it was time he was on?"

"Yeah. I told him. And he told me to fuck off."

"Things started going downhill rapidly," remembers Auger, "so I forgot about Rod and announced John instead. He didn't appear either. So off went Eric again, and again he returned empty-handed."

"Now what's the problem?" asked Auger. "What's going on? Where is everybody?"

"Well, I found John, but there's been an accident."

Baldry had sunk "three or four double port and brandies", and while he waited for his turn to perform, went into the dressing-room to lie down. "He had a headache," Eric continued, "it was dark in there, so fair enough.

"The next thing he knew, some guy had come wandering in, not knowing John was there, and he heaved this very big, very heavy suitcase on to the bed. It caught John right in the balls."

"After the show," Auger explains, "there was a firework display outside. Right in the middle of this, stumbling through the rose bushes and flower beds, comes old Rod and a couple of rather tasty birds. And Rod starts calling out bingo numbers at the top of his voice, as the fireworks are going off; 'on the blue 22', things like that. It didn't go down at all well, everybody was pissed off with us, and a few days later a letter arrived from the Guinness people saying they weren't going to pay us 'due to our cavalier behavior'."

Both Stewart and Long John retained their own managership throughout Steampacket's existence, so that any decisions relating to the band had to travel through three different offices – Gomelski's included. Everything, it seemed, was a potential bone of contention, but the most contentious of all, it seemed, was the fate of any recordings the band might make.

While Gomelski insisted that Steampacket be treated as a separate entity and allowed to record wherever Gomelski felt they ought to, Long John's manager, Martin Davies, demanded that everything be channelled through Baldry's existing deal with United Artists. While they fought, the band just sat around waiting, breaking up before the row was ever resolved. The only tapes that exist of Steampacket are a handful of crude studio demos, several live tapes, and a few television clips taken from "Ready Steady Go".

"For what was happening at the time in England, I think we were pretty good," says Long John today. "Looking back on it now, it seems fairly daft. There certainly wasn't anything left behind in terms of recording that was any good. The only tapes that ever came out were some rough old things Giorgio taped from a rehearsal at the Marquee. Dreadful stuff!"

According to Auger, the band had just one official recording session – and that ended in disaster. "They did the most terrible things to us," he says. "We were playing in Newcastle, when we got a call from Giorgio, saying the only available studio time was at nine o'clock the following morning, in London. So we drove 300 miles back, getting in around seven in the morning, and actually made it into the Advision studios. We did one session which was abandoned because it was just impossible. It simply wasn't working!"

Stewart complains, "If I wanted to do a new number, I had to put it forward to the 'Board' [Brian, John and Rod himself]. I never really got on with Auger all that well."

The feeling was apparently mutual, as Auger explains. "There were no big bust-ups, but a lot of niggling little incidents – the business with Julie, money of course, and also the fact that Rod was so universally uncooperative."

As the band's musical leader, Auger's duties in Steampacket ranged from making sure everybody turned up for rehearsals and gigs and driving one of the band's two vans from show to show, to liaising between the group and its managers. Rowlands and Wright, he remembers, were not too much of a problem – "they only seemed to be around when there was some money to collect" – but Gomelski and Davies were constantly at odds, usually when their unity was the thing the band needed most.

In August 1965, the Yardbirds finally broke through in the United States, and of course Giorgio Gomelski followed them Stateside. "I didn't see him for months," Auger remembers. "We spent five or six days a week on the road, and the rest of my time on the telephone, trying to keep things together: picking people up, paying the band's wages, dealing with all the problems that came up, going with John to talk to his manager and having nobody there who could take this load off me."

Even the band's own opportunity to visit America was scuppered by their internal disarray. "We could have gone with Eric Burdon and the Animals," Stewart remembered, "but John turned it down, the silly bastard." Baldry's final words on the subject have remained with Stewart ever since. "My American public isn't yet ready for me."

Despite Steampacket's own lack of studio work, each of its components – the Trinity, Stewart, Long John and Julie – all recorded solo records during their time with the band, often with Auger and the rest of the Trinity providing accompaniment.

Stewart's first effort was "The Day Will Come", released in November 1965. It arrived hot on the heels of the television premier of the now eighteen-month-old "Rod the Mod" documentary, but the exposure did Stewart little good. Neither "The Day Will Come" nor its follow-up, Sam Cooke's "Shake", sold more than a handful of copies.

He was still recovering from that disappointment when, he claims, he was fired from Steampacket. Not surprisingly, finances were at the root of the disagreement, although there is some dispute about just how and why matters finally came to a head. Certainly, with Auger wanting better pay for his role as the band's musical director, Stewart demanding more and more for his wardrobe, and the rest of the band seeking financial equity, there were seven too many hands reaching into the till. The band simply wasn't earning enough to justify its members' increasingly extravagant lifestyles.

As for Stewart's departure, according to Auger it was he who walked out, because "it looked like the whole thing was going to fall on its arse. The band was so popular that we were working an average of five nights a week over a period of nearly two years, driving all those distances and hauling gear up and down. And yet I was getting calls at 9 o'clock every Monday morning, 'Would you please come to the office, there's a problem with whoever it was we've just done a gig for.' I was pretty tired and I was getting to the point where something had to give. It was obvious we weren't going to record, there were all these arguments between the managers, I could see the writing on the wall."

The end of Steampacket came when the group was offered a three-week residency at the Voom Voom Club in St Tropez. Auger was all for it – they could treat it as a working holiday if nothing else. The only problem was, the money was so bad that they couldn't afford to take the whole group.

A meeting was called between Gomelski, Martin Davies, the band's agent, George Webb, Auger, Baldry, and whoever Rod's management chose to send along – which turned out to be no one at all. So when it came time to choose who would not be taking the trip, nobody was there to argue Stewart's case.

"His management knew about the meeting," insists Auger, "and so did Rod. But nobody showed up, and the one person who I thought would vote for Rod, which was John, didn't say a word. So that was it. In truth, we were all getting a bit fed up with Rod's antics. He never helped, wouldn't drive, was always cadging drinks, so he didn't endear himself to the band all that much, and although we laughed it off at the time, at the end of the day if someone had to be left behind, it was him.

"Rod says I fired him from the band, and when he became very big in England I couldn't pick up the papers without reading this. But that's bullshit. The truth of the matter is, *everybody* fired him.''

Bitterness still tinges Stewart's recollections of the band. "Looking back, there was never anything really original about Steampacket. We probably sold ourselves on our character more than our music. It wasn't the most original band to be in.''

Tony Secunda agrees. "Musically, they were only doing what was already happening, the songs that were already hits. There was no sense of forging new ground, or breaking through barriers. They were singing old Otis songs and Sam Cooke. I always thought Rod Stewart was a clone, singing other people's music.''

If Rod was a clone, however, what did that say for the growing number of people turning up at the band's gigs who were themselves doing their damnedest to look like Stewart? Brian Auger remembers, "I noticed a lot of them turning up at gigs, and some of them were pretty good. We called them Roddies, and I remember one night there was one standing in front of me, wearing the same brown jacket as our Roddy always wore, and I thought it was him! We were just about to go on, so I tapped him on the shoulder, 'Come on, Rod, we're on now', and it wasn't him!''

Out on his own once again, Stewart wondered what to do next. "For the first time I was really worried about what I was going to do," he fretted. "I was really into my music by then, and I felt I'd given a lot to that band.''

The failure of "Shake" only added to his despair, not only because Cooke was his idol, but also because he regarded his performance as "a crossing of the water", the moment when he finally made the transition from his shaky white-boy blues to pure unfettered soul music.

The early 1960s saw a number of American soul singers hit England, usually as part of a traveling package, and Stewart had swiftly fallen under their spell. His ultimate hero was Otis Redding, so tragically killed in a plane crash in 1967. "The first time I ever saw Otis was in 1967, on the first British Stax tour, which had Sam and Dave, Carla

Thomas and the MGs. Otis was so good he made me cry. I never met him, though, I was just a face in the crowd.

"I think anybody who wants to get into rock'n'roll has got something to learn from Otis. To any up-and-coming and budding singer, I would say, 'Listen to Otis before you listen to me, Bon Jovi or Robert Plant.'"

And he adds, "I'd have given my right arm to see Sam Cooke perform." To this day, Cooke, the black American soul man who was murdered by a jealous husband in 1964, remains Stewart's single greatest influence. For some two years, on either side of his recording "Shake", Cooke was one of the few artists Stewart was seriously listening to, later admitting, "It had to do with the way I sounded. I didn't sound at all like anybody, Ray Charles or anybody, but I knew I sounded a bit like Cooke, so I listened to him."

Stewart was once asked if he ever consciously emulated Cooke. Rod said no, adding, "If I'd done one of his numbers, I might have. But I've never sung one, probably never will. I wouldn't dare touch one of his tunes after he's sung them."

In fact, Stewart recorded two other Sam Cooke songs on the day he tackled "Shake", "Meet Me at Mary's Place" and one other, whose title neither he, nor anybody else, seems to remember. In later years, he would record several more. But in 1966, nobody cared a jot about an obscure would-be soul singer croaking his way through someone else's greatest hits. In fact, there was virtually no interest in any of Stewart's recordings, and as they slipped into obscurity, so Rod began worrying that he, too, might be headed the same way.

Guitarist Pete Bardens, however, had other ideas.

Bardens had known Stewart since the days of the Hoochie Coochie Men, when Bardens himself was leading a group called Peter B's Looners. The two bands occasionally gigged together at the Flamingo Club in Soho, and Bardens remembers, "We were more or less an instrumental band playing Booker T-type material. But the Looners just weren't diverse or remunerative enough to remain a viable proposition. So we decided to restructure."

As soon as he heard Stewart was available, Bardens got in touch. He was augmenting the Looners with a new vocalist, Beryl Marsden, a Liverpudlian, and a member of Beatles manager Brian Epstein's famous "stable of stars". Now, inspired by Steampacket, he was considering broadening things even further, and wanted Rod up front with Beryl. After all the disappointments embodied in Steampacket, Stewart could scarcely contain his excitement.

Unfortunately, what seemed straightforward to Stewart was not always so clear-cut to the people around him. When Rod first mentioned the new band to his own management team, their response was, "And how much money will *you* be getting out of all this?"

Rowlands and Wright knew that however much Stewart received from the band, it would never be enough. But at least if they could arrange things beforehand, there was a slim chance he might be kept happy. Plus, all this talk about not thinking of the money . . . that wasn't Stewart, that was blind enthusiasm. So was his repeated insistence that Shotgun Express, as the band was to be called, was all he had ever wanted from a group. How many times had they heard that line before!

It didn't help that Bardens and Stewart, swept away by the spirit of the moment, had already introduced the band to its public. They arranged a competition with the music paper *Disc*, announcing the new group's line-up and asking for suggestions for a name. After that sort of build-up, Stewart didn't want anything to get in the way.

In which case, it was probably a mistake to invite him along to one of the regular business meetings. Bardens' manager, Rik Gunnell, had a reputation as a very hard man to do business with. If Rowlands pushed him too far, who knew what might happen?

"This new band of yours is very interesting," Rowlands began slyly. "But we are by no means certain that it's the right thing for Rod to be involved in just now."

Gunnell retaliated by saying he wasn't sure whether Stewart was the right man for the band anyway. At the moment, they were simply sounding out different people. No, he wasn't in a position to give names . . . but to be frank, they were all certainly bigger than Stewart.

Back and forth went the conversation, both Rowlands and Gunnell arguing the singer's worth in the basest financial terms. He was the greatest vocalist in the world, an artist whose potential was obvious to everyone; he was a three-band loser, with a string of flop singles to his name. He was worth a fortune; he was worth no more than the clothes he stood up in. He was a dazzling showman; he was a posturing buffoon. He was worth every penny the band would earn; he was worth somewhat less than a small hill of beans. On and on it went until finally Stewart exploded into tears. "Look, am I in or aren't I?"

Poor Rod was never invited to another meeting.

Shotgun Express did finally get off the ground, but only just. This was a very fluid time in rock'n'roll; new bands were forming from the wreckage of old ones every day, and the Express was as much fair game as any other talent-packed combo.

Peter Green, the band's startling young guitarist, was the first through the door, driven out by an unfortunate romance with Beryl and a better offer from John Mayall's Bluesbreakers. But while drummer Mick Fleetwood insists that "the piss really went out of the band when Peter left", Bardens had no intention of calling it quits just yet.

Green was replaced by John Mooreshead, and the band limped on in increasing disarray.

Finally, even Bardens was forced to admit, "It just lost momentum. Phil often didn't appear for gigs, Beryl was perpetually at the hair-dresser's, Rod was always in bed, and the administration got to be too great a problem. It didn't matter where we were playing, we never left for a gig before four o'clock – so we were always late."

According to Mick Fleetwood, "We always used to go down well, because it was a good show." He remembers that at one point the Express was earning £200 a night, simply playing on the London club circuit – venues like the Marquee, the Flamingo, the Ram Jam in Brixton, and the Ricky Tick. They also had a strong, and equally lucrative, follow-ing in northern England.

But now Stewart found himself wishing that Rowlands had been a little tougher on Rik Gunnell, had maybe squeezed another few pounds out of him. For Stewart, even the mildest band argument would sooner or later get round to the sorry state of his wallet. "It's me people are coming to see, remember, but how can I look good on this sort of shit money?"

The rest of the group would retaliate by calling him lazy. Roadies had yet to come into fashion in 1966, and Shotgun Express was just one of the thousands of tiny bands still humping their own equipment around, with maybe just a couple of friends to help lighten the load.

Stewart, however, made it a creed to lift as little gear as possible, usually vanishing the moment he got off the stage, only to reappear once the work had been done. With his mike in one hand and a glass in the other, he'd ask, "Aren't you lot ready yet? I was done hours ago."

"We'd be a helluva lot quicker if you'd help out occasionally."

With that, Stewart would smooth his new jacket and simply stare in amazement. He didn't ask Bardens to carry his mike for him – why should he be expected to start lugging round organ cabinets? Why indeed.

Unfortunately for Stewart, however, that little trick worked both ways. One evening – Bardens thinks it was either in Aylesbury or Bristol – Stewart was standing at the bottom of a flight of stairs, watching the others wrestle a huge speaker cabinet into position for the descent.

Suddenly someone slipped. The cabinet teetered at the top of the stairs for a moment, then plummeted down, right on to Stewart. He wasn't hurt, but his well-known pride was, predictably, badly bruised.

Bardens says, "Stewart was extremely egotistical, and very aware of his image, and that sort of thing used to get on my nerves. He used to argue a lot with Beryl, who was a very untogether sort of person. A lot of the time he was great, and then other times he got up my nose and could be really nasty.

"I never managed to feel very close to Stewart because he always had a very biting sense of humor. It's difficult to remember specific things he said, but if he wanted to reduce someone to size he was very good at doing it and invariably it would make you laugh."

Unless, of course, you happened to be the target, or perhaps a concerned witness. Bardens remembers, "Stewart and his girlfriend went out with me and my girlfriend, and he was really rude to the girl he was with which was very embarrassing." Bardens never discovered what the poor young lady did to merit the weight of Stewart's wrath. Stewart simply wasn't the kind of person you could sidle up to later and ask, "Hey, mate, what was that all about, then?"

Not that Stewart was the only ego in the band. Bardens admits they all had their moments. "There were always a lot of moodies going on, a combination of general discontent and a feeling we weren't getting anywhere, and although we were all individually good by the standards of those days, I don't really think it worked bringing us all together. That wasn't a situation in which the group could be expected to have a very good life expectancy."

Stewart himself saw Shotgun Express as almost an extension of Steampacket, the only difference being things weren't quite so regimented. Rehearsals, even gigs, were chaotic, often marred by Beryl turning up late. Someone would rush off to telephone her – and find she was at the hairdresser's again. Keeping up with Stewart, it seemed, could be a full-time occupation.

Ironically, in view of the virtue he was later to make of such qualities, sloppiness was something Stewart could never tolerate, except, of course, if it was him being sloppy. Then, just as his managers had learned at his first recording session, Stewart could reason his way around most anything.

Bardens saw that side of Stewart more times than he cared to remember – the spoilt brat of Rod's Highbury youth, it seemed, was still very much alive and kicking.

Like Steampacket before them, Shotgun Express had little time or inclination for writing their own material, running instead through a catalog of other people's hits – "Knock on Wood", "In the Midnight Hour", "634-5789 That's My Number", and so on. Their one record, too, was a cover version. "I Can Feel the World Go Round" (released in October 1966) predictably did nothing.

The band broke up shortly thereafter. According to Brian Auger, who heard the story from Dave Ambrose, "They just couldn't get to the gigs, they were so disorganised. They had plenty of work; they just couldn't get their arses out of town. In the end, John Gunnell invited them up for a meeting, and once they had all arrived he took a piece of paper out of his desk and said, 'Now you're all here, I have something to show you. This is your contract.' He then tore it into shreds, threw it on the ground and screamed, 'Now get the fuck out of here.' And that was the end of the Shotgun Express."

Mick Fleetwood went on to rejoin Green in the Bluesbreakers, and later still became a founding member of Fleetwood Mac; Dave Ambrose linked with a revamped Brian Auger Trinity; Peter Bardens formed Camel, one of the most acclaimed bands of the early 1970s; Beryl Marsden became a solo artist; and Stewart all but excised the whole lot of them from his memory. Shotgun Express make no contribution whatsoever to the *Storyteller* retrospective, and when journalist Pete Frame brought up the subject with Stewart in 1971, the singer's response was so vituperative that it could only have been printed "if we had the bread to defend a libel case."

"I was still getting this terrible feeling of doing other people's music," Stewart later complained to the *New Musical Express*. "I think you only start finding yourself when you write your own material." In November 1966, when Shotgun Express finally bit the bullet, the opportunity to do just that was a lot closer than he ever imagined.

Throughout his career, Stewart found himself constantly crossing paths with the Yardbirds. There were those early days spent sitting in for an ailing Keith Relf; there was his association with Mike Vernon, who produced the Yardbirds; there was his time under the aegis of Giorgio Gomelski, the group's first manager. Now Woody was telling him that he ought to call Jeff Beck, the second in the holy trinity of lead guitarists who ran through the Yardbirds' ranks. The others, of course, were Eric Clapton and Jimmy Page.

Beck quit the Birds at the height of their fame. They had just scored their seventh hit with the frenetic "Over Under Sideways Down", and were caught midway through a typically explosive live set in David Hemmings' latest movie, *Blow Up*.

But Jeff was miserably unhappy. The band's newly recruited bassist, Jimmy Page, obviously had eyes for Beck's lead guitar slot, and although the Yardbirds willingly accommodated both musicians' egos, running for a short time with twin guitars, something had to give.

Rumors of Beck's departure were not helped by the Yardbirds' own office issuing, and then retracting, statements to that effect. Finally, in December 1966, he formally packed it in.

For a time, Beck later admitted, "I didn't even touch my guitar, and when I came to play again I was hopeless." Slowly he was edged back into the habit of playing, first by Jimmy Page, who recruited him for some session work, then by his manager, Mickie Most. By early in the new year, he was ready to take the plunge once again – which was when Ronnie Wood telephoned him. "Hello, mate, I hear you're putting together a new group."

He and Beck were friends from years before, back in the days when Jeff was still ploughing the west London circuit in his first group, the Tridents, and Woody was the fresh-faced guitarist with the Thunderbirds (as the Birds were originally called). The two bands had gigged together a few times, and were proud to call one another rivals.

But while Beck had gone on to international fame, Woody had simply run himself into the ground. The Birds had split six months earlier, and a brief spell in the Creation hadn't worked out at all. Ever the gentleman, Beck was happy to help him back on his feet.

Beck recalls his initial meeting with Stewart. "One slack night at the Cromwellian, there was this guy plowing into some food and getting drunk on his own: Rod Stewart. He didn't even look at me, so I went over to see what was happening. He was really drunk, so I asked him whether he was still playing with Steampacket; I'd seen him with them and he was outrageous. He said no, so I said, 'If you ever want to put a band together . . .'"

Stewart joined the group the following day, just in time to see Beck's other new recruits – bassist Jet Harris, late of Cliff Richard's backing group the Shadows, and ex-Pretty Things drummer Viv Prince – depart.

A succession of nondescript drummers came and went before Beck finally found one he liked, his fellow ex-Trident, Ray Cook. But there wasn't one bass player in town who met the guitarist's exacting standards. Finally, Beck had an idea. He had brought Woody in as a second guitarist. How would he like to play bass instead?

Woody agreed, and then promptly went round to the Sound City music store on London's Charing Cross Road to pick up a bass. The trouble was, he didn't have any money – so he stole one instead. "Five or six years later, when I was in the Faces, I went there and told them, 'I'm the guy who stole your Fender Jazz Bass and I've come here to pay you.' They were delighted."

The group's great unveiling was to come when they supported the Small Faces and Roy Orbison on a nationwide package tour. Brothers Paul and Barry Ryan completed the bill. The tour was to open at the Finsbury Park Astoria, London, on 3 March, 1967.

Unfortunately, everything that could go wrong did. The band had only rehearsed four or five times before the show – a sorry fact which

Melody Maker swiftly picked up on, reporting that "Beck seemed to have difficulty even playing a good solo."

In those days it was common for bands to play two sets a night, as Stewart remembers. "We all walked on stage for the first show in our band uniforms – we all had white jackets except Jeff, who wore a different one because he was the leader of the group – and we got through one number and the electricity went off. Someone pulled the plug and we immediately blamed the Small Faces. Jeff decided this was the end of the day; he wasn't going to stand any more of this, and walked off stage.

"I remember I wasn't too pleased either, because I looked down and saw I hadn't even done up my fly. The curtain came down, which nearly knocked Woody over, because it was so hefty. I caught him and we both did a sort of watusi off the stage."

The second show reportedly wasn't much better. The band was kicked off the tour without further ado, and with the Small Faces now beyond their grasp, a new scapegoat was sought. Drummer Ray Cook was sacked.

"It was bloody awful," Beck later complained. "Everything went wrong. Someone was looning around with the amps and the drummer lost his timing, and I was trying to be manager, agent and instrumentalist all in one go."

At the end of his stint with the Yardbirds, Jeff had approached his manager, producer Mickie Most, and, according to Most, "said . . . he wanted to be a pop star." Most told him he'd bear it in mind and when, a couple of months later, he came across a song called "Hi Ho Silver Lining", he passed it over to the ambitious young guitarist.

Most remembers the occasion. "I asked [Jeff] whether he could sing and he said, 'Not very well', but then none of the rest of the group could really sing very well either, so we recorded it for a bit of fun. Jeff's singing wasn't that good and it was a bit of a struggle with the vocals – in fact I was singing most of the chorus of 'Hi Ho Silver Lining', and I'm not much of a singer myself, so between us we almost ruined the record."

Stewart wasn't even invited along to the session, and when "Hi Ho Silver Lining" soared into the UK Top Twenty in April 1967, he was also absent from the television performance which backed up the record.

Rod, therefore, missed out on what had suddenly become a very successful time for the former members of Steampacket. In November 1967, Long John Baldry finally scored the hit single he had been striving for so long, when the majestic "Let the Heartaches Begin" soared easily to the top of the UK hit parade.

He followed it in August 1968 with "When the Sun Comes Shining Through", at exactly the same time as Julie Driscoll and the Brian Auger Trinity were topping the charts with their stunning cover of Dylan's "This Wheel's On Fire".

Watching from the sidelines, the best Stewart could point to were his performances on the b-sides of Beck's next two singles. And the fact that both "I've Been Drinking" and "Rock My Plimsoul" were aesthetically better than either of the a-sides was not much consolation.

Like "Hi Ho Silver Lining", neither "Tallyman" nor the soppy "Love Is Blue" had anything whatsoever to do with what the Jeff Beck Group was all about. Indeed, "Love Is Blue" probably ranks among the most embarrassing records a so-called superstar ever put his name to, being as it was a twee instrumental over which a syrupy chorus intoned the title.

To this day, Stewart continues to berate his old guv'nor for recording such pathetically thin material. "I just couldn't understand him. Here he was, a great guitarist and musician . . .' But Mickie Most defends the records staunchly. "Love Is Blue", he reckons, "kept the Jeff Beck Group alive. Somebody had to pay their weekly wages so it kept them working."

Beck, however, remembers things a little differently. Most, he says, "twisted my arm and I recorded three junk records. We were sticking all the good stuff on the b-sides. Rod would get to sing only on the flip side and he was getting really pissed. Quite understandably, but I wanted him to sing on the a-sides so that we could play something descriptive of what we were doing at the time."

Stewart himself later complained that all he and Woody did throughout this period was "hang around, waiting." In fact, neither of them was completely idle while Beck was off playing pop star. Still drinking, still chatting up the birds, they were also having a bloody good laugh at the songs Stewart was now tackling as a solo artist.

In 1965, Andrew Loog Oldham, the Rolling Stones' mercurial young manager, had started Immediate, the first truly independent record label in Britain, swiftly establishing it as a unique, if somewhat off-beat, outlet for talents the larger, more established labels were passing by. Stewart, he thought, would be perfect for the company.

The brightest star in the Immediate firmament was the Small Faces, a distinctly English band whose material – high-powered R & B – was so infused with music hall and vaudeville that it all but created a new musical genre. Songs like the psychedelic "Itchycoo Park" and the sing-along "Lazy Sunday" remain classics, while the almost philosophical "Donkey Rides, a Penny a Glass" stand among the greatest hard-rock songs of all time.

Stewart and Woody were very close to the Small Faces, indeed, for Rod, it was the ideal marriage – in Mod parlance a "Face" was one of the movement's trend-setters ("Small" referred to the band members' diminutive stature).

The group's principal songwriter was Steve Marriott, an ambitious London East Ender. He had met Stewart through one of Rod's old girlfriends, Jenny Ryland (who was now Marriott's wife), and had watched, with a mixture of incredulity and dismay, as Stewart meandered through the early 1960s. Finally, he sat down to help his old mate out of trouble.

"Marriott wrote some incredibly commercial things for me to record," says Stewart, and while nothing from these sessions was ever released, their very existence encouraged Andrew Oldham to start casting around for other partners for Stewart.

One was Mike D'Abo, of Manfred Mann. He had been doing a lot of work for Immediate, and was still celebrating the success of "Handbags and Gladrags", which he wrote for Chris Farlowe, when it was suggested he get together with Stewart.

The song he handed over was "Little Miss Understood", which he had originally written for Farlowe. It was a gentle piece, and at first Stewart viewed it with suspicion. But having heard the schlock Jeff Beck was up to, there couldn't be any harm in trying it out. With Woody in tow, Stewart recorded it for his next solo single.

For Stewart's managers, "Little Miss Understood" seemed the answer to their prayers. If they had any enduring criticism of Stewart, it was his constant refusal to record anything he considered "commercial", a failing which dated all the way back to the songs he rejected at his first-ever recording session. And when Stewart got it into his head that a song was so inclined, that was inevitably the end of it.

This time, though, he seemed to have swallowed his pride, or at least his scruples, and with "Little Miss Understood" having sent everyone at Immediate into raptures, Stewart was signed to a two-singles-a-year deal.

"Little Miss Understood" was released in November, to muted acclaim and few sales. Clearly a new approach, and perhaps a new partner, was needed.

Mick Jagger was also heavily involved in Immediate, and the way Stewart tells it, it was Jagger's girlfriend, Chrissie Shrimpton, who persuaded him to spend some time with the fledgling pop star.

"She got Mick to come down and make a record and we did a Carole King song that Wilson Pickett had recorded, 'Come On Baby'." (Another account of the session, related by Geoff Wright, has the team recording "Working In A Coal Mine".)

The band employed on the sessions is particularly interesting in light of later happenings. Of course, Stewart brought Woody along and introduced the breezy guitarist to Mick Jagger and Keith Richard, with whom he would be working full time in less than a decade. The sessions also joined Stewart and Woody with pianist Nicky Hopkins, who was later to join the Jeff Beck Group.

Finally, they introduced Stewart to soul songstress PP Arnold, with whom he would be sharing vocals, and who had recently enjoyed an enormous hit with "The First Cut Is the Deepest", a Cat Stevens song which Stewart himself would eventually cover.

But "Come On Baby" was doomed from the start. Just as Mike D'Abo infuriated Stewart by trying to tell him how to sing "Little Miss Understood", so Jagger too took exception to Stewart's gravelly voice. According to Wright, "There was a row in the studio with Jagger saying that Rod could not hit the high notes and that his voice wasn't right for the song."

Jagger walked out of the studio with the tapes under his arm, and shortly after he and Andrew Oldham had their final falling out. The track did not resurface for another decade, until "Come On Baby", now titled "Come Home Baby", finally appeared on an otherwise unworthy compilation album called *Rod Stewart and the Faces*.

Not surprisingly, Stewart's Immediate contract lapsed shortly thereafter, just as the Jeff Beck Group started moving back into gear. The unfortunate Ray Cook was replaced by Stewart Coombes, who himself was shunted aside for Aynsley Dunbar, and in November 1967 the band headlined a show at Brian Epstein's Savile Theatre in London. "It was the peak of flower power," Stewart remembers. "We all came on in flowers and kaftans and no trousers. Did we look a state! Aynsley was really insulted. This wasn't the blues!" Dunbar quit immediately after the show, but Stewart says, "I've nothing but good to say about Aynsley. He stayed about six or seven months and really got the band together."

Dunbar was replaced by Stewart's old mucker from Steampacket, Mickey Waller, and in this form work began on the first Jeff Beck Group album, *Truth*. "We had a great sound," reminisces Beck, "but nobody had written any songs! Rod wrote folk songs then, which wouldn't really have worked out for us, so he suggested we do 'Shapes of Things', the Yardbirds song." Having broken the ice, the band went on to create one of the most important records of the 1960s.

Beck finally decided he wasn't really cut out for all that pop star stuff, only to find that Most was thinking along the same lines himself. "He wanted to record the stuff we liked after all . . . and he couldn't do it. At least, he didn't have much notion of what it was all about."

At the same time as the Beck Group was recording *Truth* at EMI Studios on Abbey Road in North London, Most was also busy working with Donovan at Olympic Studios in Barnes. He admits that most of the real work was put in by engineer Ken Scott and the band members themselves, with Scott even earning the credit for creating the sheer roar which Beck wrung from his guitar. Remembers Most, "I said to Ken . . . 'I'm just going over to Olympic and I won't be long, so I want you to get a nice heavy guitar sound for Jeff.'" When he returned, he found Beck's amplifier locked in a cupboard, with a microphone outside.

"We used to take things like John Lee Hooker and Muddy Waters and all the great bluesmen, and play them our way, which is the way to do it," says Stewart. "As far as I was concerned, what we were doing didn't need producers, and I remember telling Jeff this. So I really don't think, with all due respect, that Mickie Most had much to do with producing the Jeff Beck Group. It was done by the four blokes in the band."

Truth was a remarkable album, the ultimate blending of the blues with which all four band members had grown up, and a new sound which, within a year or so, would be hijacked by Led Zeppelin and rechristened Heavy Metal.

Indeed, the first Zeppelin album even duplicates one of the songs from *Truth*, Willie Dixon's dynamic "You Shook Me", an act of piracy which Beck, at least, was not soon to forgive. Still, it's an intriguing opportunity to compare what were to become the two most distinctive voices of the 1970s, Stewart and Zeppelin's Robert Plant, and on this evidence there was no comparison. Stewart was streets ahead. It is also interesting to note that Most's assistant, and Beck's manager-by-proxy, was Peter Grant – who later went on to manage Zeppelin.

Stewart credits *Truth* with a lot of things, including improving his untrained voice. "The only way to improve on anything is to listen to what you've already done, and probably after I did the Beck album, then I had a collection of songs I could really listen to. I could take it home and listen to it, and I've improved since then."

Truth was not released in the UK until October 1968 (it hit America some three months earlier), so the Jeff Beck Group's British performances were undertaken primarily for audiences who knew nothing beyond Jeff's three hit singles. Producer Most remembers that the band would get them out of the way first, "and then get into all their other stuff."

It was a situation which caused Stewart, as the band's frontman, considerable grief. Because Beck had appeared on television as a solo artist, both playing and singing (or at least pretending to sing – lip-synching is an art which British pop performers swiftly learn to embrace if they are to appear on the TV with any regularity), many of the people at the shows knew nothing of Stewart, and wondered who this odd-looking geezer in the flashy clothes was.

In the United States, however, the boot was on the other foot. Virtually none of Beck's singles had made any impression there. Instead, he was remembered only as a former Yardbird, and as Stewart put it, "got himself a name as a guitarist because they were all into guitar players."

Americans, then, understood that Beck had far more important things to do than sing, and accepted Stewart on his own terms. It was the beginning of a love affair between Stewart and the USA which has continued unabated to this day.

"We were literally down to our last crumb. We had nothing left. But Peter Grant [who Most placed in charge of the band's day-to-day affairs] was smart enough to see there was an underground scene happening in America, where bands were making it without being seen on the surface – newspapers, records, none of that. So he said, 'I'm gonna put you out there.' It was a last-ditch thing, to keep the band going. We had just one set of good clothes that had to last us the whole tour!"

The Jeff Beck Group made their American debut on 28 May, 1968. They were booked for an eight-week tour, beginning with a veritable baptism of fire at the Fillmore East in New York, opening for the Grateful Dead.

The venue was packed. It seemed everybody knew Jeff Beck and what he meant to the history of rock'n'roll. As the band took the stage, Stewart felt as out of place standing alongside the guitar legend as he had in England, hanging loosely around the edge of the stage while Beck ran through his hit singles.

"I didn't feel I was very wanted from the audience standpoint," says Stewart. "I used to think, 'Well, they've only come along to listen to Jeff, so I might as well just sing along.'" Consequently, Rod Stewart made his American concert debut hiding behind an amplifier.

"I remember it like it was yesterday. Opening night at the Fillmore, and my first night ever in America, I was so nervous my voice gave out on the first line, which was 'Let me love you'. So I hid."

"In those days Woody and I used to have a little red bag we'd carry around that had a bottle of brandy or rum in it. I ran out, got the bag, had a quick shot, ran back, and picked up the mike again. At first I crouched behind the amps as I swigged, with Beck covering for me by playing a solo. There was definitely a bit of embarrassment all around, with everyone looking for the singer. But sure enough, as the brandy hit the bloodstream, back came the vocals!"

Beck laughs uproariously at the memory. "We played two numbers in a segue to open and finished with a big 'RRRARRHHHH'. Rod came out from behind the amps in a mackintosh and hat, ready to go home. I said, 'I think you can take them off. They liked it.'"

If Stewart was still nervous, it didn't show. Robert Shelton, reviewing the performance for the *New York Times*, wrote, "The group's principal format is the interaction of Mr Beck's wild, visionary guitar against the hoarse, insistent shouting of Rod Stewart. Their dialogue was lean and laconic, the verbal ping pong of a musical Pinter play." It was, he continued, "an auspicious beginning for an exciting group", and even "for one listener at least, upstaged the featured performers, The Grateful Dead."

Stewart never got that scared again; instead he developed a very cynical attitude toward the band. "Beck was the man in that band. If we died a death one night, I never used to care. 'It's not my band, it's Beck's. Too bad.' I tried, but I didn't lose any sleep if we did badly."

Beck's US record company, Epic, did little to change Stewart's mind. One evening the label bigwigs descended upon the show en masse, and after it was over made a beeline straight for Stewart.

"Hey, Jeff, you sang great! Fucking good guitar player you got in the band, too."

"It's unbelievable," Beck beamed, "we've been going down well just about everywhere, which is very encouraging. We played Detroit the other night – it was outrageous. Everyone was really enjoying themselves, and there were about thirty or forty people grooving away on stage. It was a great atmosphere."

He later commented, "It's amazing and overwhelming. It was breathtaking to go down so well on our debut. We spent a long time planning our American tour, getting things just right, and it was worth it. Even so, we didn't expect the sort of reception we were getting."

Stewart, too, found America a new experience, and not only from a musical point of view. The notion of the rock'n'roller as a one-man demolition team was still in its infancy in Britain during the 1960s. The occasional hotel room might be scarred with grafitti, the odd boarding-house landlady might find her toilets blocked with towels, but throughout these early years of musical innocence the idea of wanton destruction for destruction's sake was all but unknown.

In the States, however, things were very different. Hotels accepted bands' bookings well aware of the possible consequences, but knowing, too, that there would always be a record-company check to cover any damage. As Rod and Woody traveled the US, meeting other musicians and hearing their tales, slowly they realised that there was an entire rock'n'roll heritage of which they were ignorant. So they began to test the waters with enthusiasm.

Perhaps because Rod was already obsessed with model trains, the duo's first assaults both involved the real thing. In Washington, for instance, where the Beck Group was opening for Janis Joplin, Woody and Stewart were sitting in a restaurant waiting for their meal to arrive when they spotted a stationary locomotive on the tracks behind the building.

"So we hopped aboard," laughs Woody, "and proceeded to release the brakes. The thing just started moving. We jumped off yelling, and zoomed back into the restaurant. We hid in there while this giant locomotive rolled uncommanded into the sunset."

On another occasion, in Tucson, he says, the hotel itself had a mini-train, used for transporting guests around the hotel grounds. "It was late at night, so no kids were on it. We got it going and the next thing, whoop! Right off the tracks, tumbling down a hill."

America was different in other ways, too. Of course, Stewart had had his share of girls back home, even though, for more than five years now, he'd been living with Sarah. Even at his most obscure, blowing harp with the Dimensions, or roaring his way through "Tiger in Your Tank" with the Hoochie Coochie Men, Rod the Mod had been a prime catch, particularly with the Hoochie Coochies, when Baldry's stage act generally settled down somewhere between asexual aloofness and a very provocative gay outing.

In America, though, Stewart found himself dealing with a completely different breed of girl from those he was used to. It was the era of the Plaster Casters, the notorious Chicago-based duo whose bedtime habits included encasing their conquests' erect organs in Alginate, then casting it in plaster as a permanent reminder of their encounter. Stewart is also rumored to have taken a starring role in Jenny Fabian's film *Groupie*, a true-life (but for modesty's sake, disguised) account of the many rock stars who passed through her warm, welcoming thighs.

Another well-publicised liaison was with the GTOs – a band of hard-core groupies whose name, an acronym for Girls Together Outrageously, was bestowed upon them by producer Frank Zappa. It was Zappa, too, who hatched the notion of the five girls recording their own album, recruiting a parade of passing stars to accompany them. When the Beck Group played the Shrine Auditorium in Los Angeles, it was only inevitable that they, too, should be invited to participate.

For the GTOs, it was a thrill beyond words. Stewart, however, apparently had little interest in giving the group the benefit of his experience. "Rodney Rooster", as the GTOs christened him, spent much of the evening simply pacing forlornly around the tiny studio where the band, augmented by Beck and Hopkins, were recording. Finally, he stalked out. "There's nothing for me to do, so I'm off."

The GTOs waited until Beck finished the solo he was laying down, then wandered out into the streets of Glendale to find the sulking Stewart. He was finally located sitting on the steps outside a grade school, still pouting, and it took all the girls' powers of persuasion to drag him back to the studio, where he added some vocals to "Shock Treatment".

The Jeff Beck Group spent the rest of the week with their voluptuous hostesses, lounging around the Sunset Marquis. The homesick Rodney Rooster, however, apparently did nothing but talk about Britain and soccer!

Every night brought a new line of yummies to the stage door; each morning found a different stranger in bed alongside him. Was it, perhaps, a few too many early-morning horror shows that once prompted Stewart to admit, "I'm not too hung up on the beauty stakes. I have an eye for all customers."

Stewart had one other notable encounter on his American tour, albeit on the other side of the sheets, and that was meeting Lou Reizner. Reizner, the London-based American who headed Mercury Records' UK operation, had been at the Group's Shrine Auditorium show in Los Angeles, and admits that it blew him away. Even more exciting, though, was returning to his hotel, the Hyatt House Continental, and discovering that Stewart was registered there too.

This was one evening when the groupies took second place in Stewart's affections. Instead, he sat and listened while Reizner outlined the dream that was to become a consuming passion. He wanted Stewart to sign a solo deal with Mercury.

Stewart, however, was evasive – not because he didn't like the idea, but because he didn't know quite what to do about it. Peter Grant, the bullish future manager of Led Zeppelin, was then handling the Beck Group's affairs, and he had already let Reizner know that he considered himself to be Stewart's manager as well. Any approaches to Stewart should really be made through him.

Stewart, on the other hand, was recommending that Reizner contact Rowlands and Wright as soon as he got back to London. Instead, it was Rowlands who telephoned Reizner.

"When he called I was on the way to my hairdresser's," says Reizner. "And we did the deal walking from Chester Street to Grosvenor Square."

Negotiations continued while Reizner was having his hair cut, and with Rowlands having let it be known very firmly that Peter Grant had no connection with Stewart beyond his ties to the group, the subject inevitably moved round to money.

"At the time," says Rowlands, "Stewart had a desperate ambition – which, being Rod, he had thrown his whole heart into – and that was to get one of those do-it-yourself Marcos car kits, which you could buy for a thousand pounds and build your own sports car."

Another £250 was to be given to Rowlands and Wright, the first money they ever earned from Rod Stewart. "We didn't take a penny from him until then," says Rowlands. "Quite honestly, we didn't need the sort of sums that we'd have got by taking our percentage. He wasn't earning enough through his solo work to make it worthwhile for us financially. But we weren't thinking of his as a short-term career at all. We were all right financially, and we thought it important that Rod should be all right, too. Which he always was."

At that time, £1,250 was a lot of money for a simple advance, particularly as Stewart – despite his success with Beck – was still all but unknown.

But Rowlands yet had an ace to play. He didn't know how much truth there was in the story, but Peter Grant was claiming that Atlantic Records also wanted Stewart, and were prepared to pay handsomely for him. Reizner capitulated. He handed over the money, and almost immediately discovered something which any of Stewart's previous employers and bandmates could have told him. He was investing in a bottomless pit. Stewart bought his car, and then, as soon as the deal with Mercury was signed, promptly demanded more.

"But you've already had your advance. You bought the car."

"Yeah, but it wasn't enough. The money's all gone, man."

The wrangling went on for a full year. Mercury were desperate to get the boy into the recording studio; Stewart was equally desperate, and twice as adamant, to see some more bread. There was a house in Highgate, just five minutes from his parents', which he wanted to buy, "a detached house, like in the States with a veranda at the front. You can imagine the Stars and Stripes and a rocking chair out front."

Reizner tried to hold out, but Stewart wouldn't back down. At the time of signing for Mercury, he intimated that he was just looking for some security of his own, and that he would quit the Beck Group just as soon as he'd found it.

Now he wasn't so sure. After all, if Mercury only wanted to invest a thousand quid in him . . .

Again, Reizner broke. He went to Mercury's overall chief, Irwin Steinberg, and came away with an extra $10,000. "This boy of yours had better be good," Steinberg told Reizner.

Work commenced on Stewart's first solo album almost immediately, but it was to be a stop–start affair. Contrary to anything he may have promised in the past, Stewart was still very much a member of the Beck Group, and had no intention of giving it up. In January 1969, he returned to the States for the band's second tour.

This time Beck was opening with two nights at the Fillmore East, supporting Vanilla Fudge. Their performance, and the audience's reaction, was astonishingly powerful, and as the group came away from the stage, everybody was chattering excitedly. It seemed as though the whole world was at their feet.

"The gig ended up in what they call a nine-man jam," recalls Stewart. "The stage was full of people including Bonham, Page, Beck, me and Planty [Robert Plant] and the guy who used to play bass for Jethro Tull. We were doing 'Jailhouse Rock' and it was fucking incredible. I finished the whole thing off by sticking a mike stand up John Bonham's arse and *he* got arrested. The cops pulled him off and I ran away. We were all pissed out of our heads. The Vanilla Fudge couldn't follow it, just couldn't, they packed up that night."

A few evenings later, while Beck and Stewart were sitting around their hotel, waiting for that evening's show in Detroit, the Fudge's rhythm section, Carmine Appice and Timmy Bogert, phoned. At first they simply swapped pleasantries – "Great gig the other night, man," "Yeah, you too" – then they dropped the bombshell.

"You know, Jeff, we've been thinking. The Fudge has broken up, but we still want to work together. Now you and Stewart, the two of us, we could make a shit-hot band. Every night could be like the Fillmore."

Beck could hardly contain his excitement and neither, at first, could Stewart. The Fudge had been one of the most successful groups in the country. Think what he could do if he were a member of this hot new band! But while he was still wondering how best to break the news to Woody and Waller, Beck decided to dispense with any such pleasantries altogether. He could finish the tour with session men and so sacked them both on the spot.

"The trouble began right about the time we started doing the second album, *Cosa Nostra Beck-Ola*," Stewart later remembered. "Out of the blue, Beck suddenly decided he wanted to get rid of Ronnie and Mickey. He told me and I said it was a big mistake. Really, that was the tightest rhythm section I ever heard. But he wanted to get rid of them and I couldn't change his mind.

"So he sacked them, then he got Tony Newman on drums and we brought in an incredibly bad Australian bass player who rehearsed with us just once, the night before we went on stage. That was in Washington and we died the all-time death." The next day, says Woody, "I got a phone call from the States from Beck saying 'Come back'."

For Stewart, "after the night of the sackings, the band was never the same again." Just two weeks before the band was scheduled to play Woodstock, the Jeff Beck Group broke up for good.

"I think we would have stayed together had we played Wood-stock," he continues. "But we passed it up because we all wanted to go home. So anyway, the band broke up, Jeff didn't phone me up or anything to let me know what was going on, so I said 'fuck it' and split."

There had been a complete and overall breakdown in communication. While Stewart and Woody had grown even closer, so they had become more distanced from Beck. They were like a pair of giggling schoolgirls, said journalist Lester Bangs, and Beck was not amused. His night of the long knives soured things even further.

"It was a great band to sing with," confesses Rod. "But I couldn't take all the aggravation and unfriendliness that developed. It was getting too ridiculous for words near the end – we were trying to hide from each other all the time. One would stay at the Hilton and the others would stay at Hotel Third-on-the-Bill around the corner. Do you know that in the two and a half years I was with Beck, I never once looked him in the eye? I always looked at his shirt or something like that!"

Woody remembers on one US tour, he and Stewart were forced to share a room, "and were so desperate at times that we'd go down to Horn & Hardart, the automat, to steal eggs."

There were any number of proverbial last straws, but money was inevitably one of the heaviest. "We never got paid!" Stewart complained two decades later. "Woody and I were in the band and we never used to get paid. Jeff used to go off in the limo and have Woody and me call for a taxi!"

Then there was the new album, the awkwardly titled *Cosa Nostra Beck-Ola*. Gone were the heavy blues of *Truth*; in their stead there lay a rough, leaden approximation of Zeppelin's own brand of Heavy Metal, barbarously unleashed on such rock'n'roll standards as "Jailhouse Rock" and "All Shook Up", and quivering half-heartedly across a clutch of the band's own compositions.

With lyrics penned largely by Stewart and Woody, the new songs were weak and uninspired. Even Stewart later called them "silly". For a singer who, over the years, had so stressed the importance of writing one's own material, his first real attempt was best left unnoticed.

But what finally, and irrevocably, convinced Stewart that he and Beck had reached the end of the road was their much-vaunted meeting with Bogert and Appice.

Patiently, and with growing incredulity, Stewart sat listening to their plans for the new band, picturing their dream of a lumbering metal monster fired by Beck's guitar, with Stewart shrieking above the din. It was like all his worse musical nightmares come true. "I was completely turned off," he later remarked.

Little did Rod realise that one day he would indeed be in a band with Appice. But a lot of water was to flow under the bridge before that particular fantasy came to be.

4

___

Small Wonder

For Woody, dismissal from the Beck Group was a blessing in disguise. He was tired of making lousy wages, and having to put up with the crummy hotels which Beck believed befitted his station. He was also tired of the politics and petty power-plays which made Beck so difficult to work for. But most of all, he was tired of playing bass, even if it was behind one of the greatest guitarists in the world. He himself was a natural guitar player, and he wanted desperately to get back to his own first love.

He and Waller flew straight back to London, originally planning to stick together. There was a vague notion of doing something with Rod Stewart, once he got home. "With you out of the band," Waller said, "I can't see him sticking around very long." For now, however, they rehearsed with Leigh Stephens, once the guitarist with American psychedelic rockers Blue Cheer. Woody returned to his lead guitar, and passed his bass over to Ronnie Lane, the hedgehog-faced bassist with the Small Faces.

The Small Faces had likewise broken up a few months earlier. Steve Marriott, the band's iron-lunged Cockney warlord, had split to form Humble Pie, leaving Lane, pianist Ian "Mac" MacLagan, and drummer Kenney Jones to fend for themselves. They were still officially a band, but hadn't worked in months, their record company stunk, and they seemed to spend most of their time evading debt collectors. Mac, according to legend, kept a bottle of urine on permanent stand-by, ready to pour over any over-persistent creditors.

When Woody invited Lane along to jam, it looked as though that might really be the end of the band. But Lane wasn't too sure about the way things were going. He and Woody hit it off immediately, but Waller and Stephens didn't really impress him. Finally, after another frustrating evening spent trying to reconcile four very disparate musical styles, Lane conceded defeat. "It's just not working," he told Woody. "Why don't you come down and have a blow with the rest of the Faces?"

Woody, who'd been suffering severe doubts of his own, agreed.

"Well, it can't be much worse than this!" The next day, he and Lane met up with the remaining Small Faces.

"It was all a bit embarrassing," Lane remembers. "We were a bit rusty and it didn't sound very good, but we liked each other and there was a good alchemy there, so we persevered."

The first rehearsals took place at Lane's austere flat in Elsham Road, Kensington, then moved on to the Rolling Stones' rehearsal room in Bermondsey. "They let us have it for nothing, because they knew we didn't have any money, and we more or less had the run of the place for three or four months," Lane continues. "They just said if we ever made any money we could pay for the electricity."

Woody wisely didn't want to commit himself at first. "I went to see Steve Marriott too, because I got on really well with Steve, and I nearly formed a band with him.

"But I thought, no, Steve's going to be all right, but maybe the other three won't. They might split up and that would be a shame. So as they were still together, we had some workouts."

One of the new band's greatest problems was their lack of a vocalist. "Ronnie had a good voice," remembers Kenney Jones, "but in my opinion it wasn't powerful enough, especially after a singer like Steve Marriott. The backing vocals from Woody and Mac were making me laugh. We had a crack at it, but I kept thinking how Woody, Ronnie and Mac would make a really good backing vocals team. I wasn't trying to knock Ronnie because I knew he was a good singer, but I could see it being even better."

So could Woody, especially after he got that phone call from Beck, asking him to return. While Beck was dreaming of what he could do with Bogert and Appice, Woody was filling Stewart's head with visions of what the two of them could accomplish themselves with the Small Faces. Finally, at the airport on the way home from America, Woody came out with it. "Why don't you come with me?"

"Yeah, I can't see us staying here much longer," Stewart replied.

Rod knew he would be giving up a lot if he left Beck, both in financial and musical terms. "In the early days," he has said, "I always felt overshadowed by Jeff's guitar playing, but toward the end of the band, when we were beginning to be successful, the guitar and vocal bit used to fit like a glove, we really used to have it off tight. And if Jeff was having a bad night then I'd leap about a bit more and if I'd lost my voice then he'd do the same for me. We had a great rapport between the two of us."

But frankly, upon reflection, the Vanilla Fudge scheme seemed daft. So did the idea of continuing to work with Beck if Woody wasn't around. He knew in his own mind that he couldn't go back.

Could he actually bring himself to go forward, though? Musically, what remained of the Small Faces was fine, but on personal terms, "Let's face it," Rod sighed to Woody one night, "they treat me like a cunt." When he went to their rehearsals – not as a singer, just to sit around and listen – he could feel their hostility. Woody would try to smooth things over, but all the time there was that constant, nagging undercurrent of resentment. And fear. Rod was certain he could sense fear.

Kenney Jones later admitted that he was probably right. The band were a little afraid of him. It wasn't anything he'd done, of course, it was just that he reminded them of someone they didn't really want to think about – Steve Marriott.

Toward the end of the Small Faces, Marriott had become the dominant, and domineering, force in the band; a little monster with a giant-sized ego. He wrote the songs and he sang them. Without him, he believed, the Small Faces would be nothing. His management supported him, his friends abetted him, even the record company felt that way. And in a way, the Small Faces believed him too.

Once he was gone, says Lane, "We were just shelved. Nobody wanted to know about the three of us, because the general public usually look at the front man, they don't look behind." The question they were asking themselves now was how could they stop it all happening again? Just as they were getting back on their feet, the last thing they wanted was "another Steve Marriott". And when they noticed Stewart appearing more and more at rehearsals, of course it made them nervous.

Night after night, Rod and Woody would discuss the possibility of Stewart joining the group. They both knew it was a good idea, but Woody was reluctant to suggest it himself. 'They'd think I was just dragging my mates in. They're fragile enough as it is – best to wait for one of them to ask. I know someone will."

"I'd listen at the top of the stairs to them rehearsing," Rod reveals, "and I thought they sounded good. But there was no one singing, and they knew that as well. Ronnie Lane knew that. It was only a matter of time before they asked me to join."

It was Kenney Jones who finally took the plunge. "I kept wondering why he was there, apart from being good mates with Woody," he remembers. "But we got chatting and he said how he was fed up with the Beck Group. So one night I asked him, 'Why don't you join us?' "

It was the question Stewart had been waiting to hear, but he tried to act cool. "Yeah, I'd really like to. But what about the others?" Jones said he would have a talk with them. Woody was staying at Ten Years After guitarist Alvin Lee's cottage in Gloucester Place Mews in London, and almost every day Jones, Mac and Lane would troop round to discuss

Stewart's membership. Ronnie fought hard for his mate. Every time Marriott's name came up in conversation he would wave it away. "Rod's not like that. Don't worry."

The others wanted to believe him. They knew in their hearts that Stewart was right for them. Maybe if they could obtain a guarantee of some sort? The problem was, no one seemed to know quite how to phrase it, without causing offense.

"Okay, this is what we do," Jones, Mac or Lane would laugh. "We walk up to him and go, ''Ere, Stewart, we want you in the band, but we're a bit worried that you're just gonna stick around and make some dough, then bugger off and leave us. Any ideas how we can stop you?' "

The question, unfortunately, never got asked. That was Mistake Number One.

The next point was the distribution of songs between the band's career and Stewart's own solo outings. They'd heard the tapes that he'd recently completed, and they had to admit "there's stuff there we wouldn't mind having a bash at." They racked their brains trying to think of another situation like this – a singer with one career joining a band with another, when both of them played the same type of music. They couldn't.

"Usually, a guy'll go off and do something different," they said. "Stuff the rest of the band wouldn't touch. But we're going to be in competition with Stewart for the same songs! Isn't that going to get a bit . . . sticky?"

This too was left unanswered. Mistake Number Two.

In the end, Stewart got the job. The rest of the band just crossed their fingers and hoped everyone would muck in together. It would work out because they wanted it to. And that was Mistake Number Three – their moments of indecision would soon come bouncing back with a vengeance.

Stewart, for his part, didn't even think in these terms. He threw himself into this new group in the same way he threw himself into everything – wholeheartedly, unthinkingly, and without a care in the world. When Rowlands and Wright tried to raise the same sort of questions as the Small Faces had been asking, Rod just brushed them aside. "Ah, we'll work something out."

A few days after Stewart joined, in June 1969, the band made its in-concert debut at one of the annual summer balls that marked the end of term at Cambridge University. It was to be their first show since Marriott departed, and they had already asked Woody's older brother Art to come along as their singer. With Stewart now in the band . . . oh, what the hell, now they had two vocalists.

The place, Mac says, was packed with "Hooray Henries" – upper-class twits with no chins and fat wallets. None of them knew who this group really was, and to keep the media away from the show the band dubbed themselves Quiet Melon for the night. The audience was just there to get drunk and be loud. So, by the way, were Quiet Melon.

"Champagne, strawberries, jugs of beer and roast beef dinners," Mac fondly remembers. "The food was free and we were given a hundred quid to split between us. It was a joke. We went on without any rehearsal, with hardly any equipment, we did 'Hoochie Coochie Man' and 'I Got My Mojo Working' and 'What'd I Say'. It was a case of 'Quick, what key?' 'Doesn't matter – first one to the end's the winner.'"

The show was chaos, but the crowd loved it – so much so that when the headliner, PP Arnold, didn't turn up, the organisers asked Quiet Melon to play again, for yet another hundred pounds. "We said yes, and went on and did exactly the same numbers again. They were just extended jams, but we were loud, fast, noisy, and the Hoorays thought we were damned good."

Quiet Melon played a second gig a few weeks later, at a college in Surrey. This time, Art Wood was joined by Long John Baldry and Jimmy Horowitz, and if anything, the show was even more ramshackle than the last. But within the ranks of the band itself – Mac, Lane, Jones, Woody and Stewart – something had finally clicked. The Small Faces might never recapture the glories they had once enjoyed, but they could come very close. It was time to start looking to the future.

Mac admitted that the first order of business was to find a new name. "People know the Small Faces have split up and Steve has left." Quiet Melon was all right for a laugh, he said, but it wasn't something the group could live with. Neither was another plan they had come up with. "We thought it would be funny to release each record under a different name – Gilbert Green and the Emeralds, for instance. But it would make any kind of promotion difficult."

Ronnie Lane suggested Slim Chance – because that was the band's approximate hope of success, he laughed. Other names floated in and out of contention. But when Warner Brothers moved in to offer the group a recording contract in October 1969, the matter was taken out of their hands altogether. In Britain, they would become the Faces. And in America, they would remain the Small Faces. The band grunted their approval, then rushed out to spend their advance on a sports car each.

Lou Reizner remembers how Stewart broke the news of the Warners deal to him. "I want to record with the Small Faces," he said. "There's a deal in the offing, and I'm going to sign it."

"How can you record with them if you have a contract with Mercury?" asked Reizner. Like the Small Faces he, too, could not think of a single situation like this one.

"Oh, I'll leave Mercury," Stewart casually tossed back.

Reizner made a mental note to bring up the subject with his boss, and once again he had to call upon all his powers of persuasion, and his limitless belief in Stewart, to push Steinberg into agreeing.

It was decided that Stewart would continue with Mercury as a solo artist, but could record with the Faces for Warners. It was an unusual, if not unique, arrangement, but if Stewart was grateful, he didn't let it show. He celebrated the inking of the pact by scrapping the sessions for his new album, recorded with drummer Aynsley Dunbar, and pulling together a new group around a nucleus of Woody and Mac. Guitarists Martin Pugh and Martin Quittenton, and drummer Mickey Waller, completed the line-up. Lou Reizner was to produce, and he quickly found himself wondering more and more what he had gotten himself into.

"Rod was one of the meanest guys I have ever known," he says today. "If you were out for a meal with him, he would say, 'I want a bottle of champagne.' Then the Dom Perignon would arrive, and when the bill came he wouldn't reach for it." And his friends, it seemed to Reizner, were little better. "The guy he brought in as a drummer, Mickey Waller, was the only drummer I have ever met who never owned a drum kit. We always had to hire him one for the session."

On another occasion, Reizner brought his own guitar, a Japanese Aria, down to the studio for Stewart to use. He never saw it again. "I kept asking him to let me have it back, because it was a really good guitar. Then one time I went down to his house and said to him straight out, 'Can I please have my guitar back?' And Rod replied, 'Come on, Reizner, that's my favorite ax!' "

The album itself was to be an adventurous blending of folk, blues and straightforward rock'n'roll, harking back to Stewart's days as a struggling folkie with a version of Ewan McColl's "Dirty Old Town", then straight up to date with the Stones' "Street Fighting Man" – a song which Stewart says "was actually meant to be a tune by Little Richard called 'The Girl Can't Help It'. But during the session, for no apparent reason, I started singing 'Street Fighting Man', adding much confusion to an already bewildered band."

There was also a reunion with Mike D'Abo, with whom Stewart had worked on "Little Miss Understood" the previous year. Then, their collaboration had been soured by D'Abo's criticism of Stewart's voice, but Lou Reizner had apparently wallpapered over the cracks in their relationship. "A suggestion of mine was that we should record 'Handbags and Gladrags', because I'd heard the original version [by Chris Farlowe], I liked the song, and Mike D'Abo was a friend of mine. I thought that was a good choice for Stewart, and Mike did the arrangements." He also played piano on the track.

Reizner hints that "there were a lot of problems" over D'Abo's contribution, "and they always related to money." He seems to blame Stewart, but has never elaborated on the subject. It seems that they were the same kind of difficulties as the Faces now endured after Ronnie Lane brought in producer Glyn Johns.

Johns had worked regularly with the Small Faces, engineering several of their biggest hits. He also produced the six-track demos which landed the band their contract with Warners. Now he was demanding a two per cent royalty for his contribution to the group's new album, and Mac was having none of it.

"I thought, okay, his job was very important, but after all the sweating and straining, he was just going to come in at the end and appear at the recording session." If Mac had learned one thing from the original Small Faces, it was to be very careful with money. He could only wonder how the others might think otherwise. "This is how we landed in the shit last time. Let's not make the same mistakes again."

He found an ally in Stewart, and finally Mac got his way. Martin Birch, engineer on the ill-fated second Jeff Beck Group album, came in for a flat producer's fee.

First Step was recorded during December 1969 and January 1970, and, like Rod's album, was a veritable mixed bag. But whereas Stewart had simply drawn upon his own influences and interests, *First Step* threw four other personalities into the brew, with chaotic results.

The instrumental "Pineapple and the Monkey" was straight out of the Small Faces' catalog of throwaway b-sides; "Wicked Messenger" reflected Stewart's love for Bob Dylan; "Devotion", "Stone" and "Nobody Knows" were wistful Ronnie Lane compositions; "Flying" and "Shake, Shudder and Shiver" harked back to Woody's contributions to the Beck Group; and "Around the Plynth" was simply that band's "Plynth" taken to its logical rock'n'roll conclusion. Only one song, "Three Button Hand Me Down", really hinted at what the Faces could produce, and Stewart was perfectly justified when he later confided, "It wasn't a good album. It was a bloody awful album."

By this time, the Faces were playing live with some regularity, and not without incident. Their first show under their new name, at a USAF base near Cambridge, was marred by Stewart's decision to try to play a double bass on stage. It was a kind fate indeed that caused him to trip up as he left the dressing-room, and snap the hapless instrument's neck.

In Southampton, a sloppy fall-about set was booed by supporters of the headlining Taste, an improbably pure blues trio led by the guitar-playing genius of Rory Gallagher. In Bristol, the Faces arrived six hours early for their performance at an all-night University show, and were so drunk by the time they got on stage that they were barely able to play a note. As Stewart later said, "It wasn't exactly a day on the beach."

The reputation for hard drinking – and sloppy musicianship – which was later to stagger hand-in-hand with the Faces' "all lads together" image was not, Stewart reckons, all their own doing. It was true they usually met for rehearsals at a local pub, and that they returned when the session was over. "When we first started," says Rod, "nobody wanted to listen to us and nobody was taking us very seriously, so we decided to go round the pub beforehand. Call it Dutch Courage if you want, but that's what it was down to. It wasn't a conscious thing . . . it was just the natural way it came out – that we do like to go to the pub. There was a general smile whenever anyone played a dodgy note."

Stewart admits, however, that a lot of the Faces' high jinx were in fact their own shambolic interpretation of rock'n'roll history. "The myths of those old blues singers had a ridiculous effect. We heard about how they drank and smoked and carried on, so we thought we'd have to do the same thing." It was only later, he laughs, that he read that Muddy Waters, the greatest bluesman of them all, had a set of very strict rules for his band to abide by. They could do what the hell they liked after a show, but they'd better damn well be on time and sober before it! "If only we'd known that at the time!" Rod sighs regretfully.

But there was something else about the Faces, too, something novel. The 1970s had dawned with a sense of hideously po-faced musical seriousness. Suddenly it was fashionable for bands to play long, careful songs awash with introspection and forty-minute solos. Audiences were encouraged to stand still without moving, to applaud quietly at the end of each number, and not make a sound in between.

The Faces, though, weren't like that. They wanted their audience to shout, they needed to see people dancing and leaping about. Musically, the lashed out with short, clumsy celebrations of good times and lust. And if they fell over once or twice a night, or even once or twice per song, so much the better.

"We didn't say, 'Why don't we go out and jump all over the stage and fall about?'" says Stewart. "It was a natural reaction to what was going on around us at the time. If you want to listen to a band sounding like the record, go home and listen to the bloody record. But if you come and see us, you've got to put up with our mistakes and our silliness and everything else that goes along with us. People don't come along to see the Faces for the sound quality. They come along for the atmosphere."

And audiences responded with glee. When the band erected a well-equipped bar on stage during one American tour, the array of drinks on display received almost as much applause as the individual Faces themselves! At the end of the show, when the band reappeared for an encore, Stewart would admonish the audience, "If you ask for one encore, you're gonna have to endure at least five."

The Faces were still recording their debut, *First Step*, when Stewart's first record appeared in the stores, in the fall of 1969. *The Rod Stewart Album* was retitled *An Old Raincoat Won't Ever Let You Down* in his homeland. In America, Stewart himself referred to it as *Thin*, and Lou Reizner spent many years wondering why. It turned out, Rod later admitted, that *Thin* was his honest expectation of sales.

In later years, as the rest of the Faces feared, Stewart was to become the "star" of the group. In 1970, however, it was quite the other way round. While Lou Reizner remembers *Thin* selling no more than 100,000 copies, Stewart claims *First Step*, which followed in February 1970, hit the quarter-million mark within a month of release. When the band arrived in Toronto on 25 March for the first show of the tour, they got an instant taste of their new-found fame.

Even at the height of their popularity, the Small Faces had never visited North America, although they had been offered, and were even booked for, several tours. Now they were actually there, and discovered an audience they'd never dreamed of, a whole continent of kids that had grown up on their old records, that was well aware of the changes in the band, and prepared to love them whatever they did. Neither the down-home Canned Heat nor the MC5, who were both billed above them at the Varsity Arena, stood a chance. The Small Faces blew them all off the stage.

For Stewart and Woody, it was a repeat of their experiences with Beck. All but unknown in Britain, they had arrived in the US and were suddenly full-blown superstars. With Beck, however, they hadn't known how to react. With the Faces, they had all the moves down pat. They didn't need to make headlines – the headlines came in search of them.

In Detroit, the Small Faces went down so well over two nights that they were immediately rebooked for another three. As Stewart stood in front of the biggest crowd he had ever seen, he admitted, "Standing here, I'm shit scared and they didn't believe it," he laughs. "They all said, 'Nyah, come on', and I was really scared!"

In Boston, the headliner, organist Lee Michaels, was so angered by the constant calls for the Small Faces which continued throughout his set that he ended up playing at several times his normal volume, simply so he could be heard.

In San Francisco, a drunken Stewart got on to the top of their hired station wagon and persuaded the rest of the band to join him there. When the police arrived, the entire group was leaping up and down on the vehicle's mangled roof.

In all, the Small Faces played twenty-eight shows on that tour, and were treated like conquering heroes everywhere. At home, on the other hand, nobody wanted to know. In Britain during that summer of 1970, they played just six concerts, each one as desultory as the last. The rest of their time was spent sequestered in the studio, helping out on Stewart's next album, *Gasoline Alley*.

It was to be almost as protracted an affair as its predecessor. After more than five years, Stewart had finally parted company with Rowlands and Wright, and was now sharing the same management as the Faces – the short, stocky figure of Billy Gaff, and his partner, Jimmy Horowitz. But shortly before the Faces went to the US, an article appeared in the magazine *Record Retailer*, describing Reizner as Stewart's manager. It offered Rod just the leverage against his producer that he needed.

"If you're my manager then you've got to get me some more money," he told Reizner.

"But I'm not your manager."

"That's not what I've heard, mate. If you want me to do another album, I want more money."

"I'm still not your manager."

"And I still want more money."

Reizner agreed he would talk to Irwin Steinberg yet again, and see what he could do. But the deal he worked out with the Mercury President was only going to lead to more problems later on, and Reizner knew it. Maybe Steinberg did too, which was why he concocted it. This Rod Stewart project was getting to be a real pain in the ass.

Reizner was to be allocated $12,000 to produce Stewart's new album. Any money left over when the record was completed was Stewart's.

"It was then," says Reizner, "that Rod's Scottish ancestry truly surfaced."

Among the English the Scots have long had a reputation of being very tight with their money. Indeed, the Scots claim exactly the same thing about the English. But Reizner didn't know that, just as he didn't know that if Stewart was mean – and most people who have worked with him say he definitely is – it had nothing to do with his ancestry, but was rather due to a childhood during which his money was spent as *he* wanted. Extravagance could only be countenanced if he were the primary beneficiary. And he didn't see how putting a bit more of *this* on to one song, a bit more of *that* on another, was going to help his cause one little bit.

In the studio with Reizner, Stewart argued every point, nickel-and-diming his producer into submission. If Reizner suggested bringing in a new musician, or trying a different way of recording something, Stewart

would first want to know the cost. If it was cheaper, fine. Otherwise
. . . forget it.

Reizner was at breaking point. He needed a vacation, and by God he
was going to take one. His brother, back home in the States, was getting
married, and Lou could only imagine how Rod would react when he
learned his producer intended to be at the wedding.

Stewart was furious. "You're meant to be making a record with me!
Not buggering off globetrotting. Forget the fucking wedding, I want
you here with me."

Reizner wouldn't budge, so Stewart tried another tactic.

"Look, this record's important. We can't just rush it through like
that!" he would whine. "This album has to be great, you know it has.
The record company is expecting it and I can't do it on my own. Come
on . . ."

Reizner's response was exactly what Stewart should have expected.
"If you're so worried about things like that, maybe you shouldn't spend
so much time screwing around before we get started on things. And
I'm still going to my brother's wedding!"

Stewart couldn't believe his ears. Even when Reizner left for the airport he was incredulous, and there was nothing he could do about it!
Or was there?

Stewart had recently heard a song called "Country Comfort", written
by the anonymous-sounding pairing of Elton John and Bernie Taupin.
It had just been recorded by Silver Metre, a band which featured
Woody's old mate Leigh Stephens, and a friend of Rod's named Harry
Reynolds.

Even though he said nothing to Reizner about it, Stewart decided to
record the song for his new album, handling the production himself.
To outsiders, it was a commendable decision, Stewart pushing on with
the record at a time when other artists might themselves have taken
a couple of weeks' break. Reizner, however, saw it for what it was –
a sneaky power-play. Stewart was saying he no longer needed his
old mentor. More than that he had never needed him. Not even for
Thin.

"I wouldn't say he produced the album," Rod insists. "He sat there
and made sure we were all in tune. I didn't learn anything off him
at all. When you enter the studio for the first time to make an album,
you need someone to give you a guideline, but he didn't need to be
there."

"After that period," Reizner mourns, "we sort of lost touch."

There was, in fact, one final act of this little drama to be played out.
Gasoline Alley was brought in for just under $7,000. That left $5,000-plus
for Stewart. With the record completed, and Reizner still out of the

country, Stewart simply took the tapes home and hid them under his bed.

Reizner, of course, called him as soon as he returned to London.

"So what's happening with the album?"

"It's finished. I finished it while you were away."

"Where is it, then? I've just been down to the studio and . . ."

"Oh, it's not there. I've got it."

"Can I have it, then?"

"Sure. But I want my money first."

Now Stewart was ransoming his own record!

Not everything about the *Gasoline Alley* sessions was so serious, however. Recording one of the songs, Stewart decided that Mickey Waller's drumming was louder than the number required.

"We're going to have to move you back a little," said Rod. And as if he had just remembered the old Jeff Beck Group notion of putting certain instruments in the cupboard, he suggested Waller take his kit out into the hallway.

Waller agreed, but still, Stewart insisted, he was too loud. "We're just going to have to move you again," he said. "Let's try it a bit more down the hall."

Again the drum kit was dismantled and re-erected a few feet further from the control room. And again Stewart was not satisfied. By the time he had finished, Waller was playing his drums in the street outside the studio. It was four o'clock in the morning, and Stewart was wetting himself with laughter. There had been nothing wrong with the drum sound at all. Rod was just bored, and was trying to brighten things up a bit.

Gasoline Alley was not a very different record to *Thin*. Again it drew upon Stewart's own vast reservoir of personal experiences, and the influences of Dylan ("Only a Hobo"), Eddie Cochran ("Cut Across Shorty") and the blues artist Bobby Womack ("It's All Over Now") are all in evidence. But it was also a very personal record, reflecting much that Stewart was feeling, both about himself and his personal life.

The title track, for instance, was a very plaintive study of homesickness. The idea came from a girl Stewart met during the first Faces tour of America, at the Fillmore West. "We were talking and she said something like 'I must get home, because my mother will say "Where have you been, down Gasoline Alley?"' And I said 'What?'

"Gasoline Alley is nowhere in particular to me. It was about a feeling I had when I was in Spain, and I couldn't get back to England. I wanted to, but I didn't have the money. It's a song about going home."

"Lady Day", too, was autobiographical, "about a girl I fell in love with a long time ago and she didn't want to know me." And "Jo's

Lament", as Stewart so quaintly put it at the time, "is about a girl I put in the family way." It was a story which was to return to haunt him in later years.

Gasoline Alley was released shortly before the Faces returned to the United States in November 1970. Stewart later confessed, "I made that album on a bottle of brandy", but he could afford to say things like that. The record was a masterpiece, and it was greeted as such. Langdon Winner in *Rolling Stone* was only the most effusive of its supporters: "The two Rod Stewart albums are together the most important listening experience I've had since the Band's first album. His music speaks with a gentleness and depth which seem to heal the wounds and ease the pain. The question of which of the two albums is the better does not interest me in the least. The music and spiritual content of them both is so totally extraordinary that I really cannot separate the two in my mind.

"*Gasoline Alley* is for me merely the second volume in what I hope will be a continually expanding 'Collected Works' of a supremely fine artist."

Bearing in mind that the same magazine's Greg Marcus had said of *Thin*, "Rod Stewart has come up with a superb album . . . imagination pervades the music . . . perhaps the only LP to be released this year that reflects something of the Stones' *Beggar's Banquet* . . ." it was clear that Stewart was fast earning some very influential friends.

These new mates were out in force when the Faces returned to America that autumn, and while Stewart did his best to play down what other people saw as a fast-widening chasm between his own popularity and that of the group, clearly it would take more than noble words to repair the breach. The success of *Gasoline Alley*, which reached number 27 in the US charts, only added to the band's discomfort.

Rolling Stone was just one of the magazines to ask Stewart if he saw himself as the band's leader. Interestingly, his response was very different to the "look at me" image he was projecting. "No, very far from it. I'm not the leader." But he confessed, "It's probably something I brought upon myself because *Gasoline Alley* was so big, and I feel like a lot of people are coming to hear the numbers off that album.

"[But] I really hope they're not just coming to see me. Because we're a band, and I want people to realise it's a band up there. The other guys are strong, too, in what they do. I wouldn't be in this group if I didn't think they were equally strong." But he admitted that "On this tour it seems to be *Gasoline Alley* that we're living off."

On their first tour, the Faces had been playing to predominantly male audiences, lured along either by recollections of the Small Faces, whose US audience had been considerably more mature than the screaming teenyboppers they attracted at home, or by memories of the Jeff Beck Group.

This time around, the crowd was more mixed, and by the time the Faces reached San Francisco, even Lane, Mac and Jones were comparing their reception to their own heady days as pin-up idols. From the moment the band took the Fillmore stage, the entire left-hand side of the auditorium erupted into screaming, "silly screaming", as Stewart called it. "I was afraid to go over on that side of the stage. I was getting like five yards from the side and walking back again. I didn't fucking know what was going on!"

The rest of the group, though, certainly did. They had seen it before, with Steve Marriott. He had been the frontman, the sex symbol. "Oh my God," their expressions said when they got back into the dressing-room. "I think it's starting again."

Stewart, however, seemed typically unconcerned. He was used to women throwing themselves at him, he laughed, and besides, he was busy with a girl he'd run into in Boston, and who had now attached herself, leech-like, to the tour.

Stewart met Joanne Alice Petrie at a party in New York in 1970, during the Faces' first tour. Then, contact had extended no further than a polite handshake. "A pleasure to meet you, Joanne." She didn't even have time to reply "Call me Jo Jo" before he was gone again. "But one look into those big brown eyes and every guy I'd ever known faded in comparison. I had to see him again."

The next time they met, Stewart dropped the formality. "As I walked past the dressing-room," Jo Jo remembers, "I felt somebody goose my bum. I spun around and saw Rod pass by, wearing that mischievous grin I would come to know so well."

Jo Jo returned the compliment the first opportunity she could. She hung around backstage during the performance, and when it came time to leave, Stewart took her hand. "It was obviously his unspoken assumption that I was to be his girl for the night."

Jo Jo and Stewart were all but inseparable for the next few days, and when the tour moved on to New Orleans, he handed her an airline ticket. "Make sure you're on that plane."

For Jo Jo, dating Rod Stewart, "the sexiest man in the business", was a dream come true. And Stewart, for a while, went along with her. But he still had eyes for other women, as Jo Jo found out when she arrived at the Fillmore, back in New York.

"I got a ticket to the show and told the doorman, 'Tell Rod it's Jo Jo.'" He flagged her in, but once backstage, "I couldn't believe the scene. A battalion of the world's most famous groupies were hanging all over him. When he spotted me he immediately walked over and gave me a monstrous hug. The other girls I know didn't like what they saw."

Stewart was obviously feeling cornered. A girl toward whom he felt some affection in one corner, a roomful of potentially memorable one-night stands in the other. He should have made up his mind what to do right there and then, but instead he did what he always does in unpleasant situations. Handing Jo Jo a glass of wine, he silently stalked out of the room.

By the time he returned, his retinue had swollen even further. And try as she might, Jo Jo couldn't attract his attention. All she got from him that evening was a hurried look as she sat crying on the stairs at the end of the show. She translated it as "Sorry, luv, but what can I do?" Poor Miss Petrie could feel her heart sinking as he padded away.

The Faces had been in fine form that night, so fine that two of the songs taped during the show, including Paul McCartney's "Maybe I'm Amazed", were retained for use on the band's second album.

They had originally intended recording the songs at the Marquee in London, as Rod remembers, "but at the last minute we got a bit worried about whether we would get the support from the Marquee audience. We knew we'd go down well at the Fillmore."

The decision to do the McCartney song was Stewart's, and as Jo Jo says, "Rod always loved the Beatles and thought Paul's solo work was brilliant [McCartney's self-titled first album had just been released]." Jo Jo herself, however, has ambivalent memories of Stewart's appreciation of Macca's music.

She hadn't seen or heard from him since that night in New York. Since then, the band had returned to Europe, toured Britain and Germany, and then doubled back to the USA for their third tour in less than a year. When the party reached Boston, she made a beeline for their hotel, turning up at Stewart's room completely unannounced. At the last moment she panicked. What if he had someone else in there? She cupped her ear to the door.

"I made out the sound of heavy breathing and telltale rhythmic movements of the bed." She was furious. Petrie knew that in New York she didn't have a chance against the "hard-core babes for whom groupie was a profession." But in Boston . . . in Boston, Stewart was *hers*. Jo Jo takes up the tale. "Why, you motherfucker, I thought to myself. Who've you got in there? Screwing some little tart in my own backyard. And then I heard a guitar. The supposed lovers' tryst was the thumping beat off the solo *McCartney*." The lovers were reconciled right then and there.

Like *Gasoline Alley*, *Long Player*, the second Faces album, was less of a departure from its predecessor than a slight progression. Work on the record started at the same place Stewart had been using, Morgan Studios in London. But "it took us a long time to get the sound we wanted, and we were getting frustrated."

The band picked up and moved into the Rolling Stones' studio in Mick Jagger's house in Newbury. It was expensive. The two songs recorded there, "Bad'n'Ruin" and "Tell Everyone", ended up costing close to a thousand pounds. But this time it wasn't Stewart's money being spent, it was the record company's, and "it was worth it", he says, "because we felt that we couldn't afford to cut any corners."

Back in America, Stewart had remarked that the Faces needed to make a "really good album, a team thing" if they wanted to exorcise the ghost of *Gasoline Alley. Long Player* was not that record, but in chart terms at least it came close. America sent it racing to number 29 in the chart, just two places below *Gasoline Alley.* For a time, egos were soothed . . . but they were soon to erupt again.

So far, Stewart had been fairly even-handed with the songs he was writing. The original divide he had sensed between his solo work and the Faces' albums had closed considerably. He was well aware that songs he wrote for his own records were often just as appropriate for the Faces to do, and so far he had been working on a first come, first served basis. If he had a record to make, he'd get the songs. If there was a Faces album in the works, the band could have them instead.

But now, he saw things were changing. Ronnie Lane was just as capable a songwriter as he – maybe a little less polished, maybe a bit more prone to the slower, more sensitive type of material, but apart from that he was fine. Now, probably for the first time in his life, and certainly for the first time with the Faces, Stewart felt endangered. What if Ronnie should start writing more songs or better songs than he? There was no alternative. He was going to have to fight Lane for songwriting supremacy. And, maybe unconsciously, he began by keeping the "best" songs for himself.

Work on Stewart's third album began almost immediately after the Faces' third American tour in 1971. Once again, Woody and Mickey Waller joined him in the studio, but the only other member of the Faces present was Mac. Stewart justified himself by saying, "We really gotta separate the two issues. Put the band over there and my albums over here. And keep the music as far away from each other as we can. So we can make nice rocker-type albums with the band, and I can do a bit of smooth stuff on the quiet."

Of course, *Every Picture Tells a Story* could not be that great a departure from the Faces' own direction. That would have spoiled everything. Besides, how could the Faces play Rod's songs in concert if they didn't fit into the set? And speaking of the set, there was one number already in the Faces' repertoire that Stewart quite fancied having a go at, the Temptations' "I Know I'm Losing You".

Stewart had a special reason for wanting to get the song down on vinyl as soon as he could. Talking to *Rolling Stone* during the second American tour, Stewart mentioned that he would like to produce David Ruffin, the Temptations' vocalist. "I'd love to pick the songs he should sing, because he doesn't seem to know."

Ruffin read the interview, and when the Faces hit Detroit, the entire Ruffin family was there. "His wife, his sisters, his bass players, his mum, everybody but him. Apparently they wouldn't let him in because it was a full house and they didn't know who he was!

"After the show his wife came round and said, 'When you did "Losing You" I really cried because David missed it.'"

Stewart and Ruffin met up later in the evening, back at the hotel, and parted with Rod promising he would be in touch. So far, he hadn't had the chance . . . so he recorded one of Ruffin's songs instead. The fact that he had virtually stolen it from the Faces didn't even cross his mind.

The Faces, of course, saw things in a very different light. Even when Stewart invited them all along to play on the song, their ruffled feathers were not smoothed. They had already half-decided to record "Losing You" themselves, for their next album. Now it would just be filed away as another Rod Stewart song, and when they played it on stage it would be Stewart who got the applause. Not the Faces.

"'Losing You' could've been on a Faces album, but there are so many things that could've made a great Faces album," said Kenney Jones later. "I put the band first, which I think we should all do. [Because] then the Faces would turn out a great album. In other words, when you've got a good song, put it to the Faces first, and we'd make a great album." The alternative, of course, was that the Faces would always play second fiddle to their ambitious lead singer.

This resentment grew as Stewart's star climbed ever higher, until even the ever laid-back Woody was getting fed up. On a couple of occasions, both in the USA and in Britain – where Stewart's fame was just beginning to seep into view – promoters advertised the band as "Rod Stewart *and* the Faces", and Woody admits, "It did use to bug me a little. If people didn't know Rod was in the group, hard luck, but if it had to be forced on them, then it got a bit out of hand." Whenever they got the chance, the band would scratch out the first part of the name, so it just read "the Faces".

Of course, Stewart's great success was not doing the Faces any harm. "It used to help our attendance at concerts and everything," remembers Woody. "The public has to single out one member of the band, so why not Rod? He'd waited long enough. I never begrudged him."

"When I went in to make *Every Picture Tells a Story*, I wanted to make another *Gasoline Alley*," says Stewart. "If your last album's moderately accepted, you go in thinking, 'I'll try and do it again, but better.' Only it didn't turn out like that."

Creatively, Stewart had grown immeasurably during the year since *Gasoline Alley*, sampling his first taste of critical acclaim. He had been the center of attraction at parties, clubs and backstage at shows. And he had decided to produce himself.

Stewart was adamant that Reizner didn't do anything more than keep the band in tune, whilst finding ever more extravagant ways of spending their money. So serious was Rod in his condemnation of Reizner that when he heard that Long John Baldry was making a comeback, Stewart was on to him like a shot.

"I was being managed by Billy Gaff, and through him just signed with Warner Brothers," says Baldry. "Rod got to hear about it so he volunteered his services as producer. Warners loved the idea, and we were going to go ahead."

But things didn't quite work out as planned.

"That Christmas, 1970," says Baldry, "Rod and I went over to Billy Gaff's apartment in Pimlico for a party and Elton John was there. Now Elton had also been in one of my bands, Bluesology, and of course Rod had recorded 'Country Comfort' but they had never met.

"So we got chatting and I mentioned I was about to start the album with Rod, and Elton says, 'Oh, I'd love to get involved.' He got very excited about it, and we arranged things so Rod would produce one side of the album, and Elton the other."

"The first time I met Rod Stewart," Elton remembers, "I was still at school and Steampacket was playing at the local Conservative Club. Afterwards I went to the pub, strolled up to him and said, 'Excuse me, Mr Stewart, can I have your autograph?' Wild! He used to come on stage with a scarf around his neck and sing 'Good Morning Little Schoolgirl'. I thought he was great."

Since then, their paths had crossed on more than one occasion. The Faces' American tours had followed almost exactly the same routes as Elton's, and with the little fat pianist already established as the hottest Brit import since the Beatles, it hadn't hurt Stewart one bit when he recorded "Country Comfort" – even if he hadn't realised who wrote it.

Now they were to work together. Rod would handle "the punchy side", Elton a more relaxed selection of songs. Later, when Long John appeared on "Top of the Pops" to perform his new single, "Iko Iko", both Rod and Elton leaped up on stage with him to add backing vocals.

It Ain't Easy was a great album, recapturing much of the magic Long John had lost during his period of late-sixties pop stardom. And while it didn't particularly sell, it did lead to a second Baldry–Stewart–John collaboration, *Everything Stops for Tea*, two years later.

Stewart was especially proud of his efforts. *"It Ain't Easy* is such a good album," Stewart enthused later. "I was ridiculously pleased with it." What he really meant was that he was ridiculously pleased with his performance. In the studio, performing before his old boss and, as both Stewart and – very modestly – Baldry have acknowledged, his greatest influence, faced, too, by Elton John's fast rising star, Rod pulled out all the stops as a producer. Now he was to take the experience and apply it to his own work.

Recording *Gasoline Alley*, Stewart had somehow got it into his head to resurrect the mandolin, an instrument which barely even showed its face in folk music any more. He used it sparingly, wondering perhaps how people would react to it. On his third solo album, *Every Picture Tells a Story*, he and Woody wrote an entire song around the instrument, "Mandolin Wind": "We did that after we just came back from the States. We'd finished with the Jeff Beck Group and were on our own. I was living in Muswell Hill, Ellington Road, and I remember Andy Fraser, Free's bassist, came round. I'd been looking for a way to incorporate mandolin, which is so much a part of the Celtic heritage, on to a record."

It was one of the first songs recorded for the album, and was to become the cornerstone of the entire venture. Even when the mandolin didn't appear, its sound seemed to percolate the songs. And when it was present, the effect was electrifying. "Maggie May" was testament to that.

With the mandolin quivering alongside some catchy blue-grass fiddling, Stewart's arrangement of guitarist Martin Quittenton's melody launched the song to its now legendary status.

"It was the first up-tempo ballad I ever did," he remembered. "I always thought the mandolin was such a romantic-sounding instrument. It sounds very Italian to me. I found the mandolin guy who played on *Every Picture Tells a Story* and "Maggie May" and the fiddle player in a restaurant in London playing romantic songs from the 1930s. In the studio I would just whistle the parts for them to play. That's one thing I pride myself on, coming up with melody lines for the instruments."

Mickey Waller's flustered drumming rounded out a distinctive flavor which characterised not only "Maggie" but the entire album. "He used to turn up with just his snare, a base drum and sometimes a high hat, the most humble of equipment," Stewart recalled. "If you listen to 'Maggie May' there's no crash cymbals because he didn't use any. The early solo records were made in a random way."

The infectious melody notwithstanding, it was Stewart's lyrical content based on an incident from his past that gave the tune its unmistakable hallmark.

Back in the summer of 1961, Stewart's sexual career had taken an unexpected upturn when he joined the army of music fans heading down to historic Beaulieu House in Hampshire, for the annual Jazz Festival in the stately grounds.

Stewart attended the festival for much the same reason as he tagged along on the Aldermaston marches – for a good laugh, a lot of Real Ale, and the chance of getting laid. Even the music – and many of the greatest names in jazz would be performing – was incidental, and Stewart intended to spend an enjoyable weekend simply wandering around the tent city which had grown up in the grounds.

First, however, he had to get in. Stewart bundled down to the south coast with a group of like-minded friends, all of whom were refused entry at the gate because they looked so scruffy.

Taking their problem to a local pub, the group met with a friendly farmer who kindly pointed out a way into the grounds which had no guards whatsoever, "unless you're averse to a good stink, that is." He then directed them to a manhole, and soon the would-be jazz buffs were sploshing along through a mile or so of raw sewage looking for the next outlet, which just happened to be alongside the beer tent.

Stewart might have spent the entire weekend there, had it not been for fate and a well-built older woman lending a hand. Rod was making his way around the camp ground when suddenly "this lady got a hold of me and pulled me into her tent!" He adds, with becoming modesty, "The whole thing didn't last more than about thirty-five seconds. I don't even remember her name!" From such brief encounters as this, however, great legends do sometimes grow.

Littered with rattling, lyrical images and capped by Stewart's reedy, passionate delivery, the catchy tune became a kind of Everyman's anthem during the autumn of 1971.

Yet "Maggie May" very nearly didn't appear on the album. No one could see its potential. It was a maudlin song about a long-ago love affair, they said, no great shakes. Only at the very last minute, when somebody noticed how short the record would otherwise be, was it included. And when it came time for choosing a single – an exercise which Rod's track record so far suggested was scarcely worth losing any sleep over – it was "Reason to Believe" which got the thumbs up. "Maggie May" was buried away on the b-side.

"I was nearly persuaded to take that off the album," says Rod. "A mate I was knocking about with at the time said he didn't think it had anything melodic to offer. I sort of agreed with him but it was too late because we didn't have any more tracks. Even more important, when it came out on a single it was the b-side."

And there it might have remained, if a Cleveland DJ hadn't turned the record over one day. He played "Maggie May", played it again and again, and by one of those miraculous flukes upon which the record industry so quietly turns, other stations began to follow suit. On 17 July, 1971, "Maggie May" entered the Hot 100. And it didn't stop climbing until it had reached number one. Stewart acknowledges, "If it weren't for that disc jockey I wouldn't be here today. I'd still be digging graves in the cemetery."

In Britain, the story was very much the same. On 4 September, "Reason to Believe" crept slowly into the lower reaches of the Top 50. Two weeks later, radio stations began playing "Maggie May". For three weeks in October 1971, Rod Stewart was number one in both the UK and USA on both the singles and album charts. He had arrived . . . and the Faces had to live with him.

The band's fourth American tour took place, perhaps thankfully, just before "Maggie May" reached its peak, but already they were getting a taste of what was to come. The craziness they had come to expect from American audiences was being directed more and more at Rod, and less at the rest of the band. Night after night, it was Stewart who would stand, bathed in the spotlight, while the audience hurled tokens of their affection at him, although on most occasions the rest of the group were glad to be well out of range.

"They throw underwear," Stewart once revealed. "Lots of underwear. And socks. One night, somebody was throwing bullets at me. It was during a concert in Santa Barbara. I asked one of the roadies to keep an eye out and see who it was. Turned out it was some guy standing right near the stage, so I hit him on the head with the mike stand. That stopped him." Interviewers – and where once there had been just a handful, now there were dozens – inevitably wanted only to talk to Stewart. If he couldn't make the date, if one of the Faces offered to turn up instead, the meeting would be canceled, or would pass off in such desultory small-talk that both interviewer and interviewee knew there was no chance of such drivel ever appearing in print.

Without warning, the manhunting Jo Jo suddenly reappeared on the scene, and even she felt bowled over by the sheer force of the express train which now bore Stewart. On the last tour, she remembers, Stewart had thought nothing of breaking away from the rest of the group to go shopping, or maybe take a soccer ball out to a local park. Now there always seemed to be another piece of business to watch, another man in a suit to attend to. When Jo Jo discovered she was pregnant, she

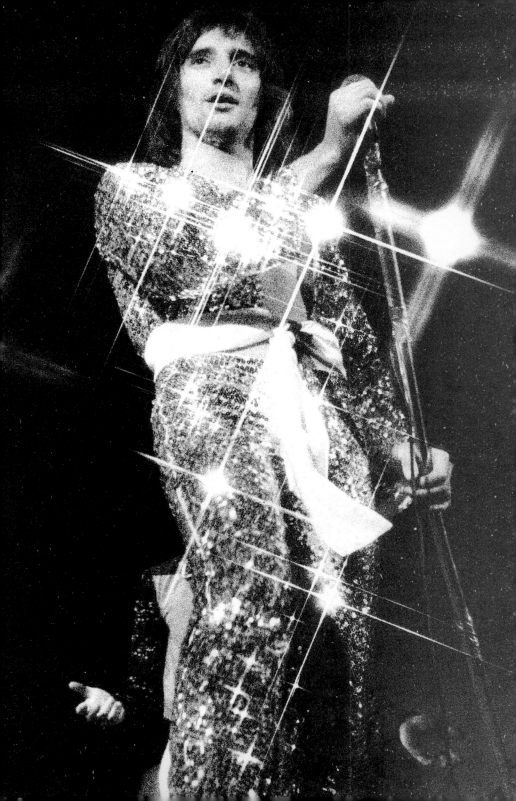

The Faces: a rare easy moment in an otherwise perpetually troubled band (left to right: Ian MacLagan, Kenney Jones, Ronnie Wood, Rod, Ronnie Lane)

The original Faces very close to the end of their tether together (left to right: MacLagan, Lane, Rod, Wood, Jones)

Ronnie Lane, a talented musician and composer who's seen his share of heart-ache

Face to face on stage with Ronnie Lane during the Faces last hurrah

Above: Rod and the two Ronnies on stage

Below: In rehearsal

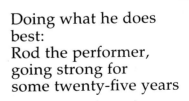

Doing what he does
best:
Rod the performer,
going strong for
some twenty-five years

Left: Ronnie Wood

Above & below left: Always the best of mates, Rod and Woody's relationship continues unabated to this day

Below: On the road: the Bob Hope and Bing Crosby of pop

could not even find time to tell Stewart about it, even if she'd wanted to.

"There was no question that it was Rod's baby," Petrie recalls. "As I hadn't been with anyone else. But there was no way I could tell him, envisioning all sorts of nasty headlines in the British tabloids. With his career about to rocket into the stratosphere, the publicity would have proved devastating. I just couldn't do that to him." Petrie eventually suffered a miscarriage.

Later, Jo Jo speculated that Stewart may indeed have believed that he'd made her pregnant. She met up with him in February 1973, while she was carrying her future husband, Denny Laine's, child, and a few months later she saw him on "Top of the Pops" performing "Oh No, Not My Baby" – his then-current hit. As he sang the little lyric, he made a gesture she recognised from their last fleeting meeting, "curving his hand over his stomach." Was it possible, she mused, that "Rod suspected the child could be his?" Probably not. Such a movement, although Petrie didn't know it, has long been English schoolboy-speak for anyone's pregnancy.

Back in May 1971, before *Every Picture Tells a Story* was released, the band played an open-air festival at London's Crystal Palace. The show, as riotously chaotic as any in America, totally failed to move an audience far more interested in soaking up the sun while they waited for the headlining Pink Floyd to appear and doodle away the evening with their soporific psychedelia.

This time around, the Faces were co-headlining the Weeley Festival with T Rex, a band which already had two runaway number ones to its credit. T Rex were due to appear last, but were late arriving at the site. The Faces were called back for encore after encore, and when T Rex did finally appear, they were all but inaudible above the continuing din.

Three weeks later, the Faces sold out the Queen Elizabeth Hall in London, one of the most prestigious venues in the capital. Two weeks later, they even gave the Who a run for their money at the Oval Cricket Ground, at a charity concert for starving Bangladesh.

What really established Stewart, however, and by association the Faces, was the string of British television appearances they made to support "Maggie May" in her frantic push up the charts. Britain at that time had only one Top Forty-oriented pop program, the eight-year-old "Top of the Pops". Aired every Thursday night at 7.30, it was a must-see for every pop-conscious teenager in the land. Its audience topped fourteen million, one quarter of Britain's total population. Virtually any record featured on the show was almost automatically guaranteed success.

But success such as that awaiting Stewart attends only the most memorable of performers, and Rod knew it. Surrounding himself with the Faces, each of whom was wielding the wrong instrument, calling disc jockey John Peel in to mime the song's distinctive mandolin lines, Stewart waited until the cameras were rolling, then produced a football out of nowhere. While the pre-recorded backing track played, he and the band simply booted the ball around the stage.

It was an outrageous performance. "Top of the Pops" was hallowed ground, a time-honored institution. Of course it was common knowledge that few of the people who appeared on the show actually sang, or played their song, but mimed to it.

But they mimed well. They didn't kick bloody footballs around. Nor did they goof off at the microphone and refuse to make even a token attempt to maintain the deception. Actually to admit to the public that there was anything phony going on was a crime which nothing could vindicate. Nothing, that is, except success. In the two decades following "Maggie May", Rod Stewart was to become one of the show's most familiar faces.

With his immediate future now secure, Stewart put himself into the market for a new home. He had broken up with the long-suffering Sarah, and after renting out his Highgate dwelling to Long John Baldry, he took a deluxe mock-Tudor house in Winchmore Hill, Stanmore.

A year later in the autumn of 1972, Rod had eyes for a mansion, a thirty-two-room Georgian monster called Cranbourne Court. "Eight bedrooms, six reception rooms, five bathrooms, kitchen quarters, a separate wing for the staff . . . Christ, think of the parties we'll be able to throw!"

The Court's previous owner, Lord Bethell, placed it on the market for £89,000. Stewart didn't even haggle over the price. His accountants had recommended that he go as high as £100,000 in their bid to stave off the ever-hungry taxman. The property even adjoined Windsor Great Park, home to the Queen herself. "It'll be great to have her as my neighbor!' Stewart would laugh. "Perhaps I can pop round on Sundays to borrow some sugar."

Set in fourteen acres of garden, Cranbourne Court boasted a roomy lodge, stable and a mammoth swimming-pool. It was, as the newspapers swiftly pointed out, the ideal home for Pop's latest Superstar.

But there was another reason for Stewart to live like a Lord. He had found himself a new Lady. On 29 July, 1972, in Los Angeles, Stewart was introduced to Deirdre Harrington, the comely daughter of an English airline pilot. When Jo Jo Petrie wondered why Stewart's calls had stopped coming and why he seemed less enthusiastic when they met up later in the tour, she put it down to the inevitable pressure of work. She had no idea that "the sexiest man in the business" had just fallen in love.

5

Skinning The Cat

"At the party," remembers Harrington, "Rod was wearing a smashing white velvet suit and looked like an advert for Omo. One girl after another kept throwing herself at him. Then I became aware that he was staring at me.

"We went to bed that night, but he fell asleep. When we got dressed, Rod put on a pair of my white knickers. It was a symbol of our closeness, he said." Stewart later admitted he enjoyed the feel of lady's underwear, a remark which fueled the growing battery of questions surrounding Rod's true sexual preference, after Dee inadvertently revealed it to the world in a newspaper interview.

"He never forgave me for that," she says, although Dee was not the only person to comment upon Stewart's predilection for ladies' underwear. Britt Ekland, recalling her years with Rod at the end of the seventies, says, "Very often he chose to wear my cotton panties on stage. Not only were they more comfortable for him, but they were seamless and invisible beneath his skin-tight trousers."

A secretary at a small London record company, Deirdre "Dee" Harrington was a young woman who would definitely stand out at most parties back in 1971. Twenty-one years old, she was tall, blonde, and, perhaps most attractive of all, looked hopelessly lost. It was her first time in America; a friend of hers, Patsy Jones, had traveled to Hollywood to stay with her boyfriend – former Apple Records executive Jack Oliver – and when he told her to bring a friend, Dee was her first choice.

While she might have *looked* lost, however, standing there wearing her home-made blue dress with yellow flowers and a pair of white clogs, feeling "dowdy and insignificant", she wasn't exactly innocent. Just a few days earlier, Harrington did a test session with a *Playboy* photographer, and she knew she had done well. If her life hadn't suddenly taken a very weird turn, she might well have gone on to a lucrative future in modelling. "Patsy and I were both trying to get work out there," says Dee. "We were also planning to go on to Tokyo from LA. We never did either."

One evening, one of Jack's friends, Kenney Jones, came over for dinner. Dee cooked, and as the evening wore on, Jones asked if she, Patsy and Jack would like to go to the Faces' end-of-tour party at Bumbles the following evening. "I didn't particularly want to see the group," says Harrington, "but I did want to see inside Bumbles, which was the place to go in Hollywood at that time." Harrington admits that all she knew about Rod was the *Every Picture Tells a Story* album which Jack played constantly.

"The evening was everything I imagined a Hollywood party would be, with beautiful suntanned people wearing glamorous and exotic clothes. I didn't know then that most of them were worthless scroungers and hangers-on. But then, I didn't know much. To me they seemed the most exciting people in the world."

The Faces naturally arrived late, draped – as usual – in a second skin of willing female flesh. "You could hardly see them for the girls," Harrington remembers. "I watched Rod as he disentangled himself from one girl after another, but they still kept throwing themselves at him. He didn't seem to be enjoying it much."

Stewart spent most of the evening glancing in Dee's direction, but it was late, very late, before he first approached her. Aretha Franklin was playing on the PA system – "There Is a Rose in Spanish Harlem."

"Would you like to dance?"

Dee said sure, and tentatively, Stewart guided her round the dance floor. "Afterwards he took my hand and led me to a dark corner where we just sat and talked." Clearly, Stewart found the young blonde secretary attractive. She was pretty, she was intelligent. And, above all, she was English.

The Faces seemed to be spending almost as much time in the US as they were in England at this point, and Stewart, even though he could not have found a more down-to-earth link with Britain than the one he had already forged with the Faces, was, quite simply, homesick.

American women, and by this time there had been more than enough of them, might have been great for some things, but when he only wanted to talk, they just didn't understand. His reference points – the TV shows he loved, the house he lived in (he was still in the Stanmore mock-Tudor), even things like how much it meant to him to be finally winning over the hearts of Great Britain – soared right over the naive American girls' heads. Dee, however, knew well what he was talking about and understood how he felt. He turned on the Little Boy Lost act, and she swallowed it whole.

From Bumbles, the two of them decided to walk to the Whisky on

Sunset Strip, not because they particularly wanted to go to a club, but because it would give them longer alone. "Walking is practically unheard of in Beverly Hills," says Harrington, "and we hadn't gone far before a police car stopped us.

"The officers said it was too dangerous for us to walk by ourselves at that time of night and offered us a lift, but we refused. Almost inevitably we got lost, and in the end we took a taxi. By the time we got to the Whisky, it was closed."

"Do you want to come back to the hotel, then?" Stewart asked. "Yes," replied Harrington after a deep pause.

"I was very strongly attracted to him. He was so different from what I had imagined. He wasn't trying to paw me – he was just a nice ordinary guy."

Back in Stewart's room, Harrington caught another glimpse of the Little Boy. Somehow the conversation got round to cars, always an obsession with Stewart. "My favorite's a Lamborghini. I just bought one." He didn't mention that he still owed Lou Reizner close to $6,000 for it, but Dee wouldn't have heard him if he had. She was too busy watching him leap up and begin rummaging through his suitcase. After a couple of minutes he emerged triumphant. In his hand there was a die-cast Dinky toy. "There, that's it!"

Around 4 a.m., Harrington announced it was time she was leaving. Stewart looked stunned. "It would be nice if you could stay," he said, but she seemed adamant. As she later remembered, "I am not a prude, but I was not in the habit of jumping into bed only a few hours after meeting a guy."

But it was late, and she remembered what the police had said about being alone on foot after dark. Dee almost convinced herself that it might be better to stay when Stewart turned on one of the famous performances which always got him his own way.

"Actually, it might be better if you did go. I feel bloody awful anyway."

"What is it?" Harrington asked, immediately concerned. "Are you alright?"

Stewart let out a groan. "I'm buggered if I know. I have a splitting headache – I think I might throw up."

Dee sat down beside Rod, now stretched out on the bed with one arm over his eyes. "You don't have a temperature."

If he did peep out from behind the hands that covered his face, or let slip a little smile of triumph, Harrington never saw it. "When Rod convinced me he really was ill, I decided to stay."

Stewart kept the act up even after he'd won. "He turned out the lights before he got undressed and we both got into bed and went to sleep. I think he felt he could hardly make a miraculous recovery as soon as we were in bed."

Instead he waited until morning. But things weren't exactly a tremendous success. "I was very tense and nervous about being in a strange hotel room with someone I really didn't know, and I kept worrying about what people would think when they found out I had stayed the night."

As Stewart got out of bed afterwards, he said, "I think that was a bit one-sided, luv."

Harrington remained by Stewart's side throughout the remainder of the Faces' stay, although she admits it wasn't all good fun and loving. There were times when the rock'n'roller-coaster raced past just a little too close for comfort.

"The parties were the worst part. I had the curious feeling that the same people were at every one. They made the same noises and even seemed to look alike. They were empty, brash and superficial, only after what they could get."

Every night, Harrington remembers, "even if he started off standing in the very center of the room, he would always end up with his back against the wall, surrounded by people telling him how wonderful he was. I used to hate seeing him trapped like that. I was relieved to get back to the hotel and discover, away from the glitter and the glory, that he really was still the same guy I had met."

The Faces' tour ended just before Harrington's holiday, and when Stewart asked her to come home with him she refused. "I think he was disappointed, but he accepted my decision and we agreed to meet again as soon as I got back. I needed some time alone to think about what had happened."

The Faces arrived home from that 1971 tour and ran smack into the heart of the "Maggie May" maelstrom, insulating themselves from the hoopla by burying themselves in work on their own third album.

Two LPs into their career, and the Faces knew that they had still to tap their potential in the studio. In concert, they had everything down to a fine art. But in the stricter confines of the recording studio, there was still something missing. Finally, Stewart said what the others had already been thinking. "What we want is a good producer. What we want is Glyn Johns."

Ever since the row over the first album, Ronnie Lane had continued singing his old engineer's praises. "When it came to the mix, Glyn would get into it like a Cadillac – a big, warm, bouncy sound. That's where he wins – he knows how to mix a record. He'll pull something out of it that you never knew was there."

Then Stewart chimed in. "It's easy enough to get my own albums together because it's all my own ideas. But with the band it's five people's ideas, and we really need a producer to act as a mediator. Glyn Johns in the only one worth having, as an engineer and producer."

And the money? Well, it wasn't Stewart's, so he didn't really care. "In the beginning, Johns wanted too much, but now we can afford him and I think he wants to do us. We don't need him and he doesn't need us, but I think the combination is a winner."

Johns, whose credentials included extended stints as engineer for the Beatles, the Who, the Stones and Led Zeppelin, leaped at the chance. Earlier in the year he had won an associate producer credit on the Who's landmark *Who's Next* album.

But there he'd had to share the glory with the band. The Faces were offering him undisputed control of the sessions, and he went at them like the devil. The band repaid him, not only with a production credit, not only with the once-disputed two per cent royalty, but also with a very heartfelt message on the album cover. "Thank you, Glyn, you made all the difference."

"As well as doing what a producer should be doing, and doing it well," remembers Mac, "he was like glue to us." Johns followed the band everywhere, immersing himself in everything that made the Faces what they were – the greatest rock'n'roll band in the country. The Stones had had their day. The Who were becoming too ambitious. Only the Faces still had the excitement, the *joie de vivre* that was rock'n'roll as it ought to be. And he recaptured every last ounce of that in the studio.

A Nod's as Good as a Wink to a Blind Horse was the album that catapulted the Faces on to almost equal footing with Stewart. Of course, Stewart's reputation had something to do with that, in Britain in particular. There, Mercury had still to release a follow-up single to "Maggie May". *Every Picture Tells a Story*, too, was old news. But people wanted more Rod Stewart, and the Faces were the next best thing. *A Nod* roared all the way to number two.

In America, however, it was a slightly different story. Both "Losing You", from *Every Picture*, and "Handbags and Gladrags", from *Thin*, had seen chart action in the wake of "Maggie May". But still the Faces made the Top Ten.

The album contained any number of indisputable Faces classics, including a barnstorming rendition of Chuck Berry's "Memphis" and the rollicking "Miss Judy's Farm". But there were also three songs by Ronnie Lane which, in the light of later events, were to be seen as peculiarly prescient. Or perhaps they were already sadly resigned.

On the first Faces album, Ronnie Lane and Woody had worked together on several songs, and for a time it looked as though a very strong writing partnership might emerge. Lane, of course, was swiftly usurped by Stewart, and now he wrote alone, creating those stirring but melancholic songs which many critics furiously denounced as having no business being on a Faces record. But in many ways they were what brought to the Faces the peculiar magic which drenched this new record.

Lane took the criticism hard, but seldom complained. Or did he? Lester Bangs, writing about one of Lane's songs on that album, *Debris*, admitted, "I have this theory that most of his songs are on at least one unhappy level addressed to Stewart." He goes on to quote from *Debris*, "We both know you got the money and I wonder what you woulda done without me hanging around." At the very least, it was certainly food for thought!

"Stay with Me", written by Stewart and Woody, was the record's focal point. "In the morning, don't say you love me," sang Stewart in his most dismissive tones, "'cos you know I'll only kick you out the door." And later, "Yeah, I'll pay your cab fare home, you can even use by best cologne, just don't be here in the morning when I wake up."

It was a song for every groupie, in every town, hanging on to every band, in the world, a vicious, misogynistic essay which, if nothing else, set the seal on Stewart's reputation for arrogance and personal carelessness. I don't want you around in the morning, "but tonight you're gonna stay with me."

The song made many people uncomfortable, particularly in America. Woodstock, that crowning achievement of the counter-culture, was less than two years old. The ideals that had grown out of the hippy generation had still to bear their fullest fruit. Women's Lib was in full swing, fighting its way up through the thickening mass of white male-dominated society. Now here was Stewart kicking it down again, proving that behind the smile, the hair-do and the good-time bravura he was as big a chauvinist pig as anyone.

"I think he had his values all screwed up," says Reizner. "When it came to discussing anything on a political level, he was almost like a child."

Stewart concedes that he is not at all political, at least in his music. When he recorded "Street Fighting Man", he remembers, "it was like I was trying to lead the revolution over here or something. [People] look too deeply into music . . . this happens a lot in America. I recorded 'Street Fighting Man' because it was a funky old number and because somebody had to hear those incredible lyrics." He looks incredulous. "Me? Lead a revolution? Get out of here!"

"Stay with Me", perhaps the most childish of all his musical outbursts, was a watershed in Stewart's battle for acceptance. Previously, over the course of three solo albums of ever-increasing sensitivity and majesty, he had at least given the impression that he cared, that he had something important to say, even if it was bound up in some kind of semi-autobiographical angst. There was something in his songs that struck a sympathetic chord – a yearning for home, for the past, for any of a thousand different things.

But "Stay with Me" was downright spiteful, a nasty slice of maggoty rancor whose cruelty was only increased by the rollicking, irresistible backing of the Faces. It was a classic rock song, no one could deny that. When it came on the radio, it was impossible not to sing along. So insidious was it that it, too, struck a chord. Its very sordidness seemed glamorous, and it was only when you actually thought about what Stewart was singing that you did a double-take.

Such philosophical misgivings did nothing to harm the single's success during the new year of 1972. It made number six in Britain, went to seventeen in the States, and in its wake the band stormed out on yet another American tour, to be followed by their first full British outing.

According to Ronnie Wood, the Faces hit the road in America at exactly the same time as the Rolling Stones launched one of their own increasingly sporadic tours. In actuality, several months separated the expeditions. The Faces toured in April 1972 and again in September; the Stones went out during June and July. But their presence hung heavy over the country nevertheless, and Woody remembers how, in Rod's eyes, a band which had once been looked up to as gods were suddenly reduced to mere rivals – in every stake imaginable.

"We'd never admit it, but the Faces were actually pretty influenced by those old farts," Woody reminisces. "We sometimes warmed up in the dressing-room by listening to the *Get Yer Ya Yas Out* album." But that was in the days when the Stones were still the undisputed Kings of Rock. By 1972, the Faces were ready to steal their crown – and a lot of their thunder.

Three years earlier, the Stones had staged the Rock'n'Roll Circus, a succession of acts taking place in a Big Top. The Faces were now producing their own variation on that theme by taking a real live circus out with them. Jugglers, motorcycle stuntmen, fire-eaters and trapeze acts preluded the band's appearance on stage, creating a spectacle which may not have had much to do with real rock'n'roll but which certainly irritated the Rolling Stones!

So did Stewart's onstage antics. As well as his wardrobe, Rod was slowly, and not always subtly, beginning to ape many of Jagger's onstage movements. The two bands also found themselves sharing the same chicks after shows. It was the groupies, rather than the time-honored dressing-room walls, which were being used to ferry messages and insults back and forth between the two bands.

Considering how many women showed up for each gig, the hard-core groupie community was surprisingly close. When the Stones got around to developing the hours of film which ultimately became the infamous *Cocksucker Blues*, one of the film's most visible, and in the context of the movie, voracious stars, Renee, remembers that every musician she met that summer – a roll-call which included members of T Rex, the J. Geils Band, Edgar Winter and the Faces – only had one thing in mind. One "very crass, famous musician" introduced himself to her with the invitation to suck his dick. "They all expect me to do something wild every time."

The rock'n'roll grapevine echoed with a Who's Who of Sexual Acrobats. In Detroit, the Plaster Casters had left behind a legacy of quite infamous abandon. Then there was the girl who liked nothing more than getting screwed by a cast of Jimi Hendrix's prick. In Seattle, there was apparently a whole line of women waiting for someone to fuck them with a fish. There was the Butter Queen, who specialised in greasing her visitors' anatomy, the GTOs . . . even dimwitted little Jo Jo Petrie had earned herself something of a reputation on the circuit.

The Stones and the Faces were never in the same city at the same time, but occasionally no more than a few weeks separated them. And that could sometimes lead to problems.

If the Faces got in first, fine. "I hope mine ends up with Jagger," someone would crack as the band compared notes on the previous night's adventures. "I'd swear she's got the crabs."

When the boot was on the other foot, however, and the Stones had been in first, things were a lot more circumspect. "Sticky buns are fine," Rod would say as he contemplated – with that charming English colloquial euphemism – going to bed with a girl fresh from another man's arms, "but I hope the old cream ain't Keith's!"

The Stones and the Faces finally met up at the Beverly Wilshire in LA. It was the first – and last – time any hotelier was to make that mistake. Both bands' entourages gathered together in Woody's room, a sumptuous suite decked out in mirrors. Every single one was smashed, and as the Faces drove away the next day, poor Woody was still calculating just how many years of bad luck he had to look forward to.

The US visit sowed more seeds of discord within the band. By now the Faces were so big that they could headline the largest venues around. Madison Square Gardens was sold out weeks in advance, and Woody – who opened the show by striking "the worst note I had ever heard" from a horribly out-of-tune guitar – remembers, "We were playing to much bigger audiences than we ever wanted to." The band was making money, but losing intimacy.

Ronnie Lane, in particular, was feeling the strain. He considered larger venues, with correspondingly higher ticket prices, a sacrifice which the band should never have made. It exploited the fans and, besides, he missed "the lovely gigs in old, shitty theaters with dirty floorboards."

Only Stewart seemed unaffected by it all. Woody told the *New Musical Express*, "Rod's had a lot of problems with success. It's taken him completely by surprise." It was a polite way of saying his head was getting very, very big.

According to Dee Harrington, however, egotism was the furthest thing from Rod's mind when he was with her.

"He was great," she says today. "He's very shy, but he's a very funny person as well, who likes a joke and can always make everybody laugh. When people refer to his egotistical side that's the performance side of him. For the first years we were together, he was just an ordinary person. He simply went out to work as a rock star. But away from that, we had this wonderful life together because he loved his privacy, and he loved his home."

Harrington moved in with Stewart in the summer of 1972, shortly before he bought Cranbourne Court. "We had to move from the house in Winchmore Hill," she says, "because on a Sunday Rod was on the guided coach tours." Regular as clockwork, packs of sightseeing tourists would motor past the luxurious, but unassuming, mock-Tudor, cameras at the ready, waiting for their tour guide to give the word. "We are now passing pop star Rod Stewart's home." Rod and Dee quickly learned to spend their Sunday mornings well away from the road!

"We used to get people coming to the door, and when I say that Rod liked his privacy, he didn't like walking out of his front door into a herd of people!"

For a time, Harrington kept her day job, but Stewart soon put a stop to that. As she got ready to leave each morning, he would roll over in bed and ask, "How can you possibly leave me?"

"Quite easy. Just watch me."

So he would wait until she got to the office, then bombard her with phone calls. "You're too good for that place," he would tell her, "and besides, I need you with me. Come on, give it up." He had, she says, "all kinds of reasons why I should stop working and move in with him. In the end, I agreed."

At last she had won admission to Stewart's inner sanctum, the first girl to do so since the mysterious Sarah. And like Sarah, Dee saw a side of him which his fans never dreamed existed. Unwashed, unshaven, Stewart would often wear the same old clothes for days on end, lounging around the house all day long, and only getting up for sex . . . or to clean the house.

"He was exceptionally houseproud," says Harrington. "He used to love dusting and polishing, especially the brass, and would vacuum the carpets almost every morning." Stewart apparently delighted in domesticity. "After he bought Cranbourne Court, for two years we decorated the house, fenced the fields, just did the things any couple does when they buy their first home together."

He was also quite a revelation in bed. "I often thought he was over-sexed," Dee admits. "Sometimes we had barely finished making love before he wanted to start again. And when he came back from tours, the first thing he wanted to do was jump into bed with me."

That, at least, was in keeping with the image. But elsewhere, "Rod was a million miles away from the public perception of a rock star," Dee laughs. "For instance, when we had visitors come down, the first thing he'd say would be, 'Right, leave your drugs outside my front door.' He was so outrageous! I wasn't even allowed to smoke a ciga-rette!" In years to come, Harrington would look back on this early puri-tanism with an emotion approaching sheer wonder.

"I always put Rod's wishes first and my own second," says Dee, "an arrangement he regarded as a divine right. But I didn't mind. After all, I loved him. In some ways, he had never grown up. He hated it if I disagreed with him and would sulk for hours. He always had to have his own way and would make an awful fuss if he didn't feel well."

She also discovered that he could be furiously jealous. "When he went on tour Rod phoned me every day and expected me to be home. If I wasn't there, he would assume I was out with another bloke. I never was. I never even looked at another guy when I was his girl."

Had she only been on speaking terms with the rest of the Faces family, Dee might well have saved herself a lot of unpleasant surprises. Unfortu-nately for her, the seething, and steadily increasing, resentment which was shooting through the rest of the group was not only reserved for Stewart. It was also applicable to anybody who Stewart seemed to care for.

"From day one," Dee recalls, "Rod told me not to get involved with the Faces' wives – Krissie Wood, Jan Jones and Sandy MacLagan. He said they were bad news, always trying to outdo each other with clothes, jewelry and things. At first I thought he was just being funny, but it turned out that there was quite a lot of ill-feeling going on there."

At the airport with the wives one time, waiting for the flight out to New York where they would be attending the Madison Square gig, Harrington remembers how she was totally ignored by everybody. "It was as if I didn't exist. I couldn't understand why they had it in for me, although I learned later that the Rolling Stones' wives reacted in a similar way to Bianca Jagger." They saw her as a threat, as someone who would side with Stewart in everything, building up his selfish resolve while he ground the group into the dirt. Of course they resented her, and to no one's surprise the dislike was mutual.

"They were always arguing about money. If one of them had a more expensive outfit than the others, for example, they would immediately accuse her husband of earning more than he should. I thought they were just pathetic."

Her opinion of the band apparently wasn't much higher. Always squabbling, always petty . . . what she didn't know was that, behind the scenes, her lover was giving the Faces more and more reasons to behave that way.

The group started work on a new album only months after *A Nod's as Good as a Wink* came out. Stewart was handling production this time, but it swiftly became apparent that it just wasn't going to work; that he was, in fact, simply creating yet another album in his own image. In the end he agreed to scrap the sessions, adding something about salvaging anything that looked good. Which may or may not have been his intention all along. "True Blue", the song that opens the fourth Rod Stewart album, *Never a Dull Moment*, was pulled straight from the abortive Faces recordings, and the rest of the band soon knew they had been had.

If Stewart had come out and simply said "Play on my record, I'm doing 'True Blue'", he knew how they would have reacted. So he approached the problem from a different direction, and then, to rub salt into the wound, he ripped three more songs from the heart of the Faces' own repertoire – Jimi Hendrix's "Angel", Sam Cooke's "Twisting the Night Away", and "I'd Rather Go Blind", an Etta James song which had been a hit for Christine Perfect four years earlier.

The band continued protesting, but what was the point? They knew exactly what he would say. "We agreed, didn't we, that the sessions were useless? I was just sweeping up what you didn't want." The Faces were reaping the rewards of their early indecision, back when they'd sidestepped the issue of distributing material.

There was only one member of the band Stewart was listening to now, only one person who had laid down any ground-rules he seemed to respect, and that, of course, was Woody. Dee Harrington marvels at how close the pair of them were. "They had a great thing going, a very tight relationship both creatively and when they weren't working." Most importantly, Rod respected what Woody had to say.

The good-time guitarist remembers, "The songs I composed with Rod, I either wrote with the Faces in mind, or him. We never used to scheme and say, 'Oh, let's save this one.' If I presented a melody to him, it was always 'This is definitely a Rod solo melody, or this is a Faces song', and if he used to say 'Oh no, let me have this Faces one for mine', I used to kick up and refuse."

100

Stewart, for his part, did not necessarily see all this as a problem. Speaking three years later, he said, "We've got more songs from *Never a Dull Moment* still with us in concert than any other album. We still play 'True Blue', 'You Wear It Well', 'Angel', and 'Twisting the Night Away'. They've stayed with us more than anything. So it says a lot for the album – it came out at the right time." The rest of the Faces just gritted their teeth and didn't dare say a word.

But Stewart did not always get things his own way. And the day somebody finally got one over on him – really got one over on him – the sniggering from his band, his friends and his management almost drove him to distraction.

In 1973 anybody purchasing the *History of British Blues* compilation album would have found a completely unknown Rod Stewart performance, "Stone Crazy", recorded with drummer Aynsley Dunbar, bassist Jack Bruce and Rod's old mate from Shotgun Express, guitarist Peter Green. The song had been recorded back in 1967, and had never been released anywhere.

Mike Vernon, who produced the recording, remembers, "Aynsley had just left Jeff Beck's group, and was putting together his own band. For a time there was talk of him and Rod staying together, particularly as nothing was happening with the Beck Group at that time, but it wasn't to be."

Former manager Geoff Wright says that such engagements were typical of Stewart, and that he was lucky there weren't more of them floating around. "We would phone him up if we had something to discuss, but he would never bother to phone us unless he had a problem. If he needed some money, he would call us up. But we never used to see him otherwise. And I think he probably did quite a lot of things we never even heard about."

Indeed he did. Back in 1969, a friend of his – "a car dealer trying to enter rock'n'roll management" is how Stewart describes him today, although it was actually disc jockey John Peel – asked Stewart to help out on some demos he was recording with a new Australian band, Python Lee Jackson. Peel had just signed them to his Dandelion record label, but they were having some problems with vocals. Stewart says he agreed to help out in return for some carpeting for his car.

His contribution was intended to be a guide vocal only, and in the normal course of events would probably never have been heard of again. But Python vocalist David Bentley never got around to recording a satisfactory vocal for the song, and while the band was keen to see a release for "In a Broken Dream", with or without Bentley singing, Peel wasn't quite so sure. A band called Chicory Tip had just hit the headlines, accused of not singing on their own hit single. The Dandelion label simply didn't need that sort of publicity.

Indeed, Peel let the band go, selling them and their tapes to the Youngblood label. And just around the time *Thin* appeared in the shops, "In a Broken Dream" – with Rod's vocal intact – was released, slightly remixed and with a hint of mellotron added.

There was little fanfare and less sales for the song, but the Youngblood label never gave up hope, and two years later, with "Maggie May" still fresh in everybody's mind, and Stewart's the most distinctive voice in the business, "In a Broken Dream" was re-activated.

As before, there was no mention of Stewart on the record label. The performance was credited to Python Lee Jackson alone. But there was no mistaking that voice. In May 1972, "In a Broken Dream" rose to the very brink of the US Top 50, selling 100,000 copies in the process. Five months later, Stewart's British fans sent it soaring even higher, to number three.

And while Python Lee Jackson was never to be heard of again – an album sank without trace, a follow-up single bombed likewise – "In a Broken Dream" remains a classic, so much so that Stewart even included it on *Storyteller*. "I was conned," he says of the experience today.

Never a Dull Moment was the archetypal "follow-up" record, an album recorded in that short space of time during which the initial euphoria of success has worn off, and the panic to recapture it has begun to creep in. As always, Stewart took the easy way out.

Never a Dull Moment, in many ways, is the identical twin of *Every Picture*, as Stewart's own liner notes admit. "Far be it from us to affiliate any previous constructions on past editions – not withstanding any resemblance between this and the last phonographic achievement . . ."

His excuses, however, didn't really fly. For the first time Stewart found himself having seriously to defend himself against some rather pointed criticism. Too much of the record simply repeated its predecessor. "You Wear It Well", the first (and in Britain only) single from *Never a Dull Moment*, rewrote "Maggie" with breathtaking skill, once again pairing Stewart's lyrics with a salty Martin Quittenton melody. But whereas "Maggie" had been refreshing and memorable, "You Wear It Well" was . . . derivative and memorable.

Jo Jo Petrie claims the song was written about her. She and Stewart had drifted apart – Jo Jo was seeing her future husband, Wings star Denny Laine, and Stewart was involved with Dee Harrington. "But if there was any doubt about how Stewart felt for me, I only had to turn on the radio and there it was, a permanent tribute for all the world to hear."

Jo Jo continues, "Rod played it for me that June before my twenty-first birthday, both of us knowing without expressing it that our relationship had come to a bittersweet end. That last night we'd come back to the hotel after the show and Stewart was heading into the shower. He put on the record and coyly said, 'I want you to hear this. You'll know what it means.'"

Petrie isolates the lyrics that mean the most: " 'Homesick blues, radical views haven't left a mark on you' – meeting Stewart all over the country, pouring out my longing to go back to Boston.

" 'When you sat there and cried on the steps . . .' – that rueful incident with the New York groupies.

" 'Remember them basement parties, your brother's karate . . .' – little snippets I'd told him about my family.

" 'Remember that you were once mine.' It still remains the most treasured gift I've ever received."

"You Wear It Well" hit the British top spot in September 1972, at the end of one of the most momentous summers in British rock history. Glam Rock, the shimmering, glistening monster spawned by T Rex, brought up by David Bowie, and adopted by everyone from Stewart's old producer Mickie Most to Elton John, exploded over the entire music scene, showering everybody in spangles and glitter. And the Faces were no exception.

Once, they had been content simply to turn out in jeans and T-shirts, their sneakers and unkempt hair bookends to a dishevelled casualness which had taken one too many backward trips through a hedge. Even Stewart, the once-immaculate Rod the Mod, had gone through his scruffy phase. It went with the image, he would say. What was the point of togging up to the nines if the rest of the band looked like bricklayers?

Lou Reizner remembers seeing Stewart one day, very obviously wearing "clothes he had outgrown. Popping out the buttons of his shirt . . . trousers that came down to just above his ankles." It was a unique look certainly, but not a particularly attractive one.

Slowly, however, the peacock began to re-emerge. He had seen Marc Bolan camp it up on "Top of the Pops", a breathtaking swirl of satin and tat. He watched pudgy little Elton change from a studious owl into comic-book fantasy. He saw David Bowie wearing a dress in *Rolling Stone*. It was a time when effeminacy became a masculine fashion. "It's not a lady's dress," giggled the bashful Bowie. "It's a man's dress. My friend makes them for me."

Cautiously, Stewart joined in the fun. A velvet suit here, a satin suit there. In concert, he seemed to spend a lot less time falling on the floor than he used to. If the plane ride was bumpy, he wouldn't be holding a drink.

Jo Jo Petrie recalls being in a limo with Stewart when a pizza appeared on the scene. "I offered some to Rod. 'Get away from me with that!' he erupted. 'What do you think you're doing?'" Stewart reportedly spent the rest of the journey brushing imaginary specks of tomato off his jacket.

By the summer of 1972, Stewart's taste in clothes had infected many. Bernie Taupin, Elton John's lyricist, remembers that he and Stewart, for a time, were furiously trying to upstage one another in the clothing stakes. "If I got a tuxedo from Yves St Laurent, Stewart had to go and have one made exactly the same. Then I'd try to get shirts made the same as his."

A lot of Stewart's reborn fashion sense, says Woody, was lifted from Mick Jagger. "Mick's running joke – and it was true – was, 'I see Rod's wearing the same pyjamas this year that I wore last year.' The feather boa, the cheesecloth outfits – Mick was right. "It didn't even look good on Rod most of the time!"

Matters came to a head, Woody continues, when Jagger turned up at a Faces show at Newark's Roosevelt Stadium and spent the entire evening standing behind an amplifier out of sight of the audience, gesticulating wildly at Woody and exhorting him to look at what Rod was wearing. "It's mine! It's mine!" he was shrieking, and while Woody did try to ignore him, it was impossible. How can you fail to notice when the vocalist from the Greatest Rock'n'Roll Band in the World is pulling faces at your lead singer?

The Faces weren't impressed by the new fashions, but Stewart quickly made it plain he didn't care for their objections. Like children rebelling against their mother's taste in trousers, the Faces were dragged kicking and screaming into the heart of this latest sartorial revolution.

Out went the faded denims, in came pricey flowing flares and elephantine bell-bottoms. Out went the comfy T-shirts, in came Mr Fish shirts and Carnaby Street neckerchiefs. Proudly disrupted hair was spiked and glossed and spiked again. On the fashionable battlefields of British Pop, the Faces may never have made front-line troops. But they were still a great-looking (if reluctant) band of guerrillas.

That their new shiny threads hadn't really changed things one iota became evident when work on the next album began, in the autumn of 1972.

Stewart did not even show up at the studio for the first two weeks of recording, and when he did arrive, all he did was complain. Ian MacLagan remembers, "We had most of the tracks finished and he'd be on a real downer. He'd say, 'I don't like that', and it was like being up in front of a teacher. It was very disheartening.

"All right, some of the tunes were in the wrong key, but how were we supposed to know what key to put them in? We put them in the key they were written in. And when it came down to Stewart singing them, either he didn't like the words because he hadn't written any, or he didn't like the tune or he didn't like the key or he didn't like the way we played it, so it virtually meant that most of the tracks were blown out."

One song, "Ooh La La", he says was recorded four times – "and the first one's still the best."

Stewart himself remained dismissive about the album, even to the extent of hammering it in the music press. Glyn Johns, who was again producing, has equally harsh memories of the sessions. But unlike Stewart, who simply lashed out at the Faces, Johns knows exactly where the blame should lie.

"Rod Stewart saw himself as a solo artist far more than he did as lead singer with the Faces. I found him impossible to work with, and I disliked him intensely – still do, although I tried not to let that affect what was going on in the studio. I did my level best to hold the group together, and make it a band, and possibly that was where I went wrong.

"Maybe I should have just recognised that Stewart wasn't ever going to be that way, and left it at that, but in fact it got rather distasteful in the end, and his ego just became absurd. I don't think he really took much interest in the Faces, because he was far more involved in his solo career."

Stewart had even stopped hanging around with the lads. Instead, he won admission to a far more exclusive club, that clique of musicians who behaved like, and were dubbed, a new rock aristocracy. Elton John remembers, "There was me, Stewart, Ringo Starr and Gary Glitter. Others came and went, but Stewart, Gary and I were the nucleus. You'd see our picture in *Melody Maker* with a caption saying, 'Yes, it's the same old crew again'."

It was Long John Baldry who passed on to Elton one of Rod's darkest secrets – that forgotten feminine pseudonym which had been scrawled across the Eel Pie bathroom wall – and Elton delightedly took to using it wherever, and whenever, he could. Stewart retaliated by rechristening him Sharon, and before long their respective managers, John Reid and Billy Gaff, had also been renamed – Beryl (after the actress Beryl Reid) and Bridie respectively.

"It was just like being schoolboys, really," says Bernie Taupin. "You did the same thing every night – went to a club and got legless while your car waited outside. Then you drove around, pulling people's shoes off in the car and throwing them out." One night, it was old Gary Glitter's toupee which disappeared into the dark. Another night, "we took some poor guy's trousers off, threw them over a pawnbroker's sign and left them there. Silly, cruel things like that."

The gulf between Stewart and the Faces was only forced wider by the singer's elevation into élite company like this. The Faces had a fighting loyalty to one another, and if one of them was going to rip off someone's trousers, they were all going to have a go. Once the Faces had presented a united front to the world. Now that face was shattering. And *Ooh La La*, as the new Faces album came to be called, was to suffer because of it. One side of the record was dominated by Stewart, the other side by the laid-back Ronnie Lane. It was a precarious arrangement at best. If Stewart disliked something Lane had done, he had no reservations about coming out and saying it, and like as not the song would be scrapped. But when the boot was on the other foot, then Stewart would dissolve in tantrums and tears, and even if he never said it, the rest of the group knew what was on his mind right then. "I made this group . . . I am this group. If it wasn't for me . . ."

Stewart was as aware as everyone else that the blade swung both ways, that without the Faces behind him he would never have had the gall to tour, would never have made it across to America, might never have recorded anything more than an album or two before finally slipping into obscurity. If he had made the Faces, then the Faces had made him. But he would never admit that, and they could never make him listen. "Fucking prima donna," they would mutter as he stalked away after yet another petty squabble. "Fucking big-headed arsehole prima donna."

Even Stewart's occasional shows of loyalty cut no ice within the now embittered collective. According to John Rowlands, "After Stewart hit the jackpot with *Every Picture*, we received an offer from Gordon Mills' company Management, Agency and Music, guaranteeing Stewart a sum of one million pounds for a year's work."

Although he and Geoff Wright were no longer representing Rod, they put the offer to him. "But he turned it down saying he would prefer to continue working with the Faces."

Rowlands and Wright couldn't understand what he was thinking at first. Only later did the answer appear. Throughout his career, Stewart had always worked with a band. It was all he knew. More than that, it was a safety net, a way of insulating himself from failure. If he was in a band and he had a bad night, there was any number of people he could blame. But if he was on his own, he was done for. And besides, as he told Rowlands and Wright, solo artists have to put up with a lot more crap than band members. Beginning with payrolls.

Stewart was, however, aware that as a solo artist his drawing power would be at least equal to the Faces, and when Lou Reizner reappeared to offer him a starring role in an all-star production of the Who's rock opera *Tommy*, Rod was seriously tempted.

Reizner, however, swiftly found himself regretting that he had been so quick to try to rebuild the broken bridges between Rod and himself.

He had assembled a fabulous cast for the show. Pete Townshend appeared as the Narrator, Sandy Denny of Fairport Convention was the Nurse, Steve Winwood played Captain Walker, Maggie Bell the mother, John Entwistle portrayed Cousin Kevin, Ringo Starr was Uncle Ernie, and Stewart the local lad whose pinball crown Tommy topples. "And the only problems I had with any of the artistes was with him."

In fairness to Stewart, he had been very unsure whether he even wanted to be involved in the project. Journalist John Pidgeon, who accompanied the Faces on their 1972 British tour as an unofficial roadie, remembers seeing Stewart in a Dundee hotel, worrying about the show. "It was clear he wanted to be persuaded," Pidgeon recalled, amazed that with just two days to go before the 9 December show, Stewart was still contemplating not turning up!

Rod's uncertainty communicated itself to Lou Reizner in a very different way. Everybody else involved in the production had taken it as a compliment that they had been invited to participate in a venture which promised not only a great stage show, but also a two-album soundtrack record.

Not so Stewart. All he wanted to know was, "What's in it for me?" And it didn't matter what Reizner offered, it was never enough.

Finally, Reizner remembered that he did have one thing Stewart coveted, something which all the money in the world could not have ordinarily bought. It was a 1932 Rolls Royce, expertly restored, lovingly preserved, and valued then at around $10,000

"Tell you what. You appear in the show and I'll give you my car as an advance against royalties."

"I rather hoped you'd say that," replied Rod.

Stewart would be performing just one song on the soundtrack, the near-anthemic "Pinball Wizard". It should have been a simple session. Reizner would provide the arrangements and the backing track, all Rod had to do was turn up and sing.

Stewart, however, apparently didn't see it that way. The album's recording deadline was looming, but date after date was cancelled as Rod remembered other "pressing engagements". And when he did finally turn up, his performance sounded so lackluster that Reizner wanted to scrap it and start over. But there was no chance of ever doing that, he would just have to make do with whatever he'd got.

Stewart knew he'd made a bad job of it; close to twenty years later, writing the liner notes to his *Storyteller* compilation, he simply said, "I have no opinion of this rendition of the song first made popular by the Who."

Of course, he vindicated himself on stage; ever the professional, often the perfectionist, he turned in a devastating performance that night at the London Rainbow. But for Reizner, it was the last straw. "In conversation he would always put down the producer and people in the music business generally," he said shortly after. "Rod forgot that I was very instrumental in his career – and he never gave me the credit for that. In every interview Rod Stewart ever did once he became successful, he always put *something* down."

Back in December 1971, just five months after Rod and Dee Harrington had met, Stewart announced their engagement. "I was very shocked about that," Dee remembers. "We'd only been together a short time, it seemed very sudden. But we had been together almost constantly, and were very, very happy."

Lou Reizner was backstage at Madison Square Gardens when Stewart broke the news, and he says, "I thought that was a bit of an old-fashioned thing to say. No one gets engaged any more – they either get married or they don't."

But Stewart was old-fashioned. He even seemed to believe in the long, long engagements which had once seemed so "proper". Or so it looked to Dee. A year later, she was still knocking around the vast mansion Stewart had bought in Windsor, wondering what on earth she could do to keep busy. "As time rolled by and Rod didn't say anything more about marriage, I began to think, 'Hmmm, maybe not.' It was trendy to just live together during the seventies, nobody was in any hurry to rush up the aisle, and Rod was no exception."

Part of the problem, she later revealed, was Cranbourne Court. "Neither of us knew what we were taking on," she says. "It seemed that we would never be able to get the builders, decorators and carpet-layers out of the place."

In the early days, they treated the old house almost like the children they one day hoped to have. Nothing was too good for it. Stewart and Harrington became well-known faces on the London antique circuit, carefully shopping for just the right pieces which would turn a simple room into a stately time capsule. One room would be decked out in Georgian style, another in Victorian, and so on.

Each had its own unique color scheme, as well. The enormous entrance hall was decked out with black and white tiles; the music room – for Stewart a cherished ambition come true – a tasteful yellow. The dining-room they painted white and blue, the sitting-room black and red. A formal drawing-room was decorated with Chinese screens. And the billiard room was decked out in the red, blue and green tartan of the Stewart clan – a pattern, Stewart proudly noted, which was shared by the Royal Family! The regimental pipers of the Scots Guards wore this tartan, and King George V, the present Queen's grandfather, referred to it as "my personal tartan".

That same room housed Stewart's growing collection of silver, gold and platinum discs, an incongruous intrusion which, almost single-handedly, announced that this was not the residence of some great and noble lord, but just a common pop star, living out his dreams of aristocratic grandeur.

"I went down to Windsor," says Reizner, "and they had these Tiffany lights hanging down over the dining table. It was all very ostentatious. You would ask him how many rooms there were in the house and he'd say, 'I don't really know.'" But even he had to admit, "It was the kind of place where you would expect to find a country squire."

What he didn't know, however, was that the squire and his lady were becoming rather restless.

They had a new, modern kitchen installed, but too often Dee would be cooking for herself . . . either that, or cleaning up after Stewart, "who seemed to use every pot and pan just to boil an egg." Often she was so bored she would give the kitchen staff the evening off, just so she could busy herself with the washing up!

"After a while I began to get the feeling that we were living in a sort of luxurious prison, cut off from normal life and the real world outside.

"We couldn't just fool around together with no clothes on, like other young couples might do, because we were always frightened one of the staff would come into the room." Although they reveled in being so cut off from the outside world, at other times, Dee admits, "I felt we had no privacy, even in our own home."

She decided to grin and bear it. Dee was bored, but at least she was bored in comfort. The phrase "a bird in a gilded cage" only entered her mind when her spirits were at their very lowest.

Stewart, on the other hand, found an escape route which he simply couldn't explain to his fiancée. If she wanted to know how he was dealing with his demons, she would have to find out for herself.

6

One Man Band

In December 1972, the Faces launched their first full British tour. They went out nervous, wondering what they would find. They came home in triumph, well on their way to becoming rock'n'roll legends.

Nothing, on that tour, had been too good, or too outrageous. At every venue, a special clause in the band's contract demanded a crate of Liebfraumilch be waiting in the dressing-room. In addition, the band's label, Warner Brothers, was expected to post a man at every venue, to make sure everything went according to plan and to calm things down when it didn't.

It was a sensible precaution. To this day Woody is proud of the band's reputation as rock's rowdiest fivesome: "Although Keith Moon was famous for turning hotel demolition into an art form the Faces pioneered it." He has lost count of the hotels that banned them after one too many televisions took a trip from a top-floor balcony, and even today there are establishments that still bolt their doors and turn out the lights when they hear that Ronnie Wood is in town.

"We'd have parties where we'd round up tons of people – even strangers – just to see how many we could fit into one room. Naturally, at least one person would be in a drunken stupor, fall over, and set a whole thing off, with people toppling over like dominoes. In fact one guy once literally went through a door, leaving behind the shape of his body – like in a comic book."

Another favorite pastime was to harass manager Billy Gaff, as if he didn't already have enough to worry about! Rod, Woody and as many other people as they could round up enjoyed nothing more than to invade Billy's room in the middle of the night. Woody recalls, "We'd get the keys from reception and burst in, yelling our heads off. We'd turn his bed over on top of him, pull his pants off, flood the bathtub and disconnect all the lights. He'd be crawling around in the pitch dark, shouting, 'If you don't (CRASH) stop this right now (KERPLUNK) I refuse to carry on working with you (BOING).'"

He would then sit in horror as all the furniture disappeared out of a window. Usually an unopened window as well.

The 1972 British tour was to be as exuberant as any other, but as Woody is at pains to point out, it wasn't always the Faces' fault when things got out of hand. Sometimes it was the little man from the record company.

In Dundee, fans wrecked the first half-dozen rows of seating as they danced, jumped and battled with one another when Rod emptied a sackful of footballs over the crowd. Each one was stamped with the name of the band's next single, "Cindy Incidentally", and those kids were going to get one even if they had to rip out six rows of seating to do it. Journalist John Pidgeon reported, "When the hall emptied, the front rows of the stalls were nothing but a mess of sticks and horsehair stuffing."

Pidgeon had been invited on to the tour as an unofficial roadie, and intended to keep a simple diary of events. He ended up maintaining a catalog of near-constant destruction.

In Blackpool, for instance, the party was shepherded into an anti-quated boarding-house which should have been condemned years earlier. There were no lights in the corridor, the phones were all out of order, the bedside lights wouldn't work, the heating was on the fritz, and the bath was full of very suspect pubic hairs. Two of the band's roadies tried to fix a few things, but the place looked even worse for their efforts. When the Faces left, their truck accidentally demolished half the wall outside the hotel.

In Liverpool, one roadie was nearly jailed after he punched out a hotel night porter who wouldn't let him take a girl to his room. The rest of the crew retaliated with an unpaid £60 brandy bill, and a record-company executive had half his car windows smashed. In Sheffield, though, all hell broke loose.

Kenney Jones and Ronnie Lane had returned to London early, and for a short time the original plans for a party were left in the lurch. But slowly, party spirits returned, and with them an irresistible urge to visit their minder from Warners. Led by Woody, Mac and Stewart, the entire Faces entourage descended upon his room, just as he was trying to persuade two visiting females to join him in bed. Woody and Stewart promptly hauled one of them into a wardrobe. As she made her escape, Mac started demolishing an armchair. Things rather went downhill from there.

"Cindy Incidentally", the promised new single, was released early in 1973, and predictably returned the band to both the US and UK charts. The new Faces album, *Ooh La La*, followed in April, and even with

Stewart continuing to badmouth it at every opportunity ("It's a bloody mess!" he told an astonished *Melody Maker*), it too was a major success – particularly in the US, where its release coincided with the next Faces tour.

Dee Harrington saw the band off at the airport, then returned home to Windsor and solitude. She thought about going out with friends, but knew that wasn't such a great idea. Rod would be calling her every day, as usual, and Dee knew from experience it was best to be around when he did. On the few occasions she had missed his call, he retaliated with a host of accusations, of which rampant infidelity was perhaps the mildest. What had once seemed a sweet gesture on his part had now become yet another bar on her cage. So she simply sat and counted the hours until his return.

When he did finally breeze back, however, she didn't know him. "Rod came back from that tour completely changed," remembers Harrington. "I don't know what went on out there, but I do know when he came home he was not at all the same man."

Dee met him at the airport and straight away she noticed something very different about him. He was wearing black eye make-up for a start, something he had always sworn not to do, no matter how "fashionable" it became. "Make-up's for girls," he would laugh dismissively. "Girls and poofters. And you wouldn't want your old man looking like a fucking poofter, would you?" There he was sitting in the passenger seat of Dee's Rolls looking for all the world like a blasé millionaire panda.

Wisely, Harrington didn't say a word. It was odd, she thought, but if it was what Stewart wanted to do . . . All she wanted was to get him home. Dee knew what would happen next.

To her surprise, once there Stewart barely glanced at his collection of cars, gleamingly washed and serviced; didn't even notice that she'd had the house cleaned from top to bottom. "He didn't take much notice of the animals either, which was very unusual for him. We had four horses, two dogs, a cat and a parrot, and he always used to make a fuss over them. Now they just seemed to annoy him."

That evening she suggested going down to the local for a drink. Stewart, who'd barely said a word since he got home, shook his head. Instead he sent the chauffeur out with a pitcher. "I can't be bothered to go out. We'll drink at home." Dee instinctively knew that meant *he* would drink at home. She could do whatever the hell she liked.

Night after night, this same strange ritual was played out in front of her. First the pitcher of beer, and when that was finished, lashings of fine port and brandy. Often she would go up to bed leaving Stewart in a chair with a glass in one hand, and when she got up the next morning, he'd still be there. The only sign that he'd moved in the intervening hours was the pile of empty bottles he'd accumulated overnight.

Stewart seemed racked by self-doubt. Two or three months ago, he'd been carefree, raucous, cock of the walk. His records sold in telephone numbers. "I could fart in a bathtub and I'd still be number one," he'd joked, and Dee knew he was right. But now he didn't seem quite so sure. Night after night, he would thumb through a heap of well-worn records, picking out a Van Morrison or a Stevie Wonder, a Bob Dylan or Bobby Womack, and play it over and over again. "I wish I could make a record like that," he'd say. "I wish that just once in my fucking life I could make a record that bloody good." He wasn't even talking to Dee any more. He was talking to himself.

On other occasions he would flop into an armchair by the window and just stare into nothing for hours. Or perhaps wander listlessly through that great house, through the rooms where he and Dee had once hidden out, calling "Where are you?" to one another at the top of their voices. Now when she spoke, he would invariably snap at her. Or even worse, ignore her completely.

"Rod refused to answer the telephone or see anyone," says Dee. "He seemed incapable of making even the simplest decisions. His only pleasure was his train set." Back when they first moved into the house, Stewart had knocked a hole through the wall of two rooms and filled the place with trains. "I make all the carriages myself," he once bragged. "I have a room with a twenty-one-foot by two-and-a-half-foot track where I can shunt engines. I have my own workbench as well, so that I can do my own repairs." Now, although he sat with them all day, she couldn't even get him to talk about his trains. And if Dee tried to rekindle his old spark of enthusiasm when she showed an interest in his hobby, he would simply shut her out.

Part of the problem, she knew, was money. Stewart had earned well in the last few years, but the taxman was breathing down his neck. That was bothering him so much that he wasn't even paying his staff their full due. He grew steadily more paranoid about his money, totting everything up on a pocket calculator as if he was certain everyone was ripping him off.

"The gardeners were allowed to stay overtime, but at the end of the week, when they asked for their money, he would say he didn't believe they had really worked and refused to sign the checks," says Dee. Often she would have to plead to get him to pay them.

Slowly, Dee began to piece together some of what had happened. Midway through the American tour, Ronnie Lane announced that he'd finally had enough. "He was a person of quick and thorough decisions," said Woody. "He used the old cliché 'I'm leaving the group'. We all laughed . . . but we all knew it was true."

Everyone had seen it coming. There was no reason on earth to be surprised, but for some reason Stewart was and he blamed himself. "I could have made it work. I should have made it work." He knew deep down that there was no way things could really have been any different. But he had achieved the impossible once already, rising from grave-digging to the very pinnacle of pop stardom. Surely one more miracle hadn't been too much to hope for?

"Rod used to be so organised about his work," recalls Harrington, "but the Faces were quite the opposite. They used to record either at Olympic or Barnes, so every morning Rod would drive out at ten, and say he'd call me that evening and be home for dinner. He was regular as clockwork on that. But then I began to notice he was coming home earlier and earlier, in a bit of a mood. He'd say, 'I just can't sit in a pub drinking all day and then record all night. We're not getting anything done.'

"The Faces' albums were a real burden for him, it was all beginning to get too much. What nobody seemed to realise was that he was con-tracted to make two albums per year, one solo and one with the band. The others had only one, and it was beginning to get too much for him. His records were easy – he'd call in Woody, Martin Quittenton and Mickey Waller, write, record, and that was it. But it was a massive struggle to get the rest of the group in to work when he wanted to. If Rod was trying to take over the Faces, it was for their own good – it was the only way they'd ever get anything done."

Lane himself was less than diplomatic about the situation. "I was writing a lot of stuff and there was a bit of hemming and hawing when I presented it to the Faces. I got pissed off with it in the end because I felt I was contributing a lot more than other factions of the band, to put it bluntly. It was getting very hard to get everyone together.

"Stewart had his career, I think that's what it was. The whole band was built around Rod and he wasn't one hundred per cent there. I didn't mind being in the back-up band at all, but I do mind when you can see something and it's not coming off." Lane refused to get into slagging off his old bandmate, though, and it was left to journalist Lester Bangs to publish what he thought would have made a far more appropriate goodbye.

"Dear Rod: It was so considerate of you to pull the rug out from under me in such a charming way: nobody else noticed. It's also very nice you could fit all of us in the band into your busy schedule of ascending stardom, which after all must proceed like clockwork or Elton John might get there ahead of you.

"I suppose in the end it really is nobody's fault the way things turned out, but right now I'm too bitter to do more than punch your face in.

Unfortunately, you're an ex-football player and I'm a scrawny little runt, so it's tough shit about that, too." The imaginary letter was signed "Fuck off, Ron".

Lane reluctantly completed the American tour, but agreed to play just three more gigs, at the Edmonton Sundown theater at the beginning of June. They would be his farewell to the fans.

Stewart's world took a nasty jolt when Ronnie Lane quit. But Dee Harrington's was about to explode. She had discovered why Stewart had so suddenly changed at the first of those Sundown shows.

Backstage that evening, Harrington walked into the ladies' room and found Stewart "huddled over something in front of the mirror. He jumped up in surprise and I saw, to my horror, that he had white powder all over his nose."

"Get out! You're not supposed to be in here," roared Stewart.

"Yes I am! Take a look at the door!" Dee pointed to the glowing "Ladies" sign. "You're in the wrong bloody room!"

But it was Harrington who stormed out. "I couldn't stand the sight of what was going on in there. My head was reeling."

The show, like the other two at that venerable and now demolished old theater, went well. The Faces' very reputation allowed Stewart to roll and reel and forget lyrics. If maybe he did it a bit more that evening, nobody noticed – it was surely all part of the act.

Still, he cut a strange figure. He was heavily made-up, and the expression-killing mascara around his blank, beady eyes looked totally, obscenely out of place on his usual laughing face. He draped his lanky form in sparkling sequins, necklaces, feather boas and chiffon. And when, toward the end of the show, he stood stock still in the spotlight, arms raised to conduct the audience as they sang in perfect harmony to "Angel" and "Maggie May", he looked to all the world like a pathetic old drag queen taking her bows. A very bad, cheap drag queen.

The Faces' first choice as a replacement for Lane was Andy Fraser, once bass player with Free, the pioneering hard-rock band whose greatest hit, "Alright Now", Stewart would one day butcher on his *Camouflage* album. Fraser, however, turned them down. So did the Jamaican Phil Chen, a former member of Jimmie James and the Vagabonds. Others still were turned down by the Faces themselves, as Kenney Jones remembers, "We went through some very good bass players, but they really weren't fitting in, and we were definitely looking for someone who fitted."

Then one day Tetsu Yamauchi appeared. Japanese-born, he too had been a member of Free, where he had, in fact, replaced Andy Fraser. "He came round after we'd tried a few other bass players," remembers Jones, "and he'd sit in silence because he didn't have the language together that well. But we had another play and then suddenly he opened up as a person and we decided to pick him."

Unfortunately, it wasn't going to be that easy. Somehow, the British Musicians Union got it in their heads that Tetsu had no right to work in Britain. What they meant, in those last months of Conservative government now sounding out the potential of protectionism as a platform for re-election, was that he had no right to work with the Faces. A terse statement from the Union announced, "There are enough British musicians out of work without bringing in 'foreigners' to fill any vacancies."

Tetsu's arrival was a mixed blessing for Stewart. On the one hand, it confirmed his dominance of the group; great bassist though he was, Tetsu possessed none of the creative juices which Lane had unleashed with such devastating power. Now there was only one songwriter competing for album space. On the other, the MU dispute focused attention on the band at a time when Stewart was least able to deal with it. Harrington remembers, "Whenever the telephone rang, I had to lie for him and say he was out. It didn't matter who was calling, or what it was about. His record company sometimes telephoned six or seven times a day and he always refused to speak to them."

A doctor diagnosed Stewart as suffering from nervous exhaustion, and a projected European tour early that summer was indefinitely postponed. Hopes that a new Stewart solo album might emerge during 1973 were also dashed, and Mercury hurriedly released a compilation, *Sing It Again, Rod*, to plug the unexpected gap. Such was the demand for a new Rod Stewart album that even this uninventive collection sold close to a million copies within two months of release.

It was mid-July before the Faces were sighted again, stumbling through a European tour over which Stewart's disillusion and depression hung like a shroud. The following month, the funeral party returned to England, and Tetsu made his British debut at Doncaster's Top Rank club on 17 August, 1973. To thwart the Musicians Union, still baying for Tetsu's head, the show was not even advertised.

A night or so later, a second secret gig was staged at the Hard Rock in Manchester. It ended when Kenney Jones collapsed on stage. He, too, was suffering from nervous exhaustion.

The band was in pieces, and Jones's collapse was the final straw. A terse statement from the group's management announced that they would be playing just one more gig in Britain, at the annual Reading Festival, and would then turn their backs on the country for good. The stance taken by the Musicians Union left them little choice.

The ultimatum seemed to do the trick. In September, two weeks after the Faces headlined the Reading Festival, the Central London branch of the Musicians Union recommended that Tetsu file a new application for membership. This time it was accepted. A few days later, the Faces set out on a five-week tour of America.

The tour could not have come at a worse time for Stewart. His already precarious self-esteem was at an all-time low, and he was convinced that he was losing his magic. It didn't matter that *Sing It Again, Rod* had just given him his third successive UK number one. It was only a grim reminder of how great he had once been. Surely a better gauge of how low he had sunk in the public's estimation came when the new Faces single, "Poolhall Richard", was released in Britain, in October 1973.

It climbed no higher than number 17, and yet "Poolhall Richard" was pure Faces magic, a raucous rocker that reaffirmed the band's good-time image, bounding along behind a classic, joyful Stewart vocal which totally belied the pessimism, even paranoia, of the lyric.

Rewriting the Who's "Pinball Wizard" around a poolhall king, from the point of view of a challenger, "Poolhall Richard" perhaps revealed more about Stewart's current state of mind than anything he had ever written.

'Losing all my money and I'm getting tired," he sang, and enviously added, "His reputation's bigger than gasoline." But the real killer is "He wants my lady too." Who "he" really was, Stewart wasn't saying. But Dee could have told him. It was the faceless monster consuming him from within that heap of gleaming white powder. It was fame, and the devastation it was wreaking on him. "Poolhall Richard" was nothing more than a desperate cry for help.

The US did little to brighten his spirits. Warner Brothers had already announced that they didn't consider "Poolhall Richard" to be "singles material" in America, while *Sing It Again, Rod* had been his worst-performing album since *Thin*, not even making it into the Top Thirty. There had to be some way of pulling his career back on track.

Stewart and the band had brought along a rather significant new toy on this tour, Polaroid cameras. Since the British shows the previous year, trashing hotel rooms had become a highly publicised way of life. But now Rod was bored with simple destruction. "We don't do that now," he said. "I don't know what it proved. It's an idiotic way of having a party."

Journalists who heard this wondered what they could do with their headlines. "Rock's Bad Boys Reform?" That was hardly the sort of story a scandal-hungry public wanted to hear, not at a time when both the Who and Led Zeppelin were taking tales of rock'n'roll debauchery to new limits. And Rod knew it. He paused while his first sentence sank in, then continued with a smile, "Our new thing now is dirty pictures.

We each have our bird and our Polaroid and in the morning we compare pictures."

The American press didn't really make too much of a fuss about this. Many of the people interviewing the Faces were old fans, and they'd been let into that secret long before, when a poster included with *A Nod's as Good as a Wink* unfolded to reveal a few of the band's more presentable snapshots.

But their British counterparts had a field day. "Pop Star's Porno Polaroids!" they bellowed, and they even had the pictures, most of them cut out of the same freebie poster. It was tabloid reporting in the time-honored fashion, and it dominated the UK press for days.

"I went into hiding for five days after that," Stewart remembered. "My Dad rang up and asked, 'Where's my son?' I didn't dare see him." He was twenty-eight years old, he said, and his father still swatted him if he misbehaved.

Dee Harrington, of course, couldn't see what all the fuss was about. She already knew about Rod's peepshow Polaroids. Besides, she had a far better secret than that! Stewart was also making private pornographic movies as well.

"I had to lie naked on the bed and follow his instructions to act sexy, although I could never take it seriously like he wanted me to, and always spoiled it by giggling," she describes.

"I was not really very keen to be a star of his blue movies, but he was in such a state during that time that I would have done almost anything to humor or help him."

Stewart was by now virtually at the end of his tether. He knew how the press would respond to his latest revelations, but he needed to test them regardless. Five years can be an awfully long time in rock'n'roll. Since Stewart had broken through with the Faces he had seen any number of his peers lose first their magic, then their fame. Marc Bolan, one of the biggest stars the UK had seen since the Beatles, was lucky now to make the Top Thirty. Gary Glitter, the Sweet, Slade . . . when "Maggie May" broke through, they had all been at the very top of the heap. Where were they all now?

By letting slip about the pictures, he was reassuring himself that he was still headline news, that people still cared what he did. Two years later, Elton John would do much the same thing when he publicly announced he was gay. It wasn't news – most of his friends had known it for years. But it got the press excited, and that was all that counted.

Yet at the same time he was supplying the media with ammunition guaranteed to wound him, Stewart continued retreating ever deeper into his own private hell. His fans, he knew now, still cared for him.

But everybody else – his friends, his family, even the music industry itself – seemed out to get him.

First, there was that nasty business with the Musicians Union over Tetsu. Then, in the States, he had tried without success to postpone an interview with a teen magazine. The interviewer turned round and threatened to expose him to 40,000 readers as a stuck-up sham unless he met with her.

Even his pet parrot was against him, mimicking Dee's voice so well that when they were arguing the bird would start up, shrieking abuse and laughing uproariously. Stewart didn't know what to do, so he reportedly locked the poor bird in the safe.

Now Harrington herself was at it. Stewart arrived home one day to find that she had taken all of his records out of the jukebox in the kitchen, crossed out his name on the label and scratched ROD THE SOD on them instead. He made out he didn't care, but inside he was seething.

Dee was fast becoming intolerable to live with, he thought to himself. Always crying, always arguing, always going on and on about drugs. Once, during a particularly vicious argument, she picked up a heavy statue from the mantelpiece. For a moment he thought she was going to heave it at him. Instead, her eyes focused on a small packet of cocaine hidden beneath it. "So it's in the house now, is it?" she screamed. And so it went.

When they went out, it was usually separately. Stewart himself spent a lot of time either with Billy Gaff or with Bernie Taupin, who lived in Wentworth, only a couple of miles down the road. It was a good arrangement. When Taupin fell out with his wife, Maxine, he would crash at Stewart's for the night. And when Stewart fell out with Dee – "they were always fighting," remembers Bernie – he would stay with the Taupins.

On the rare occasions when Rod and Dee did appear together in public, it would inevitably end in a scene. "One evening," says Harrington, "at a reception for Paul and Linda McCartney at the Café Royal in London, Rod tripped in and out of the toilet. Every now and again he would catch my eye. I knew what he was doing, and he knew what I was thinking. No words needed to pass between us – but for me the evening was ruined."

On another occasion, Harrington and Stewart went to Tramps, where Rod was meeting Denis Law, the soccer star. The pair were planning to record a duet together, a version of "Angel", for inclusion on an album called *Scotland Scotland*, a celebration of the Scottish team's qualification for the 1974 World Cup soccer tournament. A few other footballers were there as well, says Harrington, "and they were all talking football. I was sitting there happily when Ryan O'Neal, the film star, came up and asked me to dance.

"When I came back, Rod went across to the bar, ordered a pint of beer, came back and threw it all over me."

Harrington retaliated with her champagne glass and then, grabbing his hair so he couldn't escape, whacked him as hard as she could.

Stewart went to hit her back, and when O'Neal moved in to stop him he caught the blow instead. The waiters soon joined in and Stewart lashed at them as well, then stormed out of the club.

Dee followed him into the street, screaming abuse at the top of her lungs. Stewart, though, gave as good as he got. "If you want to be seen with film stars, go off with him. He certainly won't look after you like I do!"

Desperately, Harrington searched for somewhere to turn. Her own father was right out. A retired RAF officer, he liked Rod well enough, but was hardly the person to take this problem to. Neither were Stewart's parents, although they certainly had an idea of what was going on. Instead she turned to Elton John, whose friendship with Stewart, masked though it was by a constant outward display of bickering and rivalry, now rivaled Woody's in intensity. Elton was a frequent caller at Cranbourne Court. Together, he, Rod and Dee would watch football, have dinner, or just sit around chatting.

Down to earth, calm – Dee even called him one of the few "normal" people she knew – Elton knew what Rod was experiencing. He may even have been having problems coming to terms with his own success. He was just coming down from his greatest triumph yet, the *Goodbye Yellow Brick Road* album and tour. John had performed before royalty, and had achieved a lifetime dream when he became Vice-President of Watford Football Club. But deep down he was lonely and confused, and when Dee arrived at his Virginia Water home, just ten minutes from Cranbourne Court, he was always ready with the tea and sympathy.

"I often went over just for the comfort of talking sensibly to some-one," says Harrington. "Elton's mother was usually there, and his life seemed so homely compared with our existence behind those high walls."

Elton, she says, "was always very good to me. I'd tell him all my troubles, how worried I was about Rod, and he would put his arms around me and say, 'Don't worry, Dee, it's only a phase he's going through. He'll get over it.'"

Ironically, Rod also turned to Elton for support. Night after night the two superstars would sit and talk, shedding every last trace of their media invulnerability and pouring their hearts out in earnest – Rod and Reggie (Elton's real name is Reginald), Phyllis and Sharon. Stewart would sigh, "God, I wish I could be like you," not perhaps comprehending Elton's own difficulties. "You've got everything."

Then he would count off all of Elton's stellar accomplishments. There was his secure future in a band he could trust. The Elton John Group was wholly under the compassionate pianist's control, with none of the terrible in-fighting and brawling that vexed the Faces. There was Beryl, as Rod insisted on calling Elton's manager and friend, John Reid. There was Woodside, Elton's luxurious home, a far cry from the upscale prison which Rod and Dee inhabited. Finally, there was Watford, the football club which Elton adored so much that he made himself chairman of the board.

Even in his darkest moments, Rod admired Elton for having sunk so much faith – and money – into Watford. They were a struggling Fourth Division team at the time, lowlier even than Brentford during Rod's days as an apprentice. But when Elton spoke of them, they could have been the greatest team in the land – an echelon to which he would, eventually, see them rise.

Stewart couldn't help but throw himself into his pudgy friend's passion. When Elton organised a benefit at the club's Vicarage Road stadium, on 5 May, 1974, Rod agreed to perform, running through a short four-song set toward the end of the evening. On other occasions, he would join Elton there when all was quiet, and the two of them would have practise kick-abouts with whichever members of the team or ground staff they could rustle up to join them.

He would come home from those little sessions exalted, but as the front door closed behind him, the despondency would hit him once again. "Can I get you anything?" Dee would ask, but Rod wouldn't reply. Instead he would slouch back upstairs to play with his trains, or sink into an armchair and just stare through the window.

Stewart's fans, however, noticed little of this. Wendy Roberts, one of the handful of girls who were frequently to be found camped outside Cranbourne Court – from where they traded good-natured insults with Elton's own gang of human watchdogs – remembers, "We used to see Rod quite a lot, and he always had a cheerful word or two for us. Sometimes he'd stop and talk on his way in or out – I think he got to know some of us fairly well. It was only later, when he and Dee broke up, and she started talking about his drug use, that we heard anything about it. He always seemed quite normal to us!"

Harrington also made a good impression on the girls. "I think she realised that we weren't a threat, weren't just a bunch of groupies out to grope Rod, so she was always pleasant to us as well. Sometimes she did seem stand-offish – we always put it down to her period, but I wonder now if that was when she and Rod had been fighting."

121

The girls spent their time swapping their own stories and fantasies, and Roberts admits that if Dee had only known the "depths" to which some of the latter adventures sank, she would probably have been horrified. "Threesomes were always my favorite," Roberts confesses. "Rod, Dee and myself. I used to dream about that happening – I knew the rough layout of the house, and could picture us doing it in almost every room." But she adds with a laugh, "Of course, if the opportunity had ever arisen, I think I would have died of fright!"

Not all the girls' fantasies, though, were so pure. One, Roberts says, used to talk of strapping Rod's anatomy to his electric train track, inching one of his powerful locomotives toward it while he gave her head. "She used to get really excited about it, and none of us doubted that given half the chance, she'd have actually done it as well!"

For Harrington, however, life behind Cranbourne's walls was somewhat less exciting. At times, she felt as though she were living with a dead man, and when she thought of her future, it was as an abyss into which her lover would just drag her down, down, down . . . There was only one way to escape. She rushed upstairs in tears, and by the time a girlfriend who was staying at the house followed her into her bedroom, Harrington had already swallowed a full bottle of Valium.

Stewart, a coward of the highest order, hid in the bathroom when the ambulance men arrived to carry her away to hospital.

"I didn't really want to kill myself," says Dee. "I just felt that if I could go to sleep for two or three days, maybe when I woke up all my troubles would have somehow gone away."

Instead, they only seemed to get worse. Harrington and Stewart could scarcely be in the same room without fighting. But when she walked out on him – as she did time after time – he would immediately be on the phone to her, sometimes in the smallest hours of the morning, begging her to come back. "It seemed we could not live apart and we could not live together," Harrington laments.

Harrington would issue her wayward boyfriend with ultimatum after ultimatum. Either the drugs go or I do. Each time she would mean it, each time she would pack her bags and storm out. And each time that little-boy-lost voice on the telephone would lure her back with the heartfelt promise to "be good".

One night, during one of those brief reconciliations, Dee and Rod were together in their local. It had not been a bad evening. They had managed not to fight or hurl abuse and accusations at one another. Anybody sitting at another table might have looked at them and thought they were just any young couple, having a quiet drink and enjoying one another's company. And then Dee erupted.

"I've had enough! As far as I'm concerned, you can shove your bloody cocaine!"

Stewart looked up, eyes wide in confusion. All conversation around them ceased, all eyes turned upon the screaming woman in the corner and her cowering, stunned escort. Rod tried to hush her. "Leave it till later, luv, please not here." But Dee ignored him.

"I don't care any more! Do what the hell you like! You've worn me out. You obviously need that stuff more than you need me. So carry on."

Harrington stormed home, not expecting to see Stewart again that night. To her surprise Rod came trailing in just a few moments behind her. "You're right," he said sheepishly. "I'm terribly sorry."

"I don't know whether it was what I said, or the way I said it," Dee later remembered, "but Rod was obviously shaken. A few nights later we were having dinner with Gary Glitter and Rod turned to him and said, 'If it wasn't for Dee, I don't know where I'd be.' I was so happy to hear him say that. He never took another sniff of cocaine for the rest of the time we were together."

It wasn't only Harrington, though, who noticed the reformed Stewart. In January 1974, a tour of Australia and New Zealand with the Faces passed off without incident. A series of British shows followed, and throughout the summer the Faces headlined major festival shows on both sides of the Atlantic.

The differences within the band suddenly seemed to have settled down too, as each member finally took the opportunity to spread his own wings. Woody was recording his first solo album, with help from Stewart and Keith Richard; he also joined with Ronnie Lane – whose own band, Slim Chance, had just enjoyed its first hit single, "How Come" – to write the soundtrack for a movie called *Mahoney's Estate*.

Kenney Jones was preparing to release a solo single on the Faces' manager Billy Gaff's own record label, GM. And Stewart had begun writing songs for his next record as well.

Back around the time of *Sing It Again, Rod*, Stewart startled the press by announcing he was only going to record one more solo album. What he actually meant was he was only going to record one more for Mercury. It was to be called *Scotland for the World Cup*, another reference to the upcoming soccer tournament.

In actual fact, Stewart's Mercury contract called for two more albums, but the wily Stewart had already figured out a way around that.

The next Faces album was to be an in-concert recording, *Coast to Coast – Overture for Beginners*. The original plan was to tape it at the Edmonton Sundown, during Ronnie Lane's last shows, but only one song from those shows, a version of the Temptations' "I Wish It Would Rain", was released, on the b-side of "Poolhall Richard". The album itself was recorded in California on the final nights of the band's December 1973 American tour.

Stewart's idea was to hand the tapes over to Mercury as a Rod Stewart solo album. Nearly all of the tracks were songs he had recorded, and the jacket itself would credit "Rod Stewart and the Faces".

It was a bizarre solution to Stewart's problems with Mercury, but even stranger was the fact that it worked. Warner Brothers, who would ordinarily have released the record, were given the rights to release the same album on cassette and eight-track cartridge only. Mercury would have all claim to the UK and the American vinyl.

To Mercury, which didn't have an inkling of Stewart's discontent, the arrangement was strange, but acceptable. Warners was game, as Stewart had promised he'd be signing to the label just as soon as the Mercury contract was done with. And in the end he did, although it took a December 1974 decision by a London court finally to sort everything out.

Released in early 1974, *Coast to Coast* was a rendition of a live Faces performance, but it was the musician credits which won the most notice. Each member of the band had inserted a line or two about himself and his colleagues, and for the first time it seemed as though Stewart had finally come to terms not only with his fame, but also with his reputation.

"Tetsu is nice, but he's foreign . . ." wrote Stewart. "Ron Wood has not got a big nose . . . Kenney has not got chickenpox and does not need a watch to keep time." Ian MacLagan "has so many teeth, when he smiles it looks like his tongue's playing the piano." And Rod himself? "He's in hospital 'cos he fell off his wallet."

After so many years of being so painfully aware of how people viewed his financial acumen, Stewart had suddenly decided to make a virtue out of it.

"I enjoy spending money, but I don't waste it," he told the *Sunday Express*. "I wouldn't say I'm mean, but there are times when I've got long pockets and very short arms."

In another interview, playing on the English euphemism for using the bathroom, he admitted, "I'm so tight I don't spend a penny. I don't mind buying a round of drinks, but I can't stand buying two." Rod reserved his most revealing comment for the tabloid-style *Record Mirror*. "Having waited so long to be successful, I found out it was a terrible anticlimax."

So was *Coast to Coast*, at least to fans who had been weaned on the magic of a Faces concert. Part of the problem was the emphasis on

Stewart's solo material, but more to the point was the inferiority of the gig itself. The *New Musical Express* review seemed to hit the nail right on the head: "When the Faces began their current incarnation, their boozy looseness helped to add some riotous vibes to a tight, powerful, hell-for-leather set. Just a little extra something to liven up the act, kind of like a rock'n'roll Dean Martin.

"Now, several gold records and a few years of gigging later, they've indulged themselves to such an extent that their music is virtually unlistenable.

"Not to put too fine a point on it, their new live album contains some of the sloppiest and most incompetent playing I've ever heard from a so-called major band."

While Mac tried to put a brave face on things, insisting that, far from unlistenable, *Coast to Coast* was the best Faces album ever, Stewart sided with the press. The album stank.

Outside the Faces, Stewart threw himself into his work. Aside from the new solo album, he was also putting together an autobiographical television documentary which he would finance himself. It was as much as Dee could do to pry him away for a holiday, in Mombasa in East Africa, that August.

It was an idyllic time. "Sometimes we talked about staying there forever, to avoid going back to all the hassles. But it was just fantasy. Rod was due to start a long European tour with the Faces as soon as he got home. He knew he had to do it and so did I."

The tour was the longest the band had ever undertaken, an ambitious fifteen-week outing which took in France, Spain, Switzerland, Germany, Belgium, Holland, Denmark, Norway and Sweden, before winding up with a series of British shows just before Christmas.

They returned to find Stewart's latest album sitting proudly at number one in the charts.

Scotland had not, in the end, won, or even come close to winning, the 1974 World Cup, and while Stewart considered renaming the record *Scotland for the NEXT World Cup*, prudence won out in the end. The record became *Smiler*, and on the cover Rod posed against a massive tartan background, wearing the biggest smile he could muster.

Smiler was an astonishing record, capturing perfectly Stewart's transition from the old folk rock'n'roller of *Every Picture Tells a Story* to the arch sophisticate he was so soon to become.

"Farewell", written by Stewart and Martin Quittenton, was at last a worthy successor to "Maggie May". "Girl from the North Country" was the most sensitive of all Stewart's Bob Dylan covers, and the token rocker, Chuck Berry's "Sweet Little Rock'n'Roller", could hold its own in any company. Another Sam Cooke song, "Bring It On Home to Me", and Pete Sears' traditional-sounding Scottish air, "Lochinvar", rounded out the "old friends" category.

Even more exciting, though, were the songs Stewart had never even hinted at before. "Natural Man" was one of the strongest tunes in Carole King's seemingly bottomless catalog, but one normally associated with female singers. "You make me feel like a natural woman," went the song's catchiest lyric.

"Dixie Toot" and "Sailor" proved that the Stewart–Wood songwriting team still had a lot of life in it, and elsewhere "Let Me Be Your Car" introduced a new partnership which, had it only been maintained, might have become as potent as any of Stewart's earlier liaisons – Rod Stewart and Elton John. Elton also appeared on the album, and once the Faces tour started, even made a special guest appearance on stage, three nights in a row.

But best of all was "Mine for Me", written as a special gift from another of Rod's pop friends, Paul McCartney, and an offering which Macca and his ever-present wife Linda belatedly gift-wrapped when they too joined Stewart onstage in Lewisham, at the start of the UK tour. If Stewart still entertained any doubts about his status, sharing the stage with a Beatle surely ended them right away.

Gary Glitter also turned up on the tour, bouncing across the stage to bellow along with the chorus of "Maggie May" at Kilburn. Everywhere, the Faces entered as champions and left as conquering heroes. They had sewn together the seams and had settled all their differences. They were a band again.

Even incidents that might once have sparked a war passed off without comment. In Glasgow, the Lord Provost came on stage and presented Stewart with the Freedom of the City. As the crowd roared its approval, Stewart beat his chest and spread his arms as wide as they would go. "My people!" he said. "MY people."

At yet another show, the band decided to invite one of their own friends on stage with them – Rolling Stone Keith Richard. Stewart could barely conceal his anger. It was his stage, his music . . . and he was being shamelessly upstaged. When Richard's solo overlapped into a verse, Stewart simply stood stock still and ran his finger across his throat. He left the hall in a separate car.

But these were just petty things, just Stewart being Stewart after all. The band was fired with an enthusiasm it hadn't felt in years, and was meeting a success it had no right to expect. The British leg of the tour was the most successful the country had seen all year, grossing over $200,000. Billy Gaff reckoned the Faces would make even more when they returned to America in the new year. Total receipts were expected to reach well over £1,000,000, a phenomenal amount for those days.

Stewart's reconciliation with real life continued when a group of people queueing for tickets to the Faces' Birmingham show was injured by a terrorist bomb blast. He and Dee made a special pre-show detour to the hospital to visit one of the more seriously hurt victims, a young boy who had been due to attend the gig. "He'd told the hospital that he was coming, but it was a surprise for the boy," remembers Dee. "Rod was so upset, so we just bobbed into the hospital before the show, it really did make that little boy's night." Whereas other people in Stewart's position would have ensured a healthy pack of photographers to capture the moment for posterity, Stewart kept the visit secret even from his own publicity people. "This was a special moment between me and a fan. It had nothing at all to do with publicity or getting your name in the papers."

Shortly before the British tour began, the Faces went into the studio to record a new single. Two days later, it was done. They had never worked so fast or so well. The song was called "You Can Make Me Dance, Sing or Anything (Even Take the Dog for a Walk, Mend a Fuse, Fold Away the Ironing Board or Any Other Domestic Shortcomings)", a hilariously unwieldy title that neatly disguised perhaps the Faces' greatest ever performance.

Neither was it a flash in the pan. The tour over, and with a few weeks to spare before they headed off to the United States, they returned to the studio to begin work on a new album.

"It was the first sign of an album being really fucking good," says Kenney Jones. "For once it had a great deal of excitement in the actual track, and the numbers were sounding nice too. All it needed was good vocals and a good mix. If we'd continued like that and finished the album instead of going to the States, we'd have made a winner."

But the States were impatient, and in February 1975 the band flew out to satisfy them. More studio time was booked in Los Angeles, and the group couldn't wait to get back to work. But just as suddenly as it had come, the moment was gone. "When we got there, it was like anything else in LA," remembers Jones. "Everyone said, 'Let's go to the studio at midnight.' As far as I'm concerned, I don't fit into that. That's my problem. I like going there at two in the afternoon.

"But I did it, I went there at twelve o'clock, only everyone's idea of twelve o'clock is actually one o'clock. Then you get all these liggers hanging about, these big guitarists and other famous people hopping in and out, and you end up talking to them for ages and nobody would be playing and it ceased to become what we wanted it to be. Everything falls apart in LA if you want to make a record."

Jones was under the impression that with the tour over, the band would return to Britain and pick up where they had left off recording. Instead, Woody rushed straight into the studio to start work on his own second solo record and Stewart announced he was remaining in the States.

The previous spring, 1974, Britain's Conservative government had finally collapsed under the weight of its own four-year ineptitude. The Socialist Labour Party took control, and with the screams of the indolent aristocracy ringing in their ears, began to undo the long-standing Conservative ethic.

Ridiculously low tax brackets were revised and raised. A new Super-Tax, slashing into the pockets of the Super-Wealthy, was planned. A new phrase entered the English language, not as a comic reference to the idle rich on their sun-soaked estates in exotic climes, but as a way of life for anybody who earned large sums of money from whatever they did. It was Tax Exile, and the way to become one was simple. It was either pay up or get out.

"The government thinks they'll tax us bastards right up to the hilt because we won't leave," Stewart complained. "But that's wrong." He was, he said, already paying a staggering seventy per cent of his earnings to the taxman, and now they wanted to raise it to ninety! "And that's bloody criminal. That's like, for a young man, paying your death duties before you die. It's just not worth living in England any more. I know I earn a lot of money, but it's taken me a long time to make it, and I intend to enjoy it."

He later told the *Chicago Tribune*, "I've got to get out of England. They take all your money. Used to be you could keep your money in banks outside the country and get around the taxes that way, but they've even closed that loophole now."

"I got a lot of criticism when I left, but at least I was honest about it," Stewart says today. "I said I was getting out for two reasons – I was in a rut in England, I wasn't coming up with any new songs or anything and I needed a change.

"But I was also being crippled by taxes. I didn't want to work my ass off and then end up someday singing in a little bar because I don't have any money."

Stewart wasn't the only person fleeing the country to escape the taxman, but he was the one the media concentrated on, particularly when both Elton John and Paul McCartney announced that they would not be forced out of their homes. "And Elton makes a hell of a lot more than Rod Stewart," snarled Lou Reizner.

But this time it wasn't just Stewart being tight-fisted. In fact, the money was only the smallest part of his reasoning. So were his songs.

He had another reason for wanting to get away from Britain. He had fallen in love again . . . and he didn't want Dee Harrington to find out. Not just yet, anyway.

7

Over The Top

When Dee Harrington first heard the reports linking Stewart with actress Britt Ekland, she was inclined to ignore them. Living with Rod for five years, she had grown accustomed to seeing his name linked with almost every woman he met, and there had been a lot of them.

During the run-up to the Faces' Christmas 1973 tour, the newspapers had a field day with Stewart's supposed involvement with model Kathy Simmonds. When the *Daily Express* contacted her for comment, Harrington simply brushed their queries aside. "Who is Kathy Simmonds anyway? I'm still engaged to Stewart, and I'm living in his house."

To which Simmonds retorted, "He is a thoroughly nice guy, very reliable and true to his word. If he says he'll call me at a certain time, he always does . . . I am not possessive, Rod is a free person and *nobody* owns him." Stewart himself intelligently kept his head down. "We are a little bit in love," he was quoted as saying, but Dee, Rod and even Kathy knew he was simply saying what the papers wanted to hear.

Indeed, Stewart was very conscious of his standing among rock's aristocracy, going so far as to employ the eminently capable publicity man Tony Toon. His job, which he started in 1972, was simply to keep Stewart in the public eye, and with a gossip-hungry press waiting on his every word, he succeeded beyond even Stewart's wildest dreams.

A voluble, almost absurdly energetic man, Toon quickly distinguished himself within Stewart's circle by referring to everybody he came in contact with as female, regardless of their gender. Both Billy Gaff and Jimmy Horowitz fast grew accustomed to Toon telephoning them in a panic because "She" wanted this, "She" wanted that. Requests for clarification only delighted Toon even more: "Oh, Miss Horowitz, Miss Gaff, it's our Miss Stewart, of course."

Ekland herself later admitted, "Toon would indulge in the slickest and cheapest of gimmicks in order to gain his client as much space as possible in the British press", and his list of triumphs was endless.

On one occasion, Toon took the beautiful Princess Mariam of Johore

along to the set of the "Russell Harty Plus" television program to meet
Stewart. Afterwards, the party went out to dinner, and the next morning
the tabloids were full of Superstar Stewart's latest Passionate Fling. And
when it was finally "over", around two o'clock that same morning, the
Princess kept her half of the bargain by offering the press a juicy dismissal: "I don't dig gravediggers any more."

Toon himself, Ekland shudders, "was totally subservient and hero-
worshipped Rod". Sometimes he would go a little too far and Stewart
would be forced to take him down a peg or two, like the time he gave
a hooker $100 to visit Rod's hotel room. She wasn't bad-looking, but
Stewart was outraged regardless. "That's the closest I got to sacking
him," Stewart later said. "Imagine me, paying for it!"

But such occasions were thankfully rare. Toon knew what his gaffer
wanted, and was more than happy to supply it. When Stewart stood
up President Ford's daughter Susan on a date, it made headlines
everywhere, although even Rod admits the whole thing was fabri-
cated. "I just couldn't get back to Washington from my tour in time
to take her out. I didn't stand her up. She thinks it's a giggle and so
do I."

There was no end to Toon's inventiveness. "Every time I got out of
bed," says Stewart, "it would be in the news. People would have parties
and they'd say, 'Let's invite the guy with the funny hair and maybe
we'll get into the papers.'"

But of all Stewart's activities, it was his romantic entanglements which
kept the tabloid press in a constant state of fascination. With or without a live-in girlfriend, Rod had suddenly become rock's most eligible
bachelor. In swift succession, models Pauline Stone, Mai Britt and
Debbie Doranck were reported to have passed through his sweat-soaked
sheets. He only had to be seen with a woman and suddenly there was
a romantic liaison. Harrington herself admits, "I got really angry only
once, when I caught Rod out in a deliberate lie. He told me he had to
go to Spain for a couple of days, to do something about our boat,
moored at Marbella.

"I didn't think anything of it – until the next day. In the newspapers,
staring me in the face, was a picture of Rod leaving London for Spain
with actress Joanna Lumley."

According to Harrington, the relationship was brief, but for her excru-
ciatingly painful, especially when she read that Stewart had said of
Lumley, "I'm desperately serious," to which Lumley replied, "I love
him to death."

Although Stewart later revealed that the affair had eventually lasted
close to two months, during which period, conveniently enough, Harrington was living alone in the Highgate mock-Tudor which Long John

Baldry had recently vacated, it was more likely that his relationship was just another enjoyable photo opportunity, nothing more. His most quotable – and quoted – comment about the glamorous Ms Lumley came after the two went out for a meal. "It was the cheapest night I have had out for some time. The meal was eight pounds, ninety pence. I thought to myself, 'There's a nice girl.'"

Stewart returned from Spain alone, vaguely apologetic but surprised that Harrington had taken the story so hard. "I was never allowed to be jealous of Rod," she says. "The gossip columns were always full of stories about him being with other women, but he got angry if I was upset. He always said his dates with them weren't important, or didn't matter." This time, Stewart insisted, he had innocently offered to take Lumley with him, not really expecting her to go through with it. "I couldn't get out of it," he complained, as though dating one of the most eligible women in show business was some kind of insufferable hardship.

"To add insult to injury," Harrington continues, "Joanna kept telephoning for weeks afterwards." At first Stewart tried to duck her calls, but finally Dee had had enough. "Joanna called and said in her most breathy voice, 'Is Rod there?' I asked, 'Who's calling', and she said, all sultry, 'Joanna'. When I finally got him to speak to her he sounded very awkward. I was humming loudly in the background – so that couldn't have helped. Then after a few minutes I said in a loud voice that she couldn't miss, 'Come on, Rod, are we going shopping or are you going to spend all day talking to her?'"

As he put the phone down, Stewart sighed in exasperation. "Why can't she get the message?" "Because," Dee answered, "people like that can't bear being shoved aside by a shorthand typist."

Britt Ekland was a very different woman from those others who had floated through Stewart's past. Three years Rod's senior, Britt-Marie Ekland was born in Stockholm, Sweden, and by the time she met Stewart had long since established herself as one of the most celebrated B-list actresses around. Just two years earlier, she had appeared as the latest, and one of the most memorable, in a long line of James Bond girls, while her most recent movie had the ironic – and, for Rod, strangely appropriate – title, *The Ultimate Thrill*.

Ekland's personal life was no less public than her professional career. Her three-year marriage to Peter Sellers had been conducted in the full glare of the media spotlight, her long-established relationship with record producer Lou Adler only marginally less so.

Britt was with Adler the first time she saw Stewart, onstage at the London Rainbow performing "Tommy", in 1972. "With his mousy-colored cactus-spiked hair, elongated mobile face and his limp figure swathed in yards of tartan, he resembled a rag doll," she says. So much for first impressions.

The following July, she ran into him again, this time at Mick Jagger's birthday party. "I couldn't resist the temptation of crushing down his spiky hair and goading him, 'Is this for real?' Needless to say, he was not amused."

In March 1975 Rod and the Faces hit LA. Ekland and Adler had now broken up, leaving the actress with two children to raise – Nikolai, fathered by Adler, and Victoria, from her marriage to Sellers. Britt was depressed, and when Joan Collins called to ask her along to the Faces gig, she didn't really want to go.

But Collins and her husband, former Apple Records executive Ron Kass, were persistent. "Come on, Britt. You've got to pull yourself together. An evening out will cheer you up."

Ekland sat through the show, but all she really remembered afterwards was the "the most poisonous of green suits" which the heavily made-up Stewart wore as he pranced around the stage. "When the concert was over, Joan and Ron led a foray of celebrities backstage to congratulate Rod on his performance. Against popping champagne corks we were properly introduced."

From the Forum, with Stewart completing the foursome, Collins and Kass led Ekland off to Luau's for dinner. Plainly they were matchmaking, but Stewart, at least, didn't seem interested. "An extrovert on stage," says Ekland, "Rod was terribly shy in private, and all through dinner he sat coyly at the table like 'Little Boy Lost', saying hardly a word." Only after a party at Cher's house did he begin to thaw out.

"I got the impression that Rod was intimidated by my image," Ekland remembers. "But slowly he came out of his shell and we found a quiet corner and immersed ourselves in conversation. Out of the corner of my eye I caught a glimpse of Ron and Joan smiling toward us, obviously feeling that their matchmaking efforts had succeeded.

"By the end of the night I knew that I would have Rod. But I wasn't going to be a one-night-stand groupie."

Stewart had, as usual, been telephoning Harrington every night in London, usually just before he went to bed. One morning, however, the telephone rang much earlier than usual. It was Rod, asking her to get on the next plane to join him in Los Angeles. "I don't like being here without you," he told her. "This is where we met. This is our special place. Please come."

Harrington, however, was strangely uncertain. Despite the recent improvement in Rod's behavior, Dee felt a sense, not of foreboding, but of finality every time she thought of him. Almost subconsciously, Harrington was preparing herself for life without Stewart. When she finally agreed to make the flight out to LA, those feelings welled up stronger than ever within her. They had met in Los Angeles, she told herself; how fitting, then, that they should part there as well.

Only when she landed in LA did the sense of almost anticipatory gloom lift. "When I arrived, I was surprised to find Rod had gone to a lot of trouble to make me feel welcome," she says. "He sent Tony to meet me at the airport, he'd rented a Mercedes for me to drive around in. Rod really was sweet." But the first major bust-up was not far away.

"As soon as we were alone in our suite, Rod wanted to make love. But I was so tired and grubby after flying from London I insisted on having a bath first."

Stewart watched as she disrobed, then exploded. A few nights earlier, Dee had gone to bed still wearing her jewelry, and had inadvertently scratched her back. Typically, Stewart didn't believe her for a moment. "Jewelry doesn't do that," he roared. "Fingernails do that!" He then launched into the tired old diatribe about her springing into an orgy of unfaithfulness the moment his back was turned.

"He wound himself up into a terrible temper," says Dee, "and he stormed out of the room. Ten minutes later he was back, acting peculiarly."

"I'm going out for a drink with Bobby Womack," he said, and Harrington, knowing how much he liked the legendary soul singer, told him she'd amuse herself until he got back. "Maybe I could go out for dinner with Tony."

Later that evening, driving back to the hotel with Toon, Harrington decided to take a detour to the Troubador Club. She had been there all those years before, on her first trip to LA, and was curious about who was appearing there.

Harrington pulled up behind a limousine, glanced up at the marquee, and was just getting ready to drive away when she saw another car pull to a halt. Out of it stepped Stewart, with a willowy blonde on his arm.

"I thought it was Krissie Wood, because I knew she was in town as well, so I parked the car and jumped out. Tony was saying, 'No, don't get out. Come on, let's get back', but it was too late because I was already out of the car and saying, 'Oh no, I've got to go and say hello.'"

She ran into the Troubador, smack into Stewart and his ladyfriend. At first Harrington didn't recognise the woman. For all her perceived fame, Britt Ekland was not yet the household face she was to become during her years with Rod. The only thing Dee knew for sure was that it wasn't Krissie Wood. She snapped.

"Have you brought me 6,000 miles just to fuck me around?"

Stewart glanced up. "It cuts both ways," he said drily, obviously still incensed over the scratch marks.

Dee retorted, "I am going to take the next plane back to London if you don't want me to stay here with you." She then turned and left the crowded, strangely hushed room.

"At first I thought it was just another groupie who had rushed in to the restaurant for Rod's autograph," remembered Britt. "But then I realised something was amiss, I didn't want to get entangled in their exchange. At the same time, I was making no claim on Rod or trying to impair his loyalties. I could not possibly know the state of their relationship and I was not going to intrude. I saw Rod trying to calm the situation but then Dee was gone and Rod came to join me at the table where I had taken discreet cover. He did not mention the incident.

"His composure in such a moment was remarkably cool. There was not the slightest trace of anxiety, although I felt strangely to blame when I learned that Dee's melodramatic departure had been the final act in the parting of their ways."

Harrington returned to the hotel and immediately started repacking. "Word of what had happened spread quickly," she says, "and people kept coming to my room to make excuses for Rod and to try and smooth things over. But I'd had enough."

True to her word, Harrington caught the first plane home, walking out, she says, "with what was left of my dignity", but still trying to figure out what had happened. "Perhaps, like a lot of insecure men, he feels he has something to prove," she said at the time. "A bit of high-class scalp-collecting is good for the ego. I'd say that Rod is on a big ego trip right now. I think he is beginning to believe his own public image. Whatever the cause, he's making a fool of himself. He's becoming better known for his amorous adventures than for his music, which is a shame."

Harrington returned to her parents' house and prepared to start life anew. And while she remembers that some nine months later Tony Toon asked her why she walked out like that – "you know Britt Ekland was just another of Rod's passing fancies" – Harrington herself knew that it was all over between her and Rod.

Stewart, stunned by her abrupt departure, deeply wounded and, perhaps, almost innocently bewildered by her hostility, fell conveniently into the first arms that opened themselves to him. It was only later that his feelings of desperate infatuation turned into the love which he and Ekland were soon to be proclaiming to the world.

But if Stewart was simply rebounding from the shattering end to what remains one of the longest-standing relationships in his life, he did so with abandon, overwhelming Ekland with his affection. And while she, at first, was not willing to throw herself so easily into a relationship with this intriguing Briton, she knew her resolve was weakening. A few nights after his showdown with Dee, Britt accompanied Rod to a party thrown by singer Joni Mitchell.

"Bob Dylan and Paul McCartney took over one of Joni's magnificent rooms and began a jam session. They wanted Rod to join them but he could not detach himself from my side."

"I don't think anyone has ever turned down the chance to jam with Bob Dylan before," Stewart later admitted to friends. "But I was so much in love with Britt."

"From that moment on," remembers Ekland, "we were inseparable, kissing and cuddling in our new-found passion. We were oblivious to the stares and embarrassment we caused."

She called him Soddy, a name that would surely have sent Dee Harrington into fits of laughter. He called her Poopy. Neither name, the couple laughingly admitted, was anything to be proud of, but they didn't care. They were too busy making love three or four times a day. Ekland compares their coupling to "two pieces of interlocking jigsaw . . . we matched physically. We were both slender, small-boned and long-legged."

Ekland's presence amused the Faces. "Got himself a real posh one this time," they'd laugh, and in moments of camaraderie which they had not known in years they mercilessly teased Stewart about his latest squeeze. "A bit flat-chested, isn't she, mate? I thought you went for the big-lunged girls," they would say, keeping it up for so long that finally Ekland herself began to wonder whether there was something to what they were saying.

"I asked Rod, 'Do you want me to have a boob job?' He was uncomplaining. He thought I was perfect as I stood. He liked my teenage figure and long blonde hair. I think the little-girl image was different for him and he liked it." Shamelessly, she reveals that he liked her to dress in virginal white stockings, panties, petticoat, a negligee, "and peel it all off like the leaves of an artichoke." In bed, he liked her to wear Patou's Joy, his favorite perfume.

Ekland fondly reminisces, although Stewart himself later contradicted her, "We would make love in all sorts of crazy places. Once, just for the kick of it, we did it on the back seat of my Mercedes which we chose to park in the long, unlit drive of my neighbor Goldie Hawn – who I'm sure would have been very understanding if she found out!"

Although he continued to doubt Stewart's true commitment to Ekland, for Tony Toon their relationship was heaven-sent. In terms of media exposure, they were the hottest couple in the world, and Toon reveled in them, coining the nickname that was to remain with them throughout their relationship – the Burton and Taylor of the seventies.

And despite her misgivings, Ekland found herself inextricably drawn into the tireless Toon's fantasy.

"I found myself almost echoing his publicity blurbs and playing on the Burton and Taylor theme. What I lacked in diamonds – and it became transparently obvious that Rod wasn't going to give me any – I compensated for by wearing the gaudiest of costumes to match those of my new pop hero.

"In our relationship, it was Rod who wore the jewelry. I bought him an eye-catching piece of carved jade, mounted on a delicate gold chain and another chain with a replica of a mouth fashioned in diamonds, a symbol of Rod's own pouting lips. I also gave him a Cartier watch, and he would borrow my gold chains, tethering them from one pocket of his waistcoat to another with safety pins." But, she mourns, "he lost most of the jewelry."

Stewart was hardly accustomed to the sort of gifts Ekland was lavishing upon him. The only jewelry he had ever owned before she appeared, he once revealed, had been thrown at him onstage. And it was all, he said proudly, "cheap. Cheap and *nasty*. I like cheap things."

Every Monday morning the couple would celebrate the weekly anniversary of their meeting. "Whoever was the first to wake would sing 'The Wedding Song' to the other," Ekland laughs. "Rod may have started this little innovation, I don't know, I can't really remember, but it showed how much gratitude we felt for finding one another."

Stewart wanted to settle down with Ekland immediately. There was an aching void in his life without Dee. Had she not stumbled across Ekland in such dramatic fashion, they might well have still been together. Stewart knew that, and desperately sought to replace her with the woman who had lost her for him. He had to prove to himself that Ekland was worth losing Dee for. His offers of domesticity were certainly his way of showing the world that he knew exactly what he was doing. Deep down inside, however, he wasn't quite so sure.

Neither was Ekland, although not because she was uncertain about Stewart's motives. "I didn't doubt that Rod loved me, but could he really accept my two children as well?"

Stewart said yes. "It's like starting out with a ready-made family, and it would be good to have kids around the house. A home isn't a home without kids."

In August 1975, six months after they had met, Ekland finally agreed to move in with him. Stewart celebrated by proclaiming his fidelity to the world.

"We've got a pact to be faithful to each other," he said. "I suppose you set yourself a goal when you've been knocking about with as many

137

birds as I've been with. Each one you find a fault in, and then you begin to think if only I could find the one that has everything.

"As far as I'm concerned, Britt's got literally everything. She's got incredible charm. She's probably the most genuine person you could want to meet in her position. She's not snobby . . . she's one of the boys, you might say. Britt's definitely left her mark on me, which I don't think any other woman has ever done before. I've never looked up to a woman or admired a woman like I do her. I've been looking for years for someone like Britt. I am in heaven. I have promised to be faithful." It was a proclamation which Ekland would later make him regret ever having uttered.

Negotiations for a home overlooking Sunset Boulevard fell through, but shortly afterwards the couple found a twenty-room mansion on Carolwood Drive in LA. "We knew we had found the house of our dreams," says Ekland. It cost $750,000, and Rod paid up without a qualm. He set aside another $100,000 in a special bank account for Ekland to use on remodeling the entire interior.

"It was a huge task and I set about making sketches of every room, planning the decor and color schemes so a distinguishable influence could be detected in the house from the moment one entered the front door."

A four-car garage was packed. Ekland still had the Mercedes Lou Adler had given her, Rod an AC Cobra, an Excalibur and, of course, the inevitable Lamborghini – a $26,000 Countach which he had air-freighted over from Rome at the cost of an additional $2000.

Ekland prided herself on passing her own peculiar love of Art Deco and Art Nouveau on to the men she loved, and Stewart was no exception. Over the next few months, Ekland shipped in a veritable warehouseful of lamps, candelabra and mirrors. Furniture was flown in from Paris. Twelve thousand dollars' worth of Old Masters were picked up at Sotheby's in Los Angeles. Crockery, linen and cutlery came from London, New York and Hong Kong. The bedroom, its centerpiece a great brass bed, was softened with blue ribbons, "to convey the coziness of a child's cot." There was also a collection of silver artichoke tables.

Ekland turned the house into a conservationist's nightmare. A pair of ornamental pelicans was made from ostrich eggs. A couple of sofas were backed with elephant tusks and upholstered in cowhide. Privately, Stewart admitted that the decor made him feel a little uncomfortable. "I don't much go for that stuff," he said of Ekland's tastes. "I mean, that style of furniture was frowned upon even in its day, wasn't it?"

But Stewart bit his lip and remained silent. To all outward appearances, the Swedish actress with her extravagant tastes and the little working-class boy from a dingy London thoroughfare were delighted. Theirs may not have been the most tasteful home, but it certainly stank of money. The wood paneling in the basketball-hall-sized living-room alone cost $30,000.

The house was not perfect, though. The terrace outside one of the first-floor bathrooms had been taken over by wild cats, which the couple had to evict. There was also a major insect problem. But slowly, over the course of several months, things came together. In the end, says Ekland, "It resembled our dream – like a shrine of our love, set amid the aromatic scent of gardenias and flowering shrubs beautifying the two-and-a-half acres of grounds providing us with a swimming-pool and paddle-tennis court."

Tony Toon was subsequently moved into a staff cottage on the grounds, all the better to feed the media with the latest hot scoops. "They're throwing a barbecue by the pool tonight," he would whisper conspiratorially into the telephone. "This is the guest list . . ."

What he didn't say was that the lovebirds rarely remained with their guests for long. Britt remembers, "We wouldn't think twice about leaving our guests to chew on their spare ribs and their conjectures while we sought the refuge of our bedroom to make love maybe for the second or third time of the day. Trying to set fresh records on the previous day's accomplishments in bed."

The only clouds on the horizon were the couple's former lovers, particularly Rod's. Ekland says, "He would refer to Lou [Adler] as 'the Rabbi', and if Sellers ever got mentioned he would be prompted to remark, 'That *old* man of yours . . . aren't you lucky to have someone at last who is young and gorgeous?'"

Harrington, on the other hand, was a much harder ghost to bury. Stewart missed her terribly, and compensated by running her down whenever he could, as if by doing so he could finally get over his love for her. Nine months were to pass between their parting and the next time they spoke, nine months during which Stewart's longing may have diminished, but his affection for her never did.

Honest to a fault, Harrington had taken no more from their lives together than she had taken into it, leaving behind even the Rolls-Royce and the Lamborghini he had lavished upon her. The only thing she wanted, and that he parted with willingly, was the horse he had bought for her.

Years later, while recording his *Out of Order* album in 1988, it was to Harrington, herself now a successful rock manager, that he turned for the song "My Heart Can't Tell You No". Written by one of Dee's clients, Simon Climie, the song gave Rod another massive hit single and, perhaps, brought out a more tender vocal than ever he intended. Thirteen years after she walked out of his life, Stewart still carried a torch for Dee Harrington. Deep down inside, maybe he still does.

Such feelings, of course, were buried deep as he and Britt set about holding court for the world's press. Stewart admitted he was considering making Los Angeles his permanent home, and perhaps even applying for American citizenship. "I love the radio stations out here," he said, "and I like the idea of being surrounded by all those musicians. But I'd like to live in Paris as well, because of the architecture and the lifestyle. And the clothes. Then again I could always live in Chicago. I hear there's an Yves St Laurent boutique there. Can't wait to get to it."

Somewhere amidst so much activity, Stewart found both the inclination and the energy to make a new record in 1975. It was, he told Britt, to be his crowning glory, a break with the past so complete and total that even his detractors would be amazed.

Even more than that, it was to be a complete break with the Faces. Not one member of the group was invited to appear at the sessions. Of all the musicians who had featured on Stewart's past albums, only one, Martin Quittenton, was asked along, and he turned it down. This new album was also to be Stewart's break with Britain – for the first time he would record in the United States – so it was no accident that he decided to call it *Atlantic Crossing*.

Stewart decided against producing it himself, instead calling in veteran producer Tom Dowd, whose name he found on so many of the records he loved during his youth – those of Wilson Pickett, Solomon Burke, Otis Redding, King Curtis and Aretha Franklin – as well as on some of the most important records of the last few years. He had also engineered three albums by Cream, establishing a relationship with guitarist Eric Clapton which kept him busy through much of the 1970s.

"Joe Smith, who was head of Warner Brothers, called me up and asked if I would like to work with Rod," Dowd remembers. "I said I'd love to, so I flew out to California to meet him."

He arrived while the Faces were still trying to get themselves together sufficiently to record their own album, early in 1975, and straight away Stewart told him he wanted to do a very different type of record from anything the band might ever conjure up. "He told me he didn't know whether he wanted to work with the Faces again," Dowd remembers, "and I said I thought they were a limiting factor."

Dowd followed Stewart down to the studio one day, and the pair sat together in the control room for an hour, listening. Dowd wasn't impressed. "If you would allow," he said as they left, "I'd rather introduce you to two or three different rhythm sections which we could use on various songs. I don't think all the songs should come out sounding the same."

140

It was a damning comment on the Faces, and Stewart knew it. But he agreed. "He asked who I was thinking about, and I said 'For the songs you're talking about that are in this tradition, I could get Steve Cropper, 'Duck' Dunn and Al Jackson'" – the legendary trio who had backed so many of Stewart's heroes during the golden age of soul. "They're friends and would be delighted to play with you.

"He looked at me and was petrified. He just went into a tizzy."

Within weeks, Stewart had recorded three songs with that hallowed line-up – the Bee Gees' "To Love Somebody", Gerry Dorsey's "Holy Cow", and Presley's "Return to Sender". Only the first of these songs has been released. It appeared on Stewart's *Storyteller* anthology, and Dowd describes the remaining pair as insurance premiums. "If all else fails, stick these out."

Dowd continues, "Rod was just overwhelmed, but then he said that he'd like to meet another rhythm section. Now he'd begun to get a little bravado about it, because he had an idea for a song with them. We went through three or four songs, and I said we'd fly down to Muscle Shoals, in Alabama, to try them out.

"At this point Rod and Steve Cropper had established a little rapport, and I said that if Rod wanted, we could take Steve along with us in case there was any breakdown in communication and Steve or I could take charge and iron out any problems."

Like the Cropper–Dunn–Jackson axis, the Muscle Shoals Rhythm Section was one of soul music's most legendary outfits, and Stewart couldn't wait to meet them. But when he did, he was convinced Dowd was having him on. "That's not the Muscle Shoals Rhythm Section," he said, taking Dowd by the arm and walking him out of earshot. "They're all white." In his mind, they should have been black!

"I said, 'Believe me, Rod, that's them. That's Roger Hawkins, Barry Beckett, and Jimmy Johnson . . . that's them.' He still said he didn't believe me, and was being adamant.

"So I said, 'All right', and I went inside and said, 'Fellas, here are the chords, key of C, run it down at this tempo', and they started doing it. Rod was standing outside the door, and he looked in and said, 'I don't believe it. They play black, but they're all white.'"

Stewart ended up recording his new album at five different studios, as far apart as New York, LA, Miami and Memphis, but it was at Muscle Shoals that Dowd remembers the most productive sessions.

"We did 'Sailing', 'First Cut Is the Deepest', and a whole pile of those things there," Stewart says, and he adds, "I recorded 'Sailing' in Alabama, a partially 'dry' state – meaning no alcoholic beverages available. I was asked to sing live at 10.30 in the morning with no lubrication for the vocal cords on hand – get my drift?"

It is a strangely off-hand way of describing the creation of a song which, as Rod himself claims, became "almost a national anthem in Britain". Stewart's father remembers attending a big soccer game at Wembley Stadium and hearing the whole crowd spontaneously burst into the song – and not for his benefit! The old man simply stood there with tears in his eyes thinking, "My son started all that!"

"Sailing" was written by Gavin Sutherland, of the British group Sutherland Brothers and Quiver, one of the most respected, if unsuccessful, bands then playing the British circuit. Stewart himself thought they were great, describing them as "one of the best bands Britain's got to offer", and even toying with recording at least part of an album with them. That idea soon went by the board, but the band swiftly overcame their disappointment. They too had released "Sailing" as a single, but it passed by all but unnoticed. "We were overjoyed when Rod recorded that song," says Quiver guitarist Tim Renwick, today one of Britain's most successful session players. "We'd been coming to the end of our contract with Island; the interest generated by Rod's recording of the song helped us get a new deal with CBS, and essentially relaunched our career.

" 'Sailing' is strange," says Tom Dowd, 'because among the group singing in the background is Bob Crewe, who used to make all those old Four Seasons records, and Cindy Bullens. Bob just happened by the studio one day when we were doing the song and I told him I needed some backgrounds for the song to make it sound like a big choir. He listened to it and said he wanted to sing on it, and ran in with about ten of his friends and here we were with a choir."

Stewart himself was brimming with enthusiasm for *Atlantic Crossing*. "I think it's the best one I've ever done, I definitely needed new blood around me. Suddenly I've seen the light of day. This is what I should have been doing two years ago. Perhaps I could be wrong; it might be a total flop and it'll be back to the drawing board. I sincerely hope it's successful, but how do you define success? Selling a couple of million albums? Or satisfying yourself?

"I don't think there's a weak track on it," he enthused. "The days have gone of fillers and things like that." And while he admitted that it seemed strange to record an album without Woody alongside him, he could not help but remark, "The musicianship is a lot more polished, which is what I really wanted. At last I've found a rhythm section I can really get into.

"My albums have been Woody's biggest source of income," he continued. "But he understands that I was getting fed up using the same backing musicians all the time. I'd been getting tired of recording, period. But going to Muscle Shoals and working with the people down there was like a new lease of life. I can't wait to do another album there, the musicianship's so incredible."

He also admitted that he had been listening to his critics. "For years everybody's been saying I should write more original material, but I'm lazy. I don't do it unless I have to and then it's at the last minute. This time, though, I was so excited about working with new people that I had five songs written before I even went into the studio – the most I'd done before was three." Asked where he got his inspiration from, he joked, "I nick it from other people."

In Britain, *Atlantic Crossing* swiftly established itself among the biggest-selling albums not only of the year, but also of the decade. It entered the charts at number one and remained there for five weeks.

"Sailing", too, turned the charts on their head. It roared into the British Top Twenty at number two, spent a couple of weeks jostling for supremacy with the Bay City Rollers, then hogged the top spot for four weeks straight. If there had ever been any doubts about Rod Stewart's superstardom, they were now behind him forever.

The United States, however, were less enthused about Stewart's change of direction. The album barely scraped into the Top Ten, "Sailing" peaking at a desultory number 68. US reviewers, too, were less than kind, complaining that Stewart's decision to divide the record into two very separate entities – side one was all rockers, side two all ballads – only exaggerated the already sterile atmosphere the album was martyred by. Had they only known that Ekland was behind the division, their wrath might never have been quelled.

Woody agreed with the charges being leveled at his old mucker. "The musicians he's used on this album are the cream," he said. "But as far as I can see it's a mistake. It's taking people from one kind of musical field and trying to turn them into rock musicians, which they're not. Rod's singing tight with a tight band, but each track is in its own vacuum."

The Faces, he continued, worked very differently. "Kenney just plays the drums the way he would have anyway, and when it comes time to rehearse Rod's old songs with the band I have to learn them all again because I forgot everything. Not exactly efficient, but it's not like sitting up in my room figuring out the chords either, because I play them instantly with the voice."

Atlantic Crossing was frankly too rehearsed, too studious, and two years later, even Stewart admitted too sterile. "There's no spark at Muscle Shoals, unless you want to turn out disco records. They can't really play rock'n'roll."

At the time, however, he bubbled over with enthusiasm for the record and his confidence seemed well placed. "This Old Heart of Mine", a reworking of the classic Temptations hit, gave him a second UK Top Four in November 1975, "I Don't Want to Talk About It" returned him to number one a full two years after *Atlantic Crossing* was released, and "Sailing" itself went to number three when it was picked as the theme music for a new television documentary, "Warship".

The only thing missing from the roll-call of hit singles was the one song which Stewart had been adamant would become a single, the raucous "Three Time Loser".

It was a controversial number, dealing with that most unromantic of sexual consequences, venereal disease. He assured Ekland the song had nothing to do with personal experience, but elsewhere bragged that he had experienced almost every word. In Chicago, he even admitted, "I had my last jab of penicillin right here!"

One line of the song referred to masturbation, and Stewart confided that he'd had to battle the record company even to be allowed to use the phrase "jacking off" in the song. "I think it's in good taste," Stewart said at the time. "You can say anything as long as it's not fuck – you shouldn't ever get that base." He prophesied that as a single it was sure to go to number one. As it was, the record company opted not to take the chance.

Because of his continued wrangling with the British taxman, Stewart was forced to launch the album to the UK press from Dublin in August 1975. If he so much as set foot in Britain, he could be hit with a massive tax bill which newspaper estimates placed as high as $1.5 million. And while Stewart insisted that "I haven't been given a bill yet and when I get it I will pay the lot", he was clearly not going to invite trouble. Instead, he preferred to subject himself to forty-eight hours of waiting around, being shuttled from one airport to another as he attempted to beat the vigilant taxman.

Visiting Sweden with Ekland, Stewart was horrified to learn that he could not catch a direct flight to Dublin. The party, which numbered fifty people, flew instead to Geneva, only to find that their flight was being diverted to London.

Landing at Heathrow Airport, Ekland hurriedly left the plane and telephoned Stewart's London lawyer to get advice on Stewart's position. "It was exactly as we expected. Once Rod crossed through immigration control, he could be detained, but remaining in the transfer section he was safe, as he had not yet legally entered the country."

Britt next rushed to the Dutch airlines desk and purchased two tickets for Amsterdam. They would reach Ireland from there even if it meant delaying their arrival for another twenty-four hours. Tensions remained high, however, even after Ekland had sorted out their escape route. When a photographer stole on board the plane and tried to take Rod's photograph, members of Stewart's entourage leaped upon him and bodily forced him from the aircraft.

The record launch party itself was a sumptuous affair, but was marred by personal bitterness. Both Ian MacLagan and Kenney Jones received invitations to the reception, but neither turned up. Instead they stayed at home and slagged off the record. "He wasn't stretching himself," Mac complained. "Deep down he hasn't changed at all, but he's into all that Hollywood thing."

Jones was even more vociferous in his condemnation of Stewart, complaining that the Faces had been intending to play a series of outdoor festivals in British football stadiums that summer. They'd had to cancel because of Stewart's tax situation, and the drummer admitted he was virtually redundant now. "He doesn't want to pay out any money so the rest of us can't earn any." Jones estimated he had lost some eighty thousand pounds in earnings, and said, "I feel pretty browned off. Ever since Rod moved to the States everything's got disorganised." He said he looked on Rod "as my friend who's gone astray."

Stewart, too, admitted that things were rapidly souring between himself and the band. "We're probably further away from each other than we've ever been," he said. "There's a lot of bullshit goes down. We have a go at each other behind each others' backs. We never say the best things about each other." And while he did admit that "when we're together we're the best of mates always", he also confessed, "If the Faces are going to break up, it'll be in the next few months. I love 'em as blokes, but we've got a lot to talk about." He claimed he couldn't remember what Tetsu looked like, and concluded bitterly, "I don't even know if our guitar player is still alive."

For the last two years, there had been constant rumors that Woody was going to join the Rolling Stones. He was very close friends with Keith Richard in particular, and in 1974 Richard, Mick Jagger and guitarist Mick Taylor, whose position in the band Woody would presumably usurp, had all helped out with his first solo album, ironically titled *I've Got My Own Album to Do*.

The possibility of Woody switching his allegiance moved considerably closer at the end of 1974, when Taylor did indeed quit the Stones, and at the Faces' Christmas party that year, every photographer in town seemed to be there, trying to catch Woody and Mick Jagger in the same frame.

Woody was characteristically modest on the subject. "I suppose that I would join the Stones in another time," he said, "a lot of my roots and influences are in that band. But it could never happen when I'm with the Faces. The Stones know that, 'cause they dig the Faces too. It's just a very tempting little carrot to be dangled."

Stewart, however, was less convinced, admitting that at one time he had been "terribly worried about Woody leaving to join the Stones." But now he was more confident about his own future, or perhaps he really didn't care that much. "This time around it's a bit of an anticlimax," he said, then added, somewhat ominously, "If Woody was to go, there would be no point in me carrying on. He's a pillar for me to lean on; we share each other's tears. But there's no doubt in my mind that Woody's here for the duration."

Part of the reason for his confidence was that joining the Stones wouldn't be much more than a sideways step for any of the Faces. "The Stones have got the history behind them," he would laugh, "but we're better-looking." And in terms of drawing power, a hair could scarcely separate the two bands. For all the internal disputes, the Faces were at the peak of their profession, the highest drawing band in the world. If money was all Woody cared about, Rod was correct; he would be stupid to walk out on the Faces.

But Woody wasn't like that, and in his heart Stewart knew it. The Faces were a band, but the Stones were an institution. Only an idiot would throw away the chance to join them!

In April 1975, with it clear that the British festival shows would not be taking place, Woody announced he was joining the Stones on a strictly temporary basis, touring the States with them and then returning to the fold. As if to bind him to his word, the Faces' office announced that with just a couple of days' rest in between, Woody would then be heading out on the Faces' next US tour that autumn. It was to be their longest trek yet, taking in the US, Japan, Hawaii, Australia, New Zealand and Europe.

But behind the scenes, it was touch and go, almost to the very last minute. The individual Faces were due to convene in Miami for rehearsals in August, immediately after *Atlantic Crossing* hit the stores, and Stewart gruffly announced, "If it doesn't work out in rehearsal, then we just won't tour. If it doesn't sound how I want it to sound, that's it. I want it to sound like something new, like the record I've made. We've got to be more disciplined and tighten up. We always looked at touring like it was party time, which it should be, but it's time we proved ourselves. It's time we took the blinders off."

Among the "innovations" he demanded was the inclusion of a tuxedo-clad string section, to be led by Jimmy Horowitz, and a second guitarist, Steve Cropper. It may have been a Faces tour, but it was going to be Rod's show. And just so there were no misunderstandings about who people were really coming to see, he wanted his own name above the Faces on the tour billing.

He was not the only member of the band who felt that this was make or break time. "If Rod decides to leave, we'll carry on by ourselves," said Mac. "The pressure is on him to leave at the moment because he's constantly being told he's a Hollywood star and a dedicated leader of fashion. Perhaps he should go solo and try it. But I think he still cares about the Faces; he's just up in the air at the moment, being feted by all the people around him. I feel hurt, but realistically I suppose it was bound to happen. Personally, I'd just like a bloody phone call or something. At present I get directives through about five different people. If he wants to act like that, he will have to hire some musicians on a wage. But since he's always changing his mind about things, he's going to find it very difficult to be the boss unless he's with friends."

Those friends were going to find their relationship growing very strained indeed as, on 15 August, the Faces prepared for their next, and possibly final, tour. The entire band, Stewart aside, loathed the string section, and even once the tour was under way they continued to argue for Mac simply to pick up a string synthesiser and duplicate the orchestral sounds himself. But Stewart was adamant. They did it his way, or they didn't do it at all. The only compromise he made was to allow Woody to substitute Jesse Ed Davis for Steve Cropper.

But was this actually the Faces' swansong? Stewart said no. "If we do bust up there's gonna be no bloody farewell tour. It'll end in a punch-up." And he joked, "We'll have the fight televised and that will be our farewell show, kicking the shit out of each other."

Despite having won – or perhaps coerced – the rest of the band's agreement, Stewart remained isolated throughout much of the tour. He and Ekland traveled separately under the ribald alias of Mr and Mrs Cockforth. The ubiquitous Tony Toon tagged along behind to see to the needs of the vast army of pressmen who had attached themselves to the expedition.

"We faced press conferences one after another, and never before had an unmarried couple put their private lives so much on the line," Ekland complains. "The newsmen cared little for Rod's music; constantly we were asked, 'When are you going to marry? Are you going to have children?'" Ekland confesses that "there were times we felt like hiding from the non-stop inquisition." One particularly irritating reporter had his notes torn up and thrown to the winds by an enraged Stewart. But it was in Chicago that he finally cracked.

The conference had been even more inquisitive than usual, and Stewart sat silently seething while Ekland blithely, and it seemed to him too candidly, answered every question. Back in their hotel room, he really let her have it.

"When they ask about our private lives, tell them to go get stuffed. It's none of their fucking business!"

Ekland retorted angrily, "How can you say that when you're throwing a press conference? Once you've invited them they are entitled to ask any questions they like."

Stewart lunged forward and seized her by the shoulders. "You do as you're damn well told!" Then he slapped her.

Ekland exploded, laying into him with all the strength she could muster. Lamps and furniture were sent flying as they battled. For those few, sudden moments, all the pressures of the past few weeks, the constant interrogation by the press, a life spent, as Ekland later put it, living in an ocean-sized goldfish bowl, erupted in a passionate fury.

Suddenly Ekland's black and silver lace dress tore apart with a resounding, deafening rip. She burst into tears and collapsed, sobbing, on to the bed. Stewart stared down at her for a moment, then fell beside her. He, too, was crying. "I'm sorry, Britt. Please forgive me." It was the couple's first fight . . . but it was not to be their last. And in between times? Well, there was always another press conference. There would *always* be another press conference.

"I suppose we are a fairly interesting couple," Ekland gushed as she and Stewart posed for yet another glossy picture spread. "I guess we are, or people wouldn't want to write about us or photograph us. That's okay, I don't mind. I think my life is really exciting."

The rest of the Faces winced at her self-importance as she continued. "It is important that people should know about you. Obviously they think that your life is a little more exciting than theirs, otherwise they wouldn't want to read about you. And if it isn't – you should make it a little more exciting." On and on she droned, and the media hung on to every word like it was gold dust.

Which, of course, it was, particularly when compared to the utterances of another rock'n'roll band on another drawn-out tour, another circus of self-indulgence and childish exhibitionism. "Seeing some of Rod's men throw breakfast trays out of their hotel windows and ripping out telephone lines was only the beginning," says Ekland. "I saw entire hotel rooms torn apart."

"In certain mid-West towns we'd get incredibly bored," explains Woody. "No one to call, nothing to do, everything closed. We had to create our own fun. We were barred from so many hotels – the entire Holiday Inn chain – that we had to check in as Fleetwood Mac lots of times."

Life, Ekland earnestly pronounced, "can deteriorate to a primitive, medieval level when traveling with a rock band." And her Rod, she soon learned, could be as primitive as anyone.

In Honolulu, the hotel management was in a flap because Helen Reddy and her husband Jerry Wald were due in, and their suite, occupied by Stewart and Britt, had still to be cleaned. In fact it hadn't even been vacated!

"I was frantically packing Rod's bags for him while he and the roadies were having a last-minute beer," recalls Ekland. "Suddenly there was a rap on the door and when I answered it a small, abusive man started ordering me to get out of the suite. He just terrified me and I was so scared that I called the switchboard to have Rod paged.

"Rod and the roadies rushed back and immediately dealt with the matter in their own unique way. Rod hissed one word – 'destroy' – and the roadies were unleashed like a pack of dogs."

For twenty minutes the road crew, by now swollen with the arrival of the Faces, rampaged through the suite. "They removed the legs from the bed, took out the television tube, detached the spray from the shower, stuffed towels down the toilet, unplugged the telephones and effectively defused the entire suite."

Mac, meanwhile, was in the hotel lobby delaying Reddy and Wald – by punching him. Wald fell backwards into a wall, bringing a painting down on his head. "It was like a scene from a cartoon," Woody later remarked. "Rod still had to get out, but we made everybody suffer for it!"

Of course, the affair was hardly up to the lofty standards of Keith Moon, who could effectively demolish entire hotels in less time than it took Stewart's lackeys mildly to dent one room, but Stewart was satisfied. "The next time they ask us to leave, maybe they'll be a bit more courteous."

"The extraordinary thing was that they were," an incredulous Ekland later said. "Rod and I returned to the same hotel a few months later and they put flowers and fruit in our room and bottles of liquor. The earlier incident was not mentioned and whether it had all been smoothed over by Rod's manager, Billy Gaff, I didn't know."

More likely, the cost of repairs was simply tacked on to the Faces' bill.

Ekland had her eyes opened in other ways, too. Cocaine, she says, "became the natural substitute for food in the small hours, when hotel restaurants were closed", and no matter how much the damaged hotel rooms cost, she claims to have seen far greater sums paid out for the devilish white powder.

"Many members of Rod's entourage [when she speaks of that final Faces tour, it is always Rod's this, Rod's that – another source of irritation among the band] appeared to survive alone on a daily ration of drugs, and like all nocturnal people they were sitting targets for the pushers."

Stewart himself, she says, was "wary about the excessive use of cocaine" – her careful use of the adjective suggests he had not yet completely given up the stuff. Ekland doesn't let on whether she knew about his earlier habit – that which had come so close to destroying his relationship with Dee Harrington – but does reveal "pot did not appeal to him, having never smoked. His one experiment with heroin caused him to vomit. The thought of plunging a needle into a vein was utterly repugnant to him."

Ekland herself was not averse to joining in the late-night drug sessions, justifying her own use as an occasional "token way to show that I was not condemning anyone for their habits." Most of the time, however, "I stayed carefully on the sidelines."

So, it seems, did the rest of the Faces. Their appearances in Ekland's own reminiscences are scant; their role in the press the tour was generating, too, was equally meager. Mac probably summed the mood up best when he revealed, "We're going into the studio in November, and if Rod isn't going to sing on the numbers, we'll do them ourselves."

Yet there were other complications which Mac had not taken into account. Woody had the time of his life touring with the Stones, admitting, "The Stones bring out the best in me. I think I'm more powerful when I'm with them. It's because they give me confidence, but it's also that added ingredient that is the Stones, although no one really knows what it is.

"I couldn't get used to the freedom to be able to do whatever I wanted. The Faces were limiting where the Stones let me rip." He didn't say anything, but everybody knew – if the Stones invited him in, he'd be off like a shot. "It's just an arrangement if I've got time," he would say, but press him for details and he readily admitted he was more than willing to make that time. "I've got to do a December tour of Europe with them for nine or ten days," he said, barely heeding what such a break might do to the proposed recording sessions.

"I don't think it will harm any relationship with the Faces. This working relationship between the two bands can only go on for so long, but while there's no tension, and while it's helping both bands, there's no reason to make a major issue out of it."

Stewart himself agreed, publicly at least. "The last time I spoke with Woody he said he wanted to combine both careers," Stewart said at the outset of the tour. "If he'd like to do another tour with the Stones after he's done his tour with us, fine. I don't really care."

Later, as the tour entered its second month, he said, "At first it seemed like we would break up. But we're playing better, it sounds tighter. I'll be honest . . . I think we'll stay together."

While Stewart conceded that if Woody left things might be different, as the tour approached its climax, even those thoughts had gone from his head. Suddenly the Rod of old, the teenager for whom the slightest whim was the greatest thing ever, was back. "It suddenly dawned on me . . . how good everybody else in the group is. Even if Woody leaves – and he should make up his mind sooner or later, though I think he genuinely does want to tour with both bands – even if he did join them, I think I would stay with the band. I'd miss him, Christ. But I've realised how good the others are."

It was one of the few times that Stewart's opinion concurred with those of the critics. "The concert at Roosevelt Stadium in New Jersey was the best I had ever seen them play, which was saying something," wrote *Creem* reporter Lester Bangs. "The string section creaked and groaned, miserably out of tune, but the whole band and particularly Rod and Wood were downright brutal, Wood chopping his guitar savagely as if to say, 'This is what you're throwing away, you son of a bitch.'"

But even as Stewart raved on about the band's new lease of life, it seemed as though the enthusiasm was suddenly draining. "I'd be willing to have a go at a Faces album," he said, but now it would not be in November. He was planning to start on his next solo album in December. *If* he completed that on schedule, *if* the band made it out to Australia, "*if* we did it nice and quiet and thought about it . . ."

Australia suddenly fascinated him. "I think we should record there. There's one incredible studio in Sydney." The pressures would be off, he continued, and the band could relax while they worked. "I just don't want anyone to be waiting for the album so they can knock it, which is what's always happened. I think now we've had enough time to think about it, to look back at what we've done, we could create something really good."

Stewart talked about producing the album himself, and boasted that he could get the whole thing done inside a month. If the band preferred to use someone else, he was happy with that, too.

The rest of the guys, though, weren't convinced. "He just likes to confuse the press," said Kenney Jones, but even he admitted, "I think it's okay now. It'll end when it's meant to end, but we're playing pretty good right now. I don't think about a break-up."

Spirits were so high that the band had even given up what had once seemed a tour-long ritual – rewriting the posters which announced "Faces 1975 Fall Tour" so that they read "Faces 1975 *Down*Fall Tour". They truly believed that they still had a chance, and when the Faces parted at the end of the American tour on 1 November and everybody went their separate ways, no one doubted that they would be meeting up again in the new year, for the next leg of the tour.

Then the rumors started. The British music press got wind of Woody having rejoined the Stones in a studio in Montreux, where they were laying down tracks for their next album. He was one of a parade of top guitarists who passed through the studio that autumn, but even as other names were touted as possible new recruits – David Bowie's ex-lieutenant Mick Ronson, blues guitarist Rory Gallagher, even Rod and Woody's old chum Jeff Beck – the suspicion grew that it would be Woody.

And that was it for Stewart. On 19 December, 1975, while Woody was touring with the Stones, the *Daily Mirror* broke the story the whole rock world had been waiting to hear – "Why Rock Star Rod Is Quitting the Faces".

Tony Toon, inevitably, led the charge. "Rod feels he can no longer work in a situation where the group's lead guitarist, Ron Wood, seems to be permanently on loan to the Rolling Stones." Billy Gaff continued, "Rod thinks the world of Ron Wood. But I have repeatedly tried to telephone Ron. I have left messages for him to call me, but I've heard nothing."

As usual, Stewart nailed the whole thing down with one unequivocal statement. "I have only just made up my mind. But I am definitely quitting this time."

Kenney Jones took the news much as everybody thought he would, bad-tempered and stoically. "I'm not bothered," he remarked. "I expect I will survive." And he did. By the end of the decade he was safely installed in the Who as the replacement for the late Keith Moon.

The news had a very different effect on Mac, who heard it in stunned silence and then said, "I won't believe he is leaving the Faces until I hear it from his own lips." He never did.

The following day, Tony Toon issued another statement. The split, he insisted, was nothing against the Stones. "Rod's just upset with Woody. He told me he was fed up with all the aggravation of the last year."

Distanced from all that was going on in the band, Britt Ekland nevertheless endeavored to grab some of the attention for herself. Casting herself, simply by the vehemence of her denials, in the position of a Swedish Yoko Ono, she said, "The Faces put the split down to Rod's burning ego, and some may have suspected that I had something to do with the decision. But I was not involved at all." Speculation which had hitherto not even glanced in her direction suddenly had a new target to home in on, especially after Woody revealed just how hurt and betrayed he himself felt.

"I didn't want to believe it at all," he says. "I thought surely he must be interested in the group, because they're the ones that go on the road, they're the ones that have to live together, have to sit through those boring hotel rooms and everything, but evidently I was wrong."

He continued to insist that the situation with the Stones remained temporary, a remark which Mick Jagger himself confirmed, and added that he had been looking forward to making at least one more album with the group. The Faces, he believed, had never achieved their full potential, and he continued, "I was willing to sit through anything until we got to the final thing that we were after, that we never reached."

Now they never would. "It wasn't until Rod made that drastic decision that it was obvious I had only one path." Within the week, the Rolling Stones office announced that Woody was now officially a member of the band.

Kenney Jones, though, was not convinced by Woody's pleas of innocence. "He wanted to join the Stones, it was obvious," he said dismissively. "And it was obvious that he liked everybody and didn't have the guts to turn round and say it in the first place. Because I think if he had done that when we were all there, I think the band would still have been together with a new guitarist. Woody always plays both ends against the middle so he doesn't lose, and it's about time everybody woke up and saw that. I'm not defending Rod at all. I'm just saying that it's not all Rod."

Two years later, however, Stewart finally revealed just how intricate had been the web which he, aided and abetted by Tony Toon, had woven.

The band had been dead on its feet for more than a year, and certainly since long before the Rolling Stones walked into Woody's life. That much at least was common knowledge. So was Stewart's desire to find a way out of the whole bloody mess.

But he was not going to be the one who ended it. He knew what the Faces meant to their fans; he knew, too, the dread punishments rock fans keep reserved for anybody foolish enough to break up a band they adore. Forever unwilling to accept the consequences of his own decisions, Stewart desperately needed a scapegoat.

"It was the timing of the announcement that really broke all ties," Ekland muses. "Rod reeled out the message through his mouthpiece Tony Toon . . . and he attempted to switch the blame for the split on to the shoulders of Ronnie Wood."

In 1977, Rod admitted, "It had nothing to do with Woody playing with the Stones. Ian MacLagan and I couldn't get on any longer. Mac and I hate each other's guts." And he added, "We would still probably have been together, just drifting on and on, if I hadn't put my foot down and said, 'That's it!'"

Some fifteen years later a more tempered, reflective Rod would comment, "I think we'd taken it as far as it could go. Ronnie always had a hankering to join the Stones and I wanted to make my own albums.

Ronnie Lane started getting disinterested and he was the life and soul of the Faces, not me or Woody. Then when he got MS that was the end of it. He showed symptoms as early as the mid-seventies but we didn't know what it was. Once he left that was it."

There was one final, pathetic piece of the drama still to be played out. With Woody still theoretically in tow, Mac, Jones and Tetsu decided that the final Stewart-less Faces album was still a possibility. Warner Brothers seemed interested, and early in the new year Tetsu flew to France to find a studio for them to work in. The remainder of the band began assembling songs.

Then Warners dropped their bombshell. They were still willing to release the album, but they needed certain guarantees. The band would have to tour when the record came out.

Woody balked. The Stones were putting the finishing touches to their own record, their first with Woody. There was no way of knowing just when in the year he would be free. He was sorry, but there really was nothing he could do.

"In that case, there's nothing we can do, either," Warners replied. The advance they had promised for the album magically disappeared. If the Faces wanted to record, they would have to do it on their own money.

And the band that had once, so many years ago, almost come to blows over paying a producer a two per cent royalty, but whose individual earnings from one tour alone approached six figures, whose wives jealously studied one another's new outfits in case one seemed wealthier than the others, but whose on-the-road drinks and damage expenses probably cost more than all four of their past albums combined, they all stuffed their hands deep into their pockets, looked at one another in dismay, and said, "Fuck that for a game of skittles, I'm going home."

The Faces were no more.

8

A Charmed Life

"I always thought money could buy freedom, but in my case money only forced me to leave home," Stewart lamented after finally abandoning Britain as a tax exile. "I'm frustrated being away from home."

Even Stewart's million-dollar LA mansion with its $125,000 worth of furnishings had all but lost its allure for the frustrated star. "Bloody earthquakes, when the house starts to shake, I have to run about and hold on to everything."

Stewart complained that he couldn't even get a decent beer, and when Ekland's career called her over to London, she returned with a measly six Party Fours – four-pint cans of bitter.

Predictably, Rod also missed Scotland and poured out his grief in a heartfelt rendition of the traditional "Skye Boat Song", which was released in 1975 under the relatively anonymous name of the Atlantic Crossing Pipe and Drum Band.

But the absolute worst thing about being stranded in America for Rod was, as he put it, "missing my soccer."

The mid-1970s were the undisputed peak for organised soccer in the United States, and Stewart had thrown himself gleefully into the media maelstrom that erupted around the most successful American team, the New York Cosmos. But even they couldn't satisfy his homesickness. "I'm sure I could play as good as a lot of guys in the Cosmos," he once remarked. "Many of them are just throw-outs from the British leagues anyway."

Stewart contented himself by flying as many members of his family as he could to Dublin where they would gather around the television and roar their hearts out whenever there was an important game being played – which, of course, meant virtually any match involving their beloved Scotland. Ekland was by his side as well, staring in awe at the rain-drenched mass of humanity which stood on the primitive grandstands, and wondering just how serious her Soddy was when he held her close and whispered, "One day, Poopy, we'll be there with them."

In April 1976, Stewart's accountants finally gave him the go-ahead to return home. Under Britain's labyrinthine tax laws, having served one full year of exile, Rod was now entitled to spend up to sixty days in Britain every year. He would still be hit with a swingeing tax – fifty per cent – but he had always insisted he didn't want to avoid paying *all* taxes; he just objected to paying the full eighty-nine per cent whack.

Ekland, and Victoria, her ten-year-old daughter, accompanied him back to Windsor. They were going to spend Easter together, Stewart said, and afterwards he gushed, "Victoria gave me and Britt an Easter egg with a note attached, saying 'To Mommy and Rod, love Victoria'. That really touched me. I felt she accepted me and that was so important."

Ekland's first sight of the rambling Stewart mansion left her reeling. She describes it carefully, her words still touched by the awe she felt when first confronted by the vast, "distinctly Victorian" hall, with its enormous rooms a "maze of paraphernalia."

Passing through the hallway, festooned with wild animal heads, she remarked, "I had the feeling the house once belonged to a big-game hunter or taxidermist. Something like a hundred bird cages housing a variety of exotic stuffed tropical birds occupied the breakfast room, which did little for my appetite."

Ekland marveled at the dining-room carpet and walls – like Rod's den, they were now a mass of tartan. An immense table seated more than twenty-five guests. The circular kitchen, she says, "was ultra-modern", while the indoor swimming-pool left her speechless, walled as it was with giant black and white prints of Rod!

Ekland was well aware that Dee had lived in the house before her, but remarks, "Her possessions had magically disappeared by the time I arrived." Her memory, however, was harder to exorcise. Many a time Stewart's parents – the tragically wheelchair-bound Elsie, stricken with multiple sclerosis, and the stern and unyielding Bob – would forget themselves and call her "Dee". Ekland, though, claims she didn't really mind and in fact got on quite well with Elsie, and while Bob was a tougher nut to crack, Britt says she learned to understand him "once I realised his basic distrust of women. Rod's dad even came to bring me tea in bed!"

Stewart himself seldom mentioned Harrington, "and when he did," Ekland remembers, "he crudely painted her as having been no more than a housekeeper who slept with him whenever the whim took him." Rod likewise boasted of his many extra-curricular relationships, and proudly informed Ekland, "Dee knew I had other women, but she didn't mind."

Stewart was obviously testing the boundaries, wondering just how far he would be able to push his luck. Britt, however, left him in no doubt as to what she expected from him. "Then that's where I am very different. I would mind a great deal. In fact, if you screw another woman while you're with me, I'll chop your balls off."

For now, though, she had nothing to worry about. Britt and Rod were all but inseparable. "We've managed to spend seven days a week together," said Stewart, and even Tony Toon had to admit he was at a loss about what to do next. The stream of willing bimbos he had funneled from Stewart's bed to the front-page headlines completely dried up. The one never went anywhere without the other. "Most of our social life is confined to private parties because we prefer it that way," commented Rod. "If we're in London and we want a lively evening, we go to Tramps" – the most exclusive showbiz club in the city.

It was ironic, then, that Stewart should title his new album *A Night on the Town*. Work on the project had commenced immediately after the Faces' final tour was finished, in November 1975. Again, Tom Dowd was at the helm, and again he surrounded Stewart with some of the best musicians available – Steve Cropper and Dick Dunne of the MGs, Eagles guitarist Joe Walsh, the Tower of Horns, and the acclaimed rhythm section of Andy Newmark and Willie Weeks.

But the extended sessions were not without problems. One night, Stewart fled the studio complaining he had a sore throat. By the time he returned home to Carolwood Drive, he was virtually speechless, and try as she might Ekland simply couldn't convince him that this was anything less than his worst nightmare come true – Rod Stewart had lost his voice. A doctor was called, but even after two extensive examinations nothing was found, and Stewart remained unable to raise his famous cords above a feeble croak.

It was not, of course, a new problem. Three years earlier, touring with the Faces, Stewart had bitterly cursed the LA air after he spent an entire show, in Anaheim, croaking. "I was on key for only *one* song," he bitched afterwards. "LA knocks me right out and it's costing me a fortune in antiseptic mouthwash!"

Stewart blamed the smog, bitterly complaining that "only an idiot would try to sing with all this bloody smog around." Tom Dowd, by now deeply concerned, immediately had the entire recording operation shifted to Caribou Ranch Studios in Colorado, where Elton John had been working for some time.

The mountain air, however, had little effect whatsoever on the patient. "Maybe the sunshine will help. Let's go to Miami," Dowd suggested. But again, nothing. Finally everybody agreed simply to return home and see what happened. And back in Los Angeles – a miracle. Stewart's voice leaped back to life as suddenly as it had left and the record was completed.

This new LP was important to Stewart for a variety of reasons. Most immediately, it was the acid test of his decision to quit the Faces, the first album he had recorded since excising them from his life.

It also marked the official debut of Stewart's own record label, Riva. Ever since the Beatles hatched their Apple master plan in the late 1960s, it had become *de rigueur* for a successful artist to create his own label identity. Some – Apple, the Rolling Stones' eponymous company, and Led Zeppelin's Swansong – operated with a degree of independence; others – Marc Bolan's Hot Wax, and Deep Purple's Purple Records, for instance – were essentially nothing more than an arm of the company to which the artist was directly contracted – in Bolan's case, EMI. Still others, like Elton John's Rocket Records, were wholly self-controlled.

Stewart made no secret of the fact that it was Rocket that inspired him to strike out with Riva, even though the label was essentially nothing more than an offshoot of Warner Brothers and would not even be represented in the United States. Since striking out on his own in 1973, Elton had enjoyed a remarkable run of success. Although it would be three years before any of John's own product would be released by Rocket, by early 1976 the company had already created one star – singer Kiki Dee – netted an acclaimed cult act – pub-rockers Stackridge – and even clocked up a number-one hit with Elton and Kiki's annoyingly wholesome "Don't Go Breaking My Heart". The company's manifesto, incidentally, pledged its signings "undivided love and devotion, a fucking good royalty, and a company that works its bollocks off".

Named after a speedboat Stewart spotted in the South of France, Riva was not to be quite so altruistic. Launched in November 1975, with Rod's "This Old Heart of Mine", eight of the first ten Riva singles featured Stewart, either solo, with the Faces (as with the summer 1977 reissue of "Cindy Incidentally"), or under his Atlantic Crossing Pipe and Drum pseudonym. While, in later years, Riva was to enjoy considerable success with a young John Cougar Mellencamp, the only artist of any real consequence to appear on Riva's distinctive lion and tartan label was Stewart himself.

If Riva was conceived as a lasting preoccupation, *A Night on the Town* highlighted the mercurial side of Stewart's character when he asked Britt Ekland to appear on one of the songs, "Tonight's the Night".

The notion of the celebrity girlfriend appearing on her boyfriend's record was a time-honored tradition which dated back to the Beatles, with John Lennon bringing Yoko along to the *White Album* sessions. Later, Paul McCartney introduced wife Linda's limited talents to his solo records; but at least she could maintain a harmony, no matter how weedy. Ekland, as she herself admits, couldn't even do that, and her reaction to Soddy's suggestion was one of horror, tempered with sheer amazement.

"But I can't sing! I've got a lousy voice!"

Stewart, however, was adamant. "You won't have to sing. You'll just talk to the music."

"It was about a young virgin who was about to be deflowered," says Britt. "I was to play the sobbing girl . . ."

Ekland continued to deliberate, and so Stewart played his winning card. "Well, if you won't do it, I'll just have to find someone else – how about Stevie Nicks?" The flaxen-haired Nicks, a member of the revitalised Fleetwood Mac, had recently split with her lover, Mac guitarist Lindsey Buckingham, and Ekland knew only too well the way Rod looked at her.

"Okay, I'll do it."

Although Ekland was called upon to provide nothing more than a few tearful utterances in French during the song's fade-out, as the time to perform grew closer she became dreadfully nervous. Finally Stewart offered her a line of coke to ease her nerves. She accepted it gratefully.

Ekland later conjectured that Stewart chose to have her speak French primarily for business reasons. France had traditionally been a difficult market for him, and Stewart had once cancelled a Paris show, officially because his voice was giving him problems, but more likely, Ekland believes, because "only half of the 8,000 seats had been sold."

But the French were far too clever to buy a record simply because someone sobs out a "Mon Dieu" or two at the end. Perhaps Stewart was simply tapping into the universal belief that the French are somehow a more sensual race than any other. Certainly this was the impression many radio stations came away with, and it was not uncommon to hear the song faded out before Ekland's big moment. One American DJ was heard to complain, "The decision came from my bosses. Their feeling is, if it's in French, it must be dirty."

There were no such problems in Britain, incidentally. The BBC, whose monopoly on the radio remained absolute despite the advent of independent broadcasters, banned the song – not because of Britt, but because of the lyric "spread your wings and let me come inside". To understand Ekland, you needed to speak French, a spokesman said. To understand Stewart, all you needed was half a brain.

Ekland was enthused by her recording debut. It went without a hitch, she says, "and I was left thinking that had I been able to sing, I might have been more successful in music than on the boards as an actress." As it was, her performance was to become something of an embarrassment to Stewart in later years.

Compiling the first volume of his *Greatest Hits* collection following his separation from Ekland, Steward included a version of "Tonight's the Night" from which Ekland's contribution had been completely erased. Only the threat of legal action from Ekland's lawyers forced Rod to reinstate the missing portion of the song, as he later admitted. "The French bird on the end is actually Swedish, and threatened to sue if not included."

Because Stewart's schedule, not to mention his British tax problems, precluded his personal endorsement of every new single, he had taken to filming short promotional films for broadcast around the world.

Video was not, at this time, the all-powerful, all-consuming monster it has since become. Rather, it was regarded by many people as a neat little novelty, and Stewart threw himself into the field with considerable gusto. Three years before Queen's "Bohemian Rhapsody" ushered in what we now call the Video Age, Rod was filmed performing "Oh No Not My Baby". The following year, he went on location to the Scottish highlands for "Farewell", still one of his most moving and, in the wake of his imminent exile, poignant performances.

By 1976, almost every Rod Stewart single was accompanied by a video, and "Tonight's the Night" was no exception. Set in the sumptuous firelit drawing-room at Carolwood, it features Stewart sprawled in an armchair, mouthing the song's unquestionably romantic lyrics to a willowy blonde – probably, but not definitely, Ekland. Her face is never on camera, nor is she seen to speak, and rumor swiftly spread that if she had, Stewart would have had to pay her quite a bit more! Ekland, however, dismisses the story out of hand. "I didn't get a dime of the multi-million-dollar royalties, and neither did I ask for one," she says. "I did it all for love."

With the album now complete, Stewart began piecing together the band he would take on the road with him that autumn. It included at least one major surprise. When Kenney Jones, his first choice for the drumseat, declined his invitation, Stewart called on Carmine Appice, the drummer who, eight years earlier, had filled Rod with dread by outlining his dream of a union between Vanilla Fudge and the Jeff Beck Group. Appice had not seen Stewart since another of his bands, Cactus, opened for the Faces on an American tour a few years later, but he leaped at the chance. After all, he proclaimed, "Rod is the best singer in the world!"

Another of the Faces' old support acts, Strider, was plundered for guitarist Gary Grainger, like Stewart an ambitious North Londoner. The British contingent was completed by Jim Cregan, the curly-haired guitarist whose first name band, Blossom Toes, succeeded Steampacket into Giorgio Gomelski's music-loving heart, and whose guitarist, Brian Godding, had married Julie Driscoll's sister. "Small world, mate!" Cregan laughed when Stewart first got back in touch with him.

Since Blossom Toes, Cregan had become, if not a household name, at least the creator of a household sound, having played the so-memorable guitar solo on Cockney Rebel's 1975 number one, "Make Me Smile (Come Up and See Me)". Stewart made no secret of what he wanted Cregan to provide – another solo as breathtaking as that one.

Philip Chen, the Jamaican-born bassist, had already turned down the chance to work with Stewart once before, when he passed over an invitation to join the Faces. He wasn't about to make the same mistake twice.

Pianist John Jarvis – at twenty-two, the youngest member of the group – was a well-known session player, recommended to Stewart by Steve Cropper and, said Rod, the first member of the band to be selected.

Lead guitarist Billy Peek was snatched away from Chuck Berry's group after Stewart saw him perform with Berry on "Midnight Special". Like Jarvis, he made his debut with Stewart during the *Night on the Town* sessions. Tom Dowd remembers exactly how the feisty American came to be chosen. "Rod was on tour in Denver with some hotchpotch band that he was experimenting with. He's sitting watching 'Midnight Special', Chuck Berry's on, and all of a sudden Berry starts singing and Rod goes, 'Who's that playing guitar?' As it pans out he sees this one little guitar player in the background doing all Chuck Berry's licks. So it's two in the morning in Colorado, and about five in the morning in Miami and Rod isn't aware of the time difference so he picks up the phone and says, 'Tom, are you watching the concert?'

"I say, 'Rod, I'm sound asleep, it's five in the morning' and Rod says, 'It can't be, it's only two o'clock and I'm watching the concert, there's a guitar player with Chuck Berry and I want him in the studio next week.' Click – and he hangs up. And I don't even know what show he's watching. Find out who the musician is on a show that's being televised in Denver – it could have been a year old! Anyway, it turned out to be Billy Peek."

Stewart was ecstatic as the group took shape around him. "The good thing about working with your own band," Stewart explained, "is that we can cut out a song whenever we want. With the Faces you couldn't do that. You'd have to go through a bloody board meeting or something. It'd take six months to get anything done. I feel like I've been wearing blinders the last five years, only using English musicians. The best people are here in America, more so than in England. The musicianship here is incredible." The use of three guitarists, incidentally, was a dream Stewart had nurtured since he first saw Fleetwood Mac back in the late 1960s. "All we need now," he joked, "is someone to stand in for Harold"

– a reference to the sixteen-inch rubber dildo which the original Mac used to introduce into their show every night!

It was a very strong band, but some observers wondered whether it was quite strong enough. Stepping into the Faces' boots would not be an easy task for even the greatest musicians in the world, particularly when they had never played together before. The Faces developed out of a camaraderie that stretched back, in the case of Lane, Mac and Jones, to their schooldays, and their onstage antics were those of people who'd been friends all their lives.

This band, though, was nothing more than a group of well-heeled sessioneers, capable of playing till your heart broke, but lacking, perhaps, that other essential ingredient of great rock'n'roll, togetherness. Only Jim Cregan seemed the correct choice. As Stewart once said, "He's as big a boozer as I am!"

Undismayed by the critical doubts, Stewart prepared a veritable baptism of fire for the new Rod Stewart Band. They would make their recording debut on the soundtrack to a new movie, *All This and World War Two*, a strange experimental film dreamed up by Lou Reizner coupling war footage with a double album's worth of Beatles songs, as interpreted by a number of artists.

Stewart was invited to contribute a version of "Get Back", and as his British tour got under way, the song, a raucous rendition of one of Lennon and McCartney's finest compositions, shot to number eleven in the British charts.

Next on the agenda was a filmed rehearsal for *A Night on the Town*, the first of two television Rod-umentaries being aired in Britain that summer. Produced by the BBC – the rival independent network's "Rod the Mod Comes of Age" was made up of archival footage – the show promised to concentrate on every aspect of his career thus far, and he gave the crew carte blanche to film whatever they liked.

The result, an in-depth warts-and-all portrait, was screened just as *A Night on the Town* was released in July 1976. The timing was exquisite, but Stewart was not particularly happy. To start with, the BBC filmed over eight hours of rehearsals, yet only one song from the new album made it on to the finished documentary. Even worse was the treatment meted out to Ekland. "Some people think Britt came over as a bit of a bitch," Stewart remonstrated. "But that was the editing of the film. I mean, you can take 'Match of the Day' and make it look good or bloody awful. She's not a bitch. She's so bloody helpful. The boys in the band all love her.

"Britt's nowhere near as bad as people make out she is. I mean, she's the most dedicated woman I've ever known when it comes to being with one guy, and I appreciate that. But there's always been a language barrier there. She doesn't speak the Queen's English, and many times when she'd try to be funny it came across as being cynical and sarcastic. Whatever happens in the future, I'll never find a better woman."

Smashing into the charts on 3 July, 1976, *A Night on the Town* was the most eagerly awaited album of the year. At one point, it seemed as though every magazine in Britain carried a Rod Stewart story, with the flamboyant singer even generating interest from the most unexpected quarters, including the homosexual magazine *Gay News*.

Rumors of Stewart being homosexual, or at least bisexual, had been common since his days with Long John Baldry. Ginger Baker remembers constantly "pulling Rod's leg" about it, and while he insists that Stewart never said or did anything to justify the rumors, they continued to circulate, often plumbing the depths of bad taste, not to mention poor judgement, as they did so.

Perhaps the most scurrilous of these naughty tales was the one that claimed that Stewart had been admitted to hospital with severe abdominal pains. His stomach was pumped, and was found to contain a large quantity of semen. There was neither foundation, nor truth, to the story, but it spread like wildfire nevertheless.

"The Cum-in-the-Belly story went all around the fucking world!" Stewart says incredulously. "What's amazing is that it never appeared in the press as far as I know. I never read it or heard it anywhere. I wasn't even in the country at the time it supposedly happened. What could it have been? A fleet of fucking sailors? Or footballers?"

The *Gay News* interview was, in actual fact, all in a day's work for Rod. Included on the new album was "The Killing of Georgie", a song Stewart wrote about the murder of a New York gay, which had been earmarked as a single. What was more natural, then, than for him to promote the record in the one newspaper that catered to Georgie, and people like him?

Much of the interview focused on Stewart's flamboyant stage act, a display which even he admitted was very "camp". He was disarmingly honest, if frustratingly non-analytical. "I suppose I did come off a bit poofy," he said of the 1974–75 tours. "But I was tired of the guy I had become with the Faces, tired of the person who didn't make very good albums."

The subject of his image came up in other, more mainstream interviews, too. The teenybop press had recently been flooding the market with Rod Stewart pin-ups, and several times the singer was called upon to defend them. He did so unequivocally, saying, "I like all that. It might look silly, but it makes me feel sensuous. Sometimes, all that praise can get embarrassing. But I'm very comfortable being a star. I rather enjoy it, in fact. I don't think you'll find many people who'll own up to that, but we're all egotistical in this business. I know I am. I look in the mirror ever so much."

The first single from the new album was, of course, "Tonight's the Night", which soared to number five in Britain some four months before it was scheduled for an American release. "Georgie" followed, and if anybody still had doubts about Stewart singing a song so obviously sensitive toward gay issues, their fears were swiftly quashed. It was held off the number-one spot by an equally unexpected pairing – Elton John and Kiki Dee.

Although John was still some months away from truly coming out of the closet, rumors of his bisexuality were even louder than those concerning Stewart's, and were given all the more credence by Elton's own utterances. Both *Playboy* and *Melody Maker* had come close to winning an outright admission. In the meantime, Britain's gays celebrated what they saw as a double triumph for themselves and their lifestyle. And Stewart was not about to spoil their fun. He didn't care what they said about him, so long as they said it about Elton as well!

To this day, Rod and Elton are both close friends and rivals. Nothing delights them more than to let fly with a stream of inventive invective every time the other is mentioned. In the mid-seventies, Stewart was obsessed with Elton's hair or lack thereof, and Elton would invariably retaliate with references to Rod's legendary meanness.

A year or so earlier, director Ken Russell approached Stewart about appearing in a film version of the rock opera *Tommy* – a courtesy extended to every member of the three-year-old Lou Reizner production. Again he would appear as the local lad whose pinball crown Tommy eventually steals, but Stewart wasn't quite sure whether the part was still right for him. Common sense should have told him better, but Stewart turned to Elton for advice.

"What do *you* think I should do?"

"I wouldn't take it, mate. I'm serious. You don't wanna get involved in all that."

"Besides," added Elton, "You had made a bad enough job of 'Pinball Wizard' last time around. What could you possibly hope to do to it this time?"

Unfortunately, Stewart took his advice. "Thanks, but no thanks," he told Russell, and was apparently surprised when Elton himself promptly, and proudly, walked into the part. With an ever-increasing barrage of insults, Stewart has been taking revenge on his perfidious friend ever since.

Andy Hill, Elton's long-time personal assistant, remembers one of Stewart's favorite tricks. "He would buy some really horrible, cheap plonk, then stick expensive labels on it, and say to Elton, 'Hey, I've got some incredible wine here, you ought to try it.' Elton and Rod had this incredible love–hate relationship. They were terrific friends, but couldn't be together without continually trying to put each other down and score points off one another."

Ekland never followed up her performance on "Tonight's the Night". Instead, she contented herself by simply helping Soddy out with his own career. "When he was composing a new song," she recalls, "he would hum odd notes into a cassette recorder and jot down lyrics on a notepad." Sometimes, she proudly adds, he would ask her for a rhyming word.

"I used to call Rod my proletarian bard, because I saw him as a street urchin writing about simple, everyday things. That part of his life Rod never left behind, and now it was to become part of his poetry."

Stewart simply shrugged. "I make the music, and she tells me if it's any good or not." It was one of several remarks which Ekland would later try to turn against him.

Warner Brothers, of course, were delighted at having both sides of pop's most talked-about couple on the record, and with Ekland only too pleased to accompany her Soddy around the world at someone else's expense, the company organised a massive promotional tour, taking the pair throughout Europe and America. Typically, it was not the new album people wanted to ask them about but their life together. And this time around, Stewart welcomed their attention.

"By now," says Britt, "Rod was preening to the newspapers. 'We've got more power as a rock'n'roll twosome than Peter Wolf and Faye Dunaway, Paul and Linda McCartney, Mick and Bianca Jagger, and we're the only two not married!'"

Typically, Stewart seemed reluctant to commit himself that far. "I think it's a little premature to put us at the altar yet," Stewart said in an interview during that spring of 1976. "But we are certainly in love. I've been looking for someone like Britt for years," he repeated for the umpteenth time. "I'm in heaven." Snuggling up alongside him, Ekland continued, "It's been a tornado courtship. My heart just keeps on thumping."

Stewart did eventually propose to Ekland, aboard an airliner flying into Stockholm, and she accepted. "There was no hurry. No urgency," says Britt, but she was "deliriously happy" regardless, "prepared to abandon my career entirely." Stewart compounded her happiness when he told the world of his intention to adopt her son, Nikolai. Later, he hinted, the couple would start a family of their own.

But just a few days later, he withdrew the offer, and in the most public forum imaginable. In an interview with an English tabloid, he scoffed, "She isn't the right woman for me. I've no plans to marry her."

The first Ekland knew of his decision was when she picked up a newspaper the following morning. What she read there hurt her more than she had dreamed possible. Stewart was sitting across the room from her as she burst into tears and threw the newspaper at him. "How *dare* you say those things when we've just built this home together?" she screamed. "If you feel like this, why go on with our relationship?"

Britt was, she commented later, on the verge of walking out on him right there and then. "But . . . well, I didn't." Instead, she put her dreams of marriage on hold while Stewart publicly apologised through an interview in the *Daily Mirror*. "I should never have said those foolish things," he mumbled apologetically. "Britt is the only woman in the world for me, and one day we will marry."

Ekland, despite her secret doubts, chose to agree with him. "I think we probably will get married one day. But not yet. At the moment we are both very involved in our individual careers, and I don't think it will do them any good to get married now."

In actual fact, as Ekland admits, her career had been on hold for over a year. "During our first twelve months together," she says, "I deliberately didn't accept any offers of work because I wanted to spend time with Rod and get our relationship off to a good start." Her last movie, *High Velocity*, had been shot during the early days of her relationship with Stewart, and he had joined her in Manila for the filming. Rod, however, absolutely hated the experience, the constant waiting around, the endless fuss and bother, and vowed never to visit a film set again.

Ekland might well have made the same pledge. Her agent, Maggie Abbott, was begging her to return to work, but Ekland didn't seem to hear her. She had already turned down Italian director Vittorio Gassman – "the only woman in the world," said Abbott, "insane enough to do so". Now, with offers of work still coming in for the recalcitrant Swede, Abbott was insistent she shouldn't make another such mistake.

Ekland had been offered a part in *Slavers*, starring Ray Milland and Trevor Howard. It was to be shot in Rhodesia, but Britt was reluctant to go, particularly with Soddy about to head out on his first ever solo tour. But this time, Abbott was adamant. "Let Rod get on with his work while you get on with yours," she demanded, and she found an unexpected ally in Stewart himself. "You'll be away for nine weeks – you'll only miss the European shows," Rod assured her. "As long as you're back for Britain, I'll survive." Ekland promised she would, although it wasn't long before she was wishing she had never agreed to leave.

Back in Los Angeles, Stewart and Ekland had been to a party hosted, in typically flamboyant style, by the band Queen. Also present was actress Susan George, and as the evening wore on, Ekland noticed, with just a tinge of jealousy, that Stewart and George had barely taken their eyes off each other all evening.

Finally Ekland had had enough and whispered to him that she was taking the car home, and waited for him to stir. He simply nodded, and carried on his conversation with the sexy starlet. Ekland quietly made her exit.

When Stewart arrived home two hours later he was plainly defensive, which in turn made him extremely belligerent. Slamming the door, he bellowed, "Why did you ditch me there like that?"

Ekland, too, was feeling more than a little cheesed off. "You saw me go. You didn't have to stay with Susan George all night." Britt couldn't explain it, but she felt as though she were fighting for her man. "Maybe he fancies Susan," she kept thinking to herself. "She has big boobs. Most of Rod's earlier women boasted well-defined breasts. What if he slept with her?" The thought whisked round and round her head.

With all the force she could muster, Britt threw herself at her errant lover, scrambling across the bed to reach him. "Suddenly I fell, hitting my head on the bed rail. I screamed with pain. I'd collected a gorgeous black eye."

The gossips, of course, had a field day. By the time the morning papers arrived, the party developed into something approaching a full-scale brawl, with Ekland "stalking out" after accusing Stewart and George of having an affair. One report even claimed she had thrown a glass of champagne over him.

Furiously, Stewart summoned Tony Toon. Neither Ekland nor the hapless promo man had seen him so angry before. "Did you put this garbage out?" he screamed, while Toon, for once totally innocent, stared at Ekland's swollen eye.

"No! I didn't say a word, I promise."

"Well, someone certainly did, and this story has your name written all over it!"

"Honest, Rod . . . Britt . . . it wasn't me! It must have been somebody else at the party."

The couple never found out who started the rumor, but once it got started, it was going to take a lot of laying to rest, as Ekland found when she picked up a newspaper during her Rhodesian sojourn. Emblazoned across the gossip column was a picture of Susan George, enjoying herself at a Rod Stewart concert.

For the record, George was quick to deny anything untoward was going on between Stewart and herself. "I was merely talking to him about tax problems," she protested, "and he asked me to say hello to his mother when I got back to England." Any talk of a romance between the two of them, she insisted, was rubbish.

But Ekland, confronted by the continual barrage of media rumor, didn't know how to react. She was still jealous of Susan George. She knew, in terms of chest measurements if nothing else, that the stunning Miss George could offer Soddy something which she definitely could not.

Ekland, however, fought to temper her jealous rage. She knew that the smallest thing could send the gossips into a feeding frenzy. "It's got to the stage that if we are apart from each other we are careful who is sitting next to us at functions because of the gossips," she told friends. Rumors of a liaison between Rod and Susan were "utter nonsense. Even when they were together, they were always with a group of people."

To make matters worse, contact between the two was difficult as Rhodesia was in the grip of international sanctions and both the mail and telephone systems were in total chaos. But when they did get through to one another, their exchanges were as tender as ever. "Why don't you send me a romantic message?" Ekland asked one night. "I miss you so much out here." Stewart said he'd see what he could come up with, and the very next day Ekland was handed a telex. It read simply, "Dear Britt. Here is the romantic message you wanted. Tired of wanking. Please come home, Soddy."

Ekland rejoined Stewart in time for the Swedish leg of the tour. "She's coming back following a telegram I sent her," Rod told the *Daily Mirror*. "I'll tell you what's in it because I know you won't be able to print it."

"He did," the paper duly reported, "and we can't."

The tour opened in Norway on 1 November, 1976. "We issued brown pants to everyone," Stewart laughed later, "as we were scared shitless! We wanted to play that first show as far from anybody as we could. We'd have played Siberia if we could. We ended up in this tiny little fishing village in Norway. The theater only held a thousand people. But it went great."

On stage, Stewart appeared even more flamboyant than ever. Draped in baggy satin, his face a mask of exotic camouflage, he strutted his way suggestively around the band, and during "Georgie", when a hastily lowered backdrop transformed the stage into a New York street scene, replete with lamp-posts, he proved he could give the most highly skilled hooker a run for her money when it came to striking a provocative pose.

From Scandinavia, the twenty-two city tour cut a broad swathe through Europe, hitting Britain in early December for the lucrative pre-Christmas gigs which the Faces had turned into a seasonal ritual. The outing would peak in Scotland in the new year. "We're playing Glasgow on New Year's Eve," Stewart boasted. "It'll be magic. Like the return of Rob Roy, or Bonnie Prince Charlie."

After that, he said, would come Australia and America. It was the

largest tour he had ever undertaken, dwarfing even the worldwide outing which the Faces had embarked upon – but never completed – in
1975, and Olympia was the most important show of his life. Not only
had the cavernous venue sold out months in advance, not only was the
Christmas Eve performance being broadcast live on British television,
to an estimated audience of 3.5 million, it was also – as Stewart well
knew – his chance to justify to his fans precisely why he had quit the
Faces, and what he could offer instead.

Rod had already put one over on the sceptics. At the beginning of
October, Ekland was awakened from a deep sleep by the phone. It was
Rod, and he sounded absolutely elated. "We've done it, Poopy!" he
bellowed down the phone, drowning the sounds of the party going on
behind him. "We're number one in America with 'Tonight's the Night'!"
He then led the band through a rousing, drunken rendition of the song,
while Ekland sat in a Rhodesian motel room, too stunned to speak.

Everybody was in high spirits. The tour had proceeded better than
anybody had dared dream. Audiences were ecstatic, the press had been
kind, and record sales were booming.

Stewart was even enjoying an unexpected hit single, after Mercury
Records reissued "Maggie May", just as "Get Back" was reaching its
peak. "Maggie May", too, made the charts, and with a reissue of "Sailing" still hanging around the Top Forty, Stewart was arguably the most
in-demand rock star in the world.

According to Ekland, however, a dark cloud hung over the proceed-
ings. Stewart was one of the biggest around, but that wasn't enough.
He wanted to be the biggest. And the man who suffered the most from
Rod's insecurity was he who already occupied that throne – Mick Jagger.

On the last Faces tour, for instance, Mick and Bianca Jagger paid him
a visit just before the New York show. "He was distinctly cold and
off-hand," Ekland recalls. At Olympia, Mick was simply downright
rude.

When Jagger and Keith Richard requested tickets to the show,
Stewart's secretary, Doris Tyler, was ordered to tell them there were
none left. So they asked for backstage passes instead and again Tyler
said no. And just in case they tried to sneak in on the strength of their
names alone, Stewart placed extra security at every door to the building.
"No one," he hissed, "*no one* is allowed in without the right pass."

What he didn't realise, of course, was just how literally the security
men would take his instructions. Among the host of passless celebrities
to be left out in the cold were a certain Miss Ekland, and two older
people, Bob and Elsie Stewart.

There were other sour – if ultimately inconsequential – notes struck
as the British leg of the tour wound its way toward its conclusion.

Stewart was in Scotland when Ekland had to make a sudden trip over to Munich. She returned to London and found she had mislaid her keys.

A hurried call to a locksmith saved the day, but the following morning she was mortified to find that someone, perhaps the locksmith himself, had passed the story on to the press. This time, though, she had to laugh. The whole world knew that Stewart was in Scotland, but here was Britt breaking into her own home, "with the sole intention of catching Rod and Susan George in bed together. I must confess," Ekland says, "it was a spectacular piece of imagination."

Britt flew up to Scotland to rejoin the tour, arriving just in time for another headline story. The Scottish police raided the band's hotel, searching for drugs and anything else they could find. Several members of Stewart's road crew were hauled away, but the really big fish – Stewart and Ekland – were not.

All it would have taken was one careless roadie, or maybe even one over-zealous copper, and everything Stewart had achieved over the years could have come crashing down around his ears. At the very least, it would have jeopardised his proposed American and Japanese tours.

But Stewart seemed unconcerned. He was, perhaps, even pleased about Inspector Knacker's midnight visit. Ever since the highly publicised Beatles/Stones arrests of the mid–late 1960s, the British police had won a reputation for only going after the biggest names in rock'n'roll. It was the superstar busts that grabbed the headlines and won promotions. If they were chasing after Stewart – "well, that's it then, boys! I've finally made it to the top!"

Stewart's reunion with Ekland was predictably brief. While Britt was in Rhodesia she had been offered another film role, starring alongside David McCallum and Patrick MacNee in a remake of *King Solomon's Mines*. Ten days' work would net her over $50,000, but it would mean parting from Soddy once again. Stewart, though, encouraged her to take it. "You'd have to be crazy to turn down that kind of bread," he said. "We can wait another ten days before resuming normal service!"

The Rod Stewart band left Britain for Los Angeles in mid-January 1977 for the remainder of their world tour. As in Britain, Stewart's star was at an all-time high. *A Night on the Town* still rested in the upper echelons of the charts, and a new single, Stewart's moving rendition of PP Arnold's 1968 hit "The First Cut is the Deepest", was ready for release.

America was to become the Rod Stewart Band's playground. Traveling to gigs, both Stewart and Appice would regale the rest of the group with tales of their own on-the-road mayhem. Every city had its own crop of special memories, be it the Vanilla Fudge's fish-fucking exploits in Seattle, or the Faces punching out pompous Jerry Wald in Hawaii.

Stewart's stories were usually the funniest, although even he would often admit, "I wish Woody was here – he can tell them a lot better than I can!"

There was the night in Sweden, for instance, when room service charged the band $100 for a plate of cheese. Before they checked out the following morning, Woody decided that the chairs in the rooms looked a bit too tall and suggested sawing the legs off. "But put them back together afterwards, so no one will know until they try sitting on them."

Both the Fudge and the Faces were a hard act to follow, but the Rod Stewart Band tried. In Lakeland, they left an estimated $5,000 worth of damage to be cleared up; in Los Angeles, the hotel grounds were left littered with shattered glasses after Appice became convinced that a wine glass, dropped from a top-floor window at the correct angle, could survive impact intact. He had even seen it happen!

"I threw a glass out the top-floor window of the Hyatt House, and the crazy thing was, it bounced. I saw it bounce right from the street into the parking lot. But no one would believe me. So I gathered up glasses from all the other rooms and we threw them out of the window. But they all broke. And when I went down to try to find the first glass, I couldn't."

Ekland, however, was not looking forward to the tour nearly as much as she pretended, particularly after her experiences with the Faces. "I was more bewildered by groupies than jealous of them," she says. "They would lay siege to the stage door, or the hotel, and throw themselves at Rod, kissing and groping him as though he were some sort of sexual messiah. Some of them were very beautiful. Others, as Rod often said, were 'scrubbers', but surprisingly many were respectable married women who simply wanted to live out their sexual fantasies with a pop star. Any pop star!"

The groupies, however, were something else entirely. They telephoned the couple's hotel suite, demanding to speak to Stewart, and if Ekland answered, their comments ranged from the pathetic – "I love Rod far more than you ever could" – to the downright evil. "They threatened to give me cocaine with broken glass in it," Ekland reveals. "And if I didn't take coke then they would doctor my cold cream which would have a nasty effect on my face."

Despite the tour, 1976 had, by Stewart's standards, been a relatively relaxed year. 1977, however, was proving to be anything but. No sooner was the tour over than Stewart was racing into the studio to commence work on his next record. He envisioned it as a double album, and after the earth-shattering reception given to "Tonight's the Night", it had to be a bloody good one.

Stewart's recorded output had gone into overdrive in the eighteen months since the Faces split. Aside from the flurry of chart-bound singles which accompanied his UK tour, no less than four compilations of old material had been issued, including a back-to-back reissue of his first two solo albums, a second volume of *Sing It Again, Rod*, called *Recorded Action Highlights and Action Replays*, and, in the US, two separate *Best of Rod Stewart* collections. Stewart himself was preparing a *Best of the Faces* album for mid-summer release on Riva.

Elsewhere, there was an album of old Steampacket recordings, the abysmal-sounding tapes which Long John Baldry remembers being made at a band rehearsal, and finally a collection of tapes dating back to Rod's very first recording session, in Poland Street in 1964, was being readied for release in America under the title of *A Shot of Rhythm and Blues*.

John Rowlands and Geoff Wright, insisting that Stewart's fans had a right to these formative recordings, were behind the release, and Rod fought desperately against the record's appearance. Backed up by journalists such as Dave Marsh, who admitted the album was "so blatantly exploitative that even a Rod Stewart fanatic like myself feels embarrassed", Stewart argued that the sleeve design, a bang up-to-date photograph of the singer, gave the impression that it was a new album.

Rod was unable, in the end, to have the release cancelled. But the adverse publicity surrounding it did have the desired effect. *A Shot of Rhythm and Blues* sank without a trace, as have several subsequent efforts to revive these historically fascinating but musically unimpressive recordings.

Still, with so many eyes focused on his back catalog, Stewart knew that his own new album needed to be a killer. But there were so many distractions. Ekland was spending more and more time away from him, either filming in exotic locations – her last job was in Swaziland – or visiting friends and family around the globe.

The strange thing was Soddy didn't miss his Poopy quite so much as he had expected to. Absence, in this case, did not make the heart grow fonder, and after more than two years of fidelity, he found his eye, if not his hands, roving more and more.

9

Boys Will Be Boys

1977 was the year of Punk. Spreading out from its base in rootless suburban London, from the same characterless avenues of meandering terraced two-ups, two-downs as the Beat Boom which Rod had so gleefully ridden, Punk was the sound of disaffected youth. Betrayed by politics, they had turned instead to rock'n'roll. Alienated by that, they had turned to rebellion.

"How can you identify with what's going on in music today?" Punk Prince Johnny Rotten demanded. Rock'n'roll stars, he roared, "stay in their narrow-minded, whimsical, pathetic little ways and never improve. You go and see them and you get exactly what you expect. That isn't entertainment."

The Punks outlined their enemies. The technical wizardry of Pink Floyd and Emerson Lake and Palmer, the bloated pretensions of the Stones and the Who, and "fucking Rod Stewart, with his Swedish tart and money coming out of his arse." For some reason, the Punks really hated poor old Rod.

Stewart had witnessed the first faint stirrings of Punk when he toured Britain at the end of 1976 and had been as shocked as anyone by the apparently mindless aggression which the first wave of Punk bands – the Sex Pistols, the Clash and the Damned – seemed to attract, even to encourage, at their concerts.

But it still came as a surprise to learn that he had been singled out as a target, as the epitome of all that had gone "wrong" with rock'n' roll.

Stewart, of course, roared back defiantly. "They say, 'Fucking Rod's gone Hollywood with a movie star', right? The cunts! I come from the same background they do. In England, all rock'n'roll comes from the working class. That's your only way of getting out of the rabble. I come from nothing. Then, all of a sudden, I'm faced with a lot of glamorous women. What the fuck am I going to do? Wouldn't your first choice be some gorgeous twenty-one-year-old blonde before it would be that sweet secretary down the hall with the thick arse?"

If the Punks wanted a stand-up, knock-down battle, Stewart could give as good as he took.

Worse than their insults, though, was the knowledge that the Sex Pistols had made the battle personal. Bragging about how the band acquired its equipment when it was first starting out, guitarist Steve Jones admitted he had taken almost all of it from the homes of rock stars, Rod's mansion in Windsor included. Two guitars had gone missing a few years before; now Rod knew where they had gone. The crazy thing was, Jones and his partner in crime, drummer Paul Cook, confessed to having been big Faces fans!

Stewart's first thought when he read all this was of revenge. And he got it, although at the time he was probably the most innocent party concerned.

The Sex Pistols' new single, "God Save the Queen", a vicious tirade against Queen Elizabeth II whose Silver Jubilee was being celebrated that June, was widely expected to go to number one in the charts, a scenario few people in the music industry cared to envisage, particularly as the record's release had been timed so that it would reach its peak in the very week of the Jubilee celebrations. Something had to be done to stop it.

John Varnom, who then worked for the Sex Pistols' label, Virgin, has no doubts as to what that something was. The national chart positions were juggled, "so that 'God Save the Queen' did not make number one." And what kept it off the pole position? "A Rod Stewart single." According to the Pistols' manager, Malcolm McLaren, CBS, who distributed both the Rod Stewart and Sex Pistols singles, agree with Varnom. "They were saying we were selling two records to every one of Stewart's," McLaren reported.

Stewart's double a-side coupling of "I Don't Want to Talk About It" and "The First Cut Is the Deepest" eventually got on to the top spot on the British charts for four weeks. Whether or not Varnom and McLaren's suspicions were justified, Rod himself was proud to relate how he struck a blow for decency and for the Queen, and without lifting a finger!

Stewart was in the studio throughout most of that spring, so Ekland took advantage of his absence to fly home to Sweden and visit her family. She returned to Los Angeles as uncertain about her future with Rod as he himself was. Several times her agent, Maggie Abbott, had called their relationship futile, and no less than Stewart, Ekland had noticed a subtle change in her own feelings. "Sometimes," she says of that visit with her folks, "I felt a twinge of guilt because I didn't think of Rod as much as I should have. When he rang it was as though I was talking to a stranger, not the man I still thought would be my husband."

Still, she did her best not to let her doubts show when she returned to Stewart's arms at the end of July. And when Stewart simply rolled over in bed at night and went to sleep, she put it down to overwork. She knew how much this new record meant to him. Besides, he had just immortalised their love once again, with a new song.

"We went out to dinner with Billy Gaff and a bunch of friends one night to St Germaine's, one of the poshest restaurants in Los Angeles. In the middle of the meal, Rod leaned over to me and whispered, 'I've written a song for you, Poopy.'

"No one," Ekland continues, "took any notice as Rod softly sang the words into my ear. My eyes filled with tears. It was the loveliest song I had ever heard."

"You're in My Heart (The Final Acclaim)", the song Stewart had just sung to her, was to be released as a single in October 1977. It would eventually race all the way to number three in Britain, number four in the US. Who could have foretold that night in St Germaine's that as fast as the record store cash registers rang up another sale of the single, Britt Ekland's lawyers would be adding another few dollars to their palimony demands?

Ironically, it was a chance encounter that spelled out the end for Poopy and Soddy. They had been invited to a party thrown by producer Alan Carr. Rod couldn't make it as he was still in the studio working on that projected double album, so Ekland decided to go by herself.

Among the guests were actor George Hamilton and his soon-to-be ex-wife Alana. Ekland and George were old friends, and when he drew her aside her first thought was, "Here comes the old charm." Instead, he told her how surprised he was to hear that she and Rod had separated. "I never thought you two would bust up."

Ekland was mystified. "But we haven't, George."

Hamilton shrugged. "I must have got it all wrong, then." Apparently, Stewart had been seen around town with one of Hamilton's old flames, Liz Treadwell. "She was driving his car and staying up at the house. In fact I saw them together only last week." What was funny, he said, was "that my ex-girlfriend should be going with your ex-guy." Realising that Ekland was caught completely off guard, Hamilton added, "I really thought you knew, Britt. Everyone else in town does."

Ekland quietly left the party and returned home. Stewart wasn't there. He would be in the studios until the small hours. But it gave her time to think . . . and to seethe.

When morning came and Soddy had to return home, Ekland stormed over to Tony Toon's cottage. "Where is Rod? He didn't come home, he didn't even call."

Toon was at his most soothingly sincere – a sure sign, Britt knew from experience, that he had something to hide. "It's alright, Britt.

Things just went on a little later than usual, and they all went down to the Hilton for drinks. Everyone got pissed, and I think Rod put his head down there for the night."

It was a pathetic excuse, and both Toon and Ekland knew it. But she continued to feign concern. "Well, you'd better find him fast," she said. "He's never done that before. I've been worried all night about him, there might have been an accident." With that she turned and walked back to the house.

An hour or so later, Stewart and his tour manager, Peter Buckland, returned. Rod was full of apologies. Ekland felt sure that Toon had already primed him, and Stewart faithfully repeated Toon's story word for word.

"Okay," Ekland replied. "But you really might have got someone to ring me. I'm feeling a wreck – I've been up all night waiting for you."

Stewart turned to leave, heading for the swimming-pool. Ekland let him get four or five paces away and then called out, "Oh, Rod, I would like to talk to you about something else."

Stewart turned and followed her into the house. He was like a small child caught with his hand in the cookie jar. Except this time it was more like the honeypot he'd been dipping into.

"Why don't you tell me about Liz Treadwell," Britt asked calmly. "I hear you have been having an affair with her, that she has been living in this house and driving your car."

Stewart slumped into a seat. "How did you find out?"

Ekland ignored him. "Have you slept with her?"

He nodded. Then it all came out. It was while Ekland was in Sweden. He'd been lonely, Liz had been there for him . . . "You know what it's like . . ."

"Well, I'm going to give you a week to decide what you're going to do. Do you love me?"

"Yes."

"Do you love Liz?"

"I don't know."

"Well, you'd better find out, because you're certainly not going to have both of us."

Stewart moved out of Carolwood almost immediately. The band had recently rented a house on Mulholland Drive, he said. He would stay there while Britt decided what she wanted to do. And then Ekland began to piece together just how deceitful her lover had been.

"Treadwell hadn't been the only light to shine in Rod's life during my absence," she reveals. "He had taken out a succession of girls." And not only while she was away. Rod had just returned from a trip to New York, discussing starring in a movie, *Jet Lag*, with Elton John. He went alone, he told her, it was strictly business, but in fact Treadwell had accompanied him. To make matters worse, Ekland discovered that the blonde Californian was still on the scene, living with Rod on Mulholland Drive.

Shattered by these developments, Ekland poured her heart out to George Hamilton over lunch. He recommended that Ekland pay a visit to his psychiatrist, a nutritionist who immediately placed her on a liquid protein diet, supplemented by vitamins. She was stressed out, he said. But she was also in a very strong legal position.

The entertainment industry had recently been shaken to the core by a California court deciding to grant Lee Marvin's live-in lover, Michelle Triola, an unprecedented fifty per cent of all Marvin's earnings from the period during which they were together.

Ekland was told that, like Triola, she had formed both a professional and a personal partnership with Stewart. And like Triola, she was entitled to fifty per cent of Stewart's earnings from the time they were together, including a $20 million deal he was about to sign, renewing his Warner Brothers contract. She might also qualify for half the couple's community assets. He suggested Ekland pay a visit to his son, a prominent LA attorney.

It was a neat family arrangement – Dad brings them in, Junior bails them out – but in her weakened, weary state, Ekland saw nothing peculiar, or even nepotistic, about it. "I was like a piece of pulp," she says. "I would sign any document that was thrust in front of me" – even one that demanded £12.5 million: three million for helping promote Stewart's career, three million in damages for fraud and deceit, and a staggering six million in "punitive damages". Stewart, this last demand insisted, had acted "with oppression, fraud and malice."

Notice of the lawsuit was served on Stewart by a private detective employed by Ekland. As Stewart was handed the documents, a waiting photographer snapped the scene for posterity.

"Filing this action is the saddest thing I've done in my life, because I love Rod more than life itself," Ekland sobbed. "But I have to let him know I'm not the type of woman who'll just sit at home while he finishes his little peccadilloes."

"The fucking amount of money she's trying to sue me for!" Stewart exploded incredulously. "There isn't that much money in the world, I'm sure! I make nowhere near that much!" Later, in a slightly more pensive mood, he admitted, "I think when a woman's been hurt as much as I hurt Britt they just become irrational and do the most wicked things. She always said she'd cut my balls off, but I didn't know what she meant. Now I know. She didn't literally mean she'd cut my balls off. She'd cut my wallet off." To the thrifty Stewart, that was probably far worse.

The day after the subpoena was delivered, Billy Gaff arrived at Carolwood, hoping to sort things out. "You can't do this to Rod," he began. "You've not got a leg to stand on. You're being a silly girl."

"Don't you ever call me silly," Ekland shot back before outlining all she had given up for Stewart. There was her home, a year of her career, there was her love, her trust. Did she need to go on? "He asked me to marry him and now you're saying I should get lost?" Her eyes flashed fire as Gaff tried to retreat.

Stewart was sorry, Gaff said. He still loved her – the other girl was gone, she didn't mean a thing to him. He wanted to start again with a clean sheet. "You know what he's like, Britt. He just got carried away. He didn't do this to hurt you."

Ekland agreed to give Stewart a second chance. But nothing had really changed. A coldness hung over them, even in bed. "There was no fire, no passion. We slept together for three nights but we lay with our backs to one another."

Then one morning, she found a phone number on the bed. It had fallen out of Rod's wallet while he dressed. Hating herself for doing it, Ekland passed the little scrap of paper on to her shrink-cum-nutritionist. The number belonged to the Waldorf Astoria in New York, he told her. The suite, one of several reserved by one of Stewart's companies, was currently being occupied by a Miss Treadwell.

Ekland got home and confronted Rod again. On 15 August, 1977 Stewart walked out for good.

The preliminary hearing in the case was scheduled for 12 September, before Santa Monica Superior Court Judge Edward Rafeedi. Both sides were on the offensive, and none more so than Rod. Having remained silent about the whole affair for almost a month, he finally exploded in print on 11 September, condemning Ekland in the most vitriolic terms.

A terse press statement declared, "Britt has been shameless in her handling of this matter. She is trying to get as much publicity out of this as she can." Stewart called her claims "absurd", and said that her estimates of his wealth were "wildly exaggerated". Ekland's claim that he had given Liz Treadwell a Lamborghini was nonsense, and her insistence that he was planning to move "most or all of his assets to Bermuda", out of reach of an American court, was no better.

Stewart denied that there had been any kind of professional partnership and said Ekland had simply gone along "for the ride" when he toured, and then stuck the knife in as deep as it would go. He also wanted the world to know that she was a lousy cook. When a journalist asked him how he would have reacted if it had been Britt out screwing around, Rod pronounced, "I'd have been off, or she'd have been kicked out of my house. But it's never happened to me, thank God, as far as I know, and I'm pretty sure I'm shrewd enough that I'd know if it ever did. That would be it. I'd say goodbye. I mean, if I can't give a woman everything, then fuck it."

Ekland retaliated by claiming that Stewart's organisation had threatened to "drag her through the dirt" if she pressed ahead with her suit. She wasn't worried about herself, she continued, but rather her children. Billy Gaff warned her that Stewart and his lawyers intended to "publicly embarrass" her "by dragging out all the personal facts of our lives", and she believed "it would be very damaging for my children to be submitted to this public laundry washing of our affairs."

She later asked that a court order be issued forbidding any mention of her past.

"He became a superstar with my aid," Ekland's thirty-six-page statement insisted. She produced press cuttings in which Stewart spoke of her influence over his music, how he turned to her for her opinion on new songs, how he once wondered aloud why she wasn't his manager.

Ekland's case against Stewart continued. She boasted that she had been responsible for doing his make-up for him, had darned his stage costumes when they were damaged by fans, claiming that she had essentially saved him money "by waiving the services of a valet and make-up girl when he was on tour." All she wanted now was to collect what she was owed.

With her devoted support, Britt argued, Poopy and Soddy had become "one of the most photographed couples in the world". As for Stewart's alleged fraud and deceit, Ekland testified that, "having developed a deep and intimate relationship, we swore an oath of fidelity to each other." Stewart had broken that oath.

Rod defended himself fiercely. "What I did was not breaking any law whatsoever. There was never a pact between us. Perhaps in a drunken moment I might have said I'd *try* to be faithful, but she knew my track record when she met me. And I did my best, but I fell short, like many of us do. I'm still a sucker for a pretty face and a pair of long legs. But I'm the only fuck-poor bastard who's ever got *sued* over it!"

The court apparently agreed with Stewart and refused to grant any of Ekland's requests for temporary orders pending a full determination of the facts. While they waited, Poopy and Soddy decided to give love another chance.

The first night of the reconciliation ended, says Ekland, with Stewart dropping her off at her door but refusing to come in. "He was like a schoolboy going out on his first date." But he remembered her birthday on 6 October, sending her fifty pink roses and a bottle of Guinness. A note attached demanded, "Drink this and fatten yourself up, girl" – Ekland had lost twenty pounds since August.

Stewart was back out on tour once again, this time in Europe, but remained in constant contact with Ekland by telephone. Night after night his pledges of undying love, his apologies and fresh affirmations of fidelity, filled Ekland's head. Convinced that this time everything would be all right, she ordered her lawyers to halt the legal action.

The couple were reunited for one night, midway through the tour. "Our love," she affirms, "instantly re-ignited, dissolving all the hate, hurt and revenge that had filled our veins for two months."

But within two weeks, Britt was back on the emotional carousel. In Florida to film the movie *The Great Wallendas*, she wondered why Rod's phone calls, once so regular, had again petered out. She wondered, too, why there were never any newspapers lying around the set. Finally she found a couple hidden away by the crew. Rod was back on the town – and back on the pull. The papers were all full of it.

Ekland called her psychiatrist who confirmed the gossip. So did Billy Gaff when he appeared at her rented condo in Sarasota, Florida. "Rod is willing to settle out of court," he told her. "You can have $200,000."

"I don't want money," Ekland told him. "I want Rod."

Gaff told her he would see what he could do.

Another reconciliation, as brief and fragile as the last, followed. Stewart wasn't even hiding his infidelities now. One night, before his show at the LA Forum, he even brought a girl home, "a floozie" as Ekland put it, and propped her up at the cocktail bar in the Carolwood lounge. Other nights he simply failed to come home altogether. He was taking cocaine again, and just as Dee Harrington had noticed, he announced it to the world with yet another dramatic image change, dying his hair pure white.

The end, however, came suddenly. Ekland was in the house alone one day when the telephone rang. It was Bianca Jagger, separated from Mick and, if the gossips were to be believed, living as bountiful a life as Stewart himself. "Is Rod coming to Spain?" she asked. Ekland, neither knowing nor caring what Jagger's motives were, hung up. That was the end.

"We aren't going to get back together," swore Stewart. "I look upon it as being a big mistake. It might be a mistake on my behalf, it could have been a mistake on her behalf. I know we were good for each other. Very good for each other. Who made the first bad move, whether it was because of what I did or because of her reaction to what I did, I don't know. It's difficult to know what to say because everything I say nowadays seems to get completely blown out of proportion and thrown back in my face."

Ekland packed her bags, gathered up Nikolai and Victoria, and flew out to Hawaii. Stewart watched as she collected her belongings together.

"Are you really going?" he asked.

Ekland replied, "There is no option, is there?"

One day, a few years later, a journalist asked Stewart why everything had turned sour, why he had taken such a great thing and destroyed it.

Stewart sighed resignedly. "Boys will be boys," he said. "Boys will be boys."

Rod's latest album, his eighth all-new release, smashed into the US and UK charts in November 1977, just as the final drama of his life with Britt Ekland was taking place. It was a startling record, perhaps his most honest collection of songs yet. Even the title, *Footloose and Fancy Free*, seemed cruelly ironic.

"I knew the title of the album before Britt and I busted up," Stewart admitted. "It must have been in the back of my mind that it was going to happen. The title is a straightforward statement of independence. I felt I'd been tied down too long and I wanted to break away. Domesticity – that's death for me!"

Stewart's dream of recording a double album had been stymied by yet another US tour, and in many ways Rod was pleased. At the same time as he denied there was any concept to the record, he confessed, "A lot of the tracks reflect what I was going through at the time with Britt." What started out as a simple rock'n'roll record was well on its way to becoming a purgative confessional.

Running through the songs he had recorded, Stewart pinpointed exactly what he meant. Of "You Got a Nerve", for instance, he explained, "Sometimes what you're writing about is what you wouldn't want to happen to you. I couldn't think of anything worse than that – the woman goes off and fucks somebody else on the other side of the world and comes back and says 'Let me in'." He paused, then added poignantly, "I wouldn't wish that on my worst enemy."

"'(If Loving You Is Wrong) I Don't Want to Be Right' really fit into what was happening. I was seeing Liz Treadwell, but Britt didn't know. The whole track was done live in the studio . . . Liz was there and I'm singing 'If loving you is wrong . . .' You couldn't help but sing it with guts."

"I Was Only Joking", on the other hand, was Stewart at his most vulnerable, a lengthy examination of his own life and those of the women he had hurt in the past. Jim Cregan, whose acoustic guitar swam so delicately alongside the lyrics, says Stewart kept the lyrics secret right up until the final minute: "The first time any of the musicians heard the lyrics was during the vocal take; Rod simply scat-sung or hummed at the appropriate places while the instrumental tracks were cut. When he finally sang the words he did it rather sheepishly, shyly glancing up at the band every few seconds to see if they thought the song was too corny. They didn't."

"I was trying to tell everybody that I'm not really a very sincere person," says Stewart. "It was pretty much an attempt to explain my lifestyle, the way I've been for twelve, thirteen years. I find it much easier to put my thoughts in a song. I don't ever write letters or make phone calls."

But the keynote remained "You're In My Heart", the sweeping proclamation of love and devotion which Ekland claims her Soddy wrote for her. And Stewart admits that she was indeed in his heart when he wrote it, but so were several other women as well.

"It wasn't totally about Britt," he confessed. "The first verse could have been about Liz Treadwell. It could have been about anybody I met in that period – and there were a lot of them. It's a very confused song in a way. It's about a lot more than just women, it's also about my love of soccer. That's why my two favorite teams [Glasgow Celtic and Manchester United] are mentioned at the end. The chorus is about Scotland. So it ends up being about three women, two football teams and a country. And the line 'You'll be my breath should I grow old' – I think that must have been about my mum and dad."

Whoever the song was about, it remains one of the most passionate, triumphant love songs ever written, as Stewart himself realised one morning in San Antonio, waking up with one of the previous night's groupies in bed alongside him. "The old sun was coming through the curtains and she says to me, 'Go on, turn the radio on.' Out comes 'I didn't know what day it was . . .' There's fucking magic in it!"

Yet *Footloose and Fancy Free* earned perhaps the worst critical reception of any Rod Stewart album to date. Already sated by the media coverage of his split with Ekland, British and American critics alike now vied with one another to savage Rod's creative endeavors.

The smallest failing was invariably picked on. A decade earlier, for instance, Carmine Appice and Vanilla Fudge had recorded a sprawling seven-minute version of the Motown song "You Keep Me Hanging On". Now Appice and Stewart were repeating the exercise almost note for note – a fact that did not pass the critics by.

Then there was "I Was Only Joking". For five minutes, Stewart poured out his heart in song, but when he came to the key line, baring his emotions for posterity, he mispronounced his own lyrics. "Posterity" became "prosperity", and for listeners who were simply looking for things to complain about, there could have been no more revealing a slip – Stewart was doing it all for the money!

With friends in Hollywood
Rod's Malibu Beach abode

Soddy and Poopy outside their palatial Beverly Hills home

Next to Liz and Dick and John and Yoko, the most talked about couple in the business depart yet another exclusive private club in Hollywood

Smiler

Chatting on the telly

Rock and Roll's bad boy
during the eighties

Rod, Kelly Emburg and their daughter
Ruby

Family man: with wife Rachel Hunter
and baby daughter Renee

With Jojo (née Petrie)

Sharing a joke with Neil Sedaka

Paying obeisance to the crowned prince
of soul, James Brown, in April 1985

Lifetime Achievement: Rod receives
his Brit Award in February 1993

To make matters worse, there was yet another tabloid scandal to weather, and this time on an even grander scale than the pornographic photographs scandal a few years earlier. Suddenly growing bored during an interview, Stewart decided to liven things up by announcing that during his teens he had fathered an illegitimate child. The mother, he said, was a Bristol beatnik.

"I've never met the child – she was adopted after birth," Stewart said, adding only that he knew her name was Sarah, and that she was born in 1963. "I was eighteen and a nobody, her mother was seventeen and from a wealthy family – way out of my class. We drifted apart, but I have a burning desire to see what she looks like. I often wonder if she turned out to be as beautiful as her mother."

The theme had dominated "Jo's Lament", one of the most popular songs on *Gasoline Alley*. He had also told the same story to Britt Ekland early on in their relationship.

The media response was as hilarious as it was inevitable, and Stewart pumped it for all he was worth. "Since that was in the papers," he deadpanned, "I haven't spoken to my parents once. I daren't phone up." Had anyone cared to check his schedule, however, they would have learned that Rod had, in fact, been with his family almost simultaneously with the breaking of the baby story.

On 23 December, 1977, Stewart flew into London for his traditional Christmas Eve concert. He arrived at Heathrow Airport considerably the worse for wear having taken a tumble on stage in San Francisco a few nights earlier, and his lip still bore the stitches.

Further, the entire first-class lounge on the plane was a shambles. The heavy stench of assorted spilt drinks hung in the air. Underfoot, the carpets were sopping wet. Butter and jam were smeared across nearly every available surface, and the airline's in-flight gourmet meals were spattered on the walls, floor and ceiling. "Rod Stewart woz 'ere," screamed the headlines the next morning.

Going back on the road breathed new life into old Rod. Emotionally drained after the events of the last few months, he worked the band to death, pulling some of the greatest performances of his career out of them. After the show, still bursting with energy, his eye would fasten on one of the dozens of nubile yummies hurrying around backstage, and rely on her to teach him how to live the life of the unattached rock star all over again.

"There is no one woman in my life at the moment who matters more than any other," he pronounced. "I'm a free man. I'm available. I'm anybody's." And he was out to prove it.

"One side of me wants to be desperately and totally in love with one woman; the other wants to be completely free of all ties. I don't know which side is the real me, and I don't know which one will control my future. But the footloose and fancy free side is in control at the moment." He wasn't in love with anybody, he said "except my band . . . and Scotland's football team."

Of course, that didn't stop the newspapers from involving him with every woman they recognised him with, including Ekland's own agent, Maggie Abbott, *Playboy* centerfold Marcy Hanson, Todd Rundgren's former beau Bebe Buell, one-time Gong Show hostess and Miss Universe runner-up Siv Aberg and, most prominent of all, Bianca Jagger.

Stewart denied that there was anything going on with any of them, but with Bianca, at least, there appeared to be more than a hint of affection. "Strangely enough, I used to hate Bianca. I thought she was a pretentious little bitch, in the way that a lot of people think Britt is a pretentious little bitch.

"But it's not true of either of them. They're so alike it's incredible. They both have exotic accents, they are both beautiful and they are both ultra-sophisticated."

Was that all there was to it, though? Or was Rod really just making use of another opportunity to upstage Mick Jagger? He didn't deny it. "I think Mick is a bit upset about it," Stewart gloated. "He goes out with Linda Ronstadt and Bianca is expected to put up with it. But when Bianca and I got together, Mick couldn't take it. Probably because the boot's on the other foot for once."

Bebe Buell, whose other famous paramours have included the likes of Elvis Costello and Cleveland punker Stiv Bator, was Stewart's occasional companion for some eight months, and she looks back on the experience with considerable distaste. "He was a little jerk. All he wants to do is go out. I don't think Rod has a domestic bone in his body. And I think that's an important part of a guy, that he can relax at home."

Buell continues with a warning to every woman who ever considered trying to tame the wild Rod. "He is a dangerous person as far as I'm concerned, if you're a woman. Because even if you go out with him once, it's plastered everywhere, and for some fucking reason he's always used it as a method of getting attention."

The "fucking reason", of course, was Tony Toon. As Bebe, Bianca, Britt, Dee and all the others well knew, Stewart only had to glance at a girl before Toon was on the phone. And it was no different when Alana Hamilton – George Hamilton's ex – appeared on the scene in December 1977.

Ironically, it was Bianca Jagger who provided the introductions, and Stewart reveals, "I was a bit nervous when I first met Alana. I had read in a paper that she'd been involved in a romance with a man called

Prince Egon von Furstenberg. He said that she was self-centered and spent hours each night with her face covered in cold cream.

"That is enough to put any man off, I nearly went home! But I stayed on and since I've met her, I haven't seen a single jar of cold cream lying around."

Hamilton herself admitted that she hadn't been particularly impressed by her first sight of Stewart either. "He just sat there looking real cocky."

The Texas-born Hamilton was about to leave for Huntsville, Alabama, where she was shooting a movie with Richard Harris, when Stewart despatched one of his employees to ask her for a date. Her response sent Rod scurrying to the phone: "If Rod Stewart wants to have dinner with me," Hamilton told the astonished lackey, "Rod Stewart can call me himself."

"Their first date was an immediate hit," says Tony Toon. "They talked by phone while she was away, and since she got back home they've been inseparable."

"She is a complete woman in all respects," Stewart declared. "For starters, she has much longer legs than me. And for the first time I found it was possible to be with a flat-chested woman. I was always a T-and-A man before. She has an IQ of 140 and can crush people with words. We are lethal together." And he concluded, "She is certainly not the latest in a series of blondes."

Alana retorted, "Maybe I'll dye my hair."

The couple hit the headlines immediately. Stewart and Hamilton were seeing the new year in at a London disco. A few tables away, Dee Harrington was sitting with friends; Rod and Alana were talking to Keith Richard and Woody.

Suddenly all eyes focused on the slim blonde woman walking purposefully toward Stewart's table. For a moment they wondered what she was going to do. It was Britt, and she looked frightfully determined and maybe a little tipsy.

Grabbing Stewart around the neck, she began showering his face with kisses. Rod didn't struggle, but he didn't respond. Instead he just looked embarrassed while the awkward scene took its course.

Alana, however, knew exactly what to do. "I said to a friend, 'I think she needs some cooling down'," she recalls. "So I poured my champagne down her back." And while Ekland reeled back to her own table, complaining loudly, Dee Harrington went into fits of laughter. It really had been too perfect!

On 22 March, 1978, Ekland finally moved the last of her belongings out of Carolwood. Within an hour, Alana was moving the first of hers in, and Stewart was telling the world, "Alana and I are fantastic together. It's really something special, and I'm happy again.

185

"She is a super girl. She does her own housework – that makes a great change from some of the women I have known. When we have parties and dinners, Alana insists on doing the washing up herself."

But what convinced him that this time he'd got it right was Alana's willingness to share her man with his other great passion – soccer. "She knows nothing about British sport, but she comes everywhere with me to watch soccer," he proudly proclaimed. In return for a holiday in Spain, she was even joining him in Argentina that summer, to watch Scotland compete in the latest World Cup tournament. "And this time, they're going to get it right as well," Stewart predicted.

Rod had every reason to feel proud of Scotland. The year before, he had confessed, "The only thing that scars me is when Scotland loses a football match, and that does happen often, doesn't it?" Since then, the team had enjoyed a phenomenal streak, taking on some of the strongest teams in Europe and South America, and winning every game. "The auld enemy", England, had fallen to the rampant Scots, and as the World Cup grew closer, Stewart made the greatest contribution he could. He entered the recording studio with the entire team, and made a record with them.

"Ole Ola" – which he adapted from an existing melody, "Muhler Brasiliera" – is not the greatest record Rod Stewart ever made, but with Scotland the only representative of the United Kingdom present in the World Cup that year, a tremendous surge of support from all over the nation lifted "Ole Ola" to number four in the British charts.

It was, however, to be the only success the Scots were to see that summer. In exactly the same fashion as they had fallen four years earlier, Scotland were eliminated after the first round. Stewart left Argentina feeling as dejected as he had once been hopeful.

But he may also have been feeling a little thankful. From the moment he arrived in Argentina, Stewart's record-company minders were constantly warning about the dangers of bandits. The huge influx of foreign football supporters into the country had seen an explosion of lawlessness amongst Argentina's more opportunistic muggers and pickpockets. "Only go to the most expensive restaurants," Stewart was told. "You'll be safe there."

Wrong! Rod and his entourage had scarcely been seated in one of Buenos Aires' swankiest eateries when, as Stewart describes the situation, a pair of would-be bandits came in, guns a-blazing. "They told everybody to put their hands on the table while they went around stealing everyone's watches!

"Then somebody in the back, one of the chefs, rang an emergency button that called the police. He got shot stone dead right in front of our eyes. Then the police came storming through about three minutes later and shouted to all of us to get down under the tables."

Resignedly, Stewart let himself be pushed to the floor, "with two great big security guards on top of me." The police shot the bandits, and everybody went back to their meals. The punchline to the tale came, of course, when Stewart and his party were handed their bill. "You must be kidding!" he told the apologetic restaurateur. "I'm not paying the bill! The restaurant has just been held up and I was nearly killed!"

Much of the summer of 1978 was to be spent recording a new album. Once again, Stewart already had a title in mind, *Blondes Have More Fun*, and having bleached his own hair to match, he was preparing to record what would become one of the most controversial songs in his career.

Parallel to the rise of Punk in Britain, the US had been swept by disco fever. The charts were riddled with it, and so persuasive was its influence that even the Rolling Stones had come on board, recording their own eight-minute "Miss You" for a summer 1978 hit single.

Stewart cursed them for having beaten him to the punch, but in other ways he was grateful. They had tested the waters and found that even all-out rock'n'rollers could carve themselves a niche in the new musical craze. Now Rod had a song which, he was certain, would out-perform the lusty "Miss You". It was called "Do Ya Think I'm Sexy?"

"The song's not about me," Stewart insisted, "although I'm certainly sexy to a point." Rather, he insisted, it was about a young couple spending their first night together. "It's not sung in the first person and your humble vocalist is not singing about himself, nor am I praising my minimal sex appeal. I am but a narrator, telling a story."

But, as Stewart himself became swiftly aware, "if ever I wrote a song which put a spanner in the works, it's this one. It was frightening, stirring up so much love and hate at the same time. Most of the public loved it; all the critics, however, hated it.

"It hurt my rock'n'roll credibility, that's for sure," he reflects today. "But I knew when I went into it that I was putting myself out on a limb. I thought, 'This is a bit of a dare, let's see what happens with it.'"

Shortly after the single's release, Stewart went on record saying "Sexy" was as good a song as "Maggie May", a pronouncement which sent the critics into the ozone. *Rolling Stone* writer Paul Nelson, who had interviewed Stewart during the previous traumatic year, says, "I don't sense that he can look into himself and judge what he's done.

"I think it was a serious answer, and that the whole time we talked he was being as honest as he could, to the point that he sometimes made himself look really terrible. This was a case where it didn't even dawn on him that his answer was really shallow or wall-eyed. He had no vision of anything."

The *Washington Post* may have described it as "finely crafted", and credited Stewart with a "sense of sloppy sophistication", but it was one of the few bright lights on an increasingly overclouded horizon.

Carmine Appice, answering criticism that Stewart had "gone Hollywood" replied, "But that's exactly what he wants – Hollywood rock'n'roll. Glamor . . . crazy press stuff. If you're in the music business and live in Los Angeles, you should go along with everything involved. It's like the movie stars lived."

The traveling stage the band carried with them emphasised the link with the Golden Age of the Silver Screen. Pure white, it was bedecked with mirrors, and shrouded by thick, lush curtains. The show would begin with David Rose's "The Stripper" piping through the sound system. Slowly the curtains would open to reveal the band, Appice in pirate drag, Stewart in a one-piece jump suit. 'We all wear crazy stage gear!" Appice bragged. But neither he, nor Stewart, seemed to understand just how alien that concept was to the decidedly anti-glamor rock establishment.

"Somewhere along the line," says writer Paul Nelson, "he's gotten this kind of Jayne Mansfield image; a really trashy, not even movie star image, but movie starlet image; a sort of male tart. And he apparently likes it."

It was pure narcissism. On the album sleeve, Stewart appeared in tight clinging leopardskin, clutching a scantily clad blonde model. The man who feared that Alana Hamilton was self-centered and vain was himself a strutting peacock, a vision of gaudy flash and gaping flesh that demanded attention, devotion and lust. "God, I was a tart back then," Stewart said a decade later. "The stink I got when I dyed my hair blonde!"

He admits, however, "I really didn't concentrate on my singing. I was definitely more concerned with showing off the anatomy than in trying to prove my vocal prowess."

Obviously people must have liked what they saw. "Do Ya Think I'm Sexy" went on to become the biggest-selling single in Warner Brothers' history, and that despite further fuel being added to the fire when a Brazilian songwriter claimed Rod had stolen the song from one of his own compositions, "Taj Mahal". In the course of the legal wranglings that followed, Stewart agreed to turn over all royalties from the song to UNICEF and to date it has generated over a million dollars for the organisation.

Alana, for her part, played down the popular conceptions about Stewart's new image. "I hate people who assume Rod is just an insolent, egotistical womaniser. He is a wonderful man – bright, funny, sensitive and kind. He doesn't resent the fact that my career is important to me.

I hate to destroy his image, but that's the man he is." And she added, "I must admit that if I had read a quarter of what's been printed about Rod it would have turned me off him completely. I would have thought he was a real jerk.

"Sure, he's been with a lot of women, many of them blonde. Look, he's single, thirty-four and enjoys life. I wasn't exactly a nun before I got married, although my menfriends didn't make the gossip columns. What do people expect Rod to be – a monk? He's not the type of guy who wants to stay home and read, and neither am I!"

She continued, "He went out with a lot of women, but he is a good-looking man. And all men like to sow their wild oats. The fact is, Rod wasn't ready to settle down until he met me. He waited until he picked the right person."

Hamilton's pronouncements, however, were drowned out by the furor surrounding Stewart's new songs. "Attractive Female Wanted" . . . "Dirty Weekend" . . . "Sexy" . . . the two songs that said the most about Stewart's state of mind in the months following Ekland's departure, the bitter "Is That All the Thanks I Get" and the mocking "Ain't Love a Bitch". Yet he remained, as he himself says, "extremely vulnerable in relationships and feelings. I am a mass of extremes, contradictions and mistakes."

One of those mistakes was *Jet Lag*, the projected movie with Elton John. The idea came about, Stewart reckoned, because John had "lost the desire to get out and play in front of 60,000 people. It's about two singers avoiding taxation by flying around in a private jet, and if it stinks, I won't make it. I ain't gonna risk my reputation coming off silly."

Besides, he did not share Elton's reluctance to tour. "I still feel like I'm sixteen," he boasted. "I can't wait to get back onstage. 'Too old to rock?' That would be the hardest pill to swallow, mate."

Turning up at Olympia for the first of his scheduled Yuletide shows, Stewart found a very public present from Elton waiting for him. A huge banner draped the building: "Blondes may have more fun, but brunettes have lots more money. Happy Xmas, love Sharon." Furious, Stewart sent a posse of roadies scurrying out to remove it. Another Olympia show, which Rod celebrated by having five giant inflated soccer balls suspended from the roof, was rudely interrupted when Elton hired a posse of marksmen to shoot them down.

After a few weeks' holiday, Stewart returned to the road, touring Australia and the US in the spring of 1979. Behind him, *Blondes Have More Fun* became his most successful album since *Every Picture Tells a Story*, finally returning him to the very pinnacle of the US charts. In Britain, however, it reached a mere number three. "We would have gone all the way if we'd toured the country," Stewart privately mourned. "But it wasn't practical."

Alana did not join Rod on the tour, remaining instead in Hollywood, discussing her own next film. "I miss him, but we talk every day on the phone. I'm not the jealous type. You can't sit at home moping. I trust him and he trusts me and it's useless sitting home eating yourself up with worry. If he's enjoying himself, that's his privilege. Not that I don't care, but you do build up a mutual trust, and I think we have that."

In January 1979, Stewart was invited to perform in a UNICEF charity concert, where he appeared alongside Kris Kristofferson. The performance was eventually cut from NBC Television's one-hour broadcast of the event, and as if to compound the wastefulness of the exercise, he came as close to death as he had ever been, or so it seemed at the time.

Flying back to LA, the plane he was traveling in was caught in heavy turbulence. Suddenly Stewart, whose reading material had lately included a slew of books about airline disasters ("I have a morbid interest in them"), was sure he was going to experience one first-hand. For a moment, he was frozen, wondering what to do, then he calmly struck the call button above his seat. "Another Bacardi and Coke, please."

Alana, beside him, shot him a glance. Rod's doctor had ordered him off the booze. The singer's liver was seriously enlarged, and, as Stewart himself put it, "I could feel my kidneys bulging out of my side. It was hardly surprising, because I was knocking back ridiculous quantities of port and brandy on an empty stomach. You just can't keep doing that for long, and survive to tell the tale. I've seen alcohol destroy more people than cocaine." While he was still able to argue that "I love the taste more than what it does. Alcohol will never kill me – but it may make me fat", he did regret the "drink first, party after" image he had so painstakingly built up over the years. Kids, he lamented, "feel obligated to get drunk before my concerts, just because they think I'm a boozer."

In recent years, health problems have caused Stewart to forswear the demon drink almost completely, but back in 1979 keeping Stewart on the wagon was a full-time occupation, and one in which Alana enlisted help from a most unexpected source.

Having already introduced Rod to the Church of Religious Science in Los Angeles, and encouraged him to develop a full-time fitness program, Alana then procured for him a psychic who promptly told Stewart that if he hadn't met Alana he'd be dead.

Psychics played a major part in Alana's life, much to the future exasperation of Billy Gaff and Jimmy Horowitz. If an airplane journey was booked, Alana had to run the flight numbers past her seer before she would agree to Rod and herself making the trip; hotel rooms had to be examined to ensure the correct "vibes"; there were, in fact, few decisions which could be made without their mystic connotations first being run past Alana's miraculous, and doubtless ultra-expensive, adviser, and as time went by her reliance on spiritual guidance only increased.

Stewart, for his part, went along with it all, agreeing to consult with the psychic when Alana deemed it necessary, and following the advice he received. But in truth, he was considerably more concerned with persuading the enchanting and strangely fascinating Ms Hamilton to move in with him at Carolwood.

Alana still maintained a second home, two miles from Carolwood, for her four-year-old son, Ashley, and a live-in maid, but promised, "If I ever did get pregnant, I would want to marry. Even though I know it's fashionable in Hollywood circles to have a baby without getting married, I don't hold with illegitimate babies. I'm still very much an old-fashioned girl in that respect. I come from a strict Southern Baptist background – my grandmother would turn over in her grave if I had a baby and wasn't married."

She declared, "I would like to have two or three children." Rod, on the other hand, was talking of just having one, "a son, born in Scotland so if he turned his mind to soccer he could wear a Scotland jersey."

In the meantime, Stewart continued the apprenticeship in parenthood which he had begun with Britt's brood, joking that young Ashley Hamilton was spoiled rotten. He threatened to find a good old-fashioned English nanny "to teach him proper discipline". Alana played along with him – "he's usually right in these matters."

Some years later, Ashley confirmed Stewart's first impressions. "Rod was good when I was little. He raised me, and was always telling my mother 'Let him go!' She was over-protective and that bothered him."

What particularly rankled Stewart, says Ashley, was Alana's reliance on "instruction tapes called *How to Raise Your Children*. While she was fussing, Rod would secretly give me a beer or chocolate. He was never particularly health-conscious!" But when such secret treats began having the inevitable effect on the boy's metabolism, Stewart's cruel response was to rechristen him Tubs.

Still, Ashley treasured the hours Rod spent patiently teaching him to play soccer and instilling in him a love of performing which, like his affection for Britain, remains with Ashley to this day. At the age of six, the boy was staging private rock'n'roll concerts in his bedroom, so private that even Alana was forbidden entry. Stewart alone would see his precocious stepson performing Rod's very own "Hot Legs". These days he is an aspiring actor.

All that remained to complete the boy's happiness, even at the tender age of four, was to be able to call Rod "Daddy". And that chance was a lot closer at hand than even Stewart was aware.

On tour in Australia, Stewart had been linked in the local press with a former Miss Australia, Belinda Green. He denied everything, and when the American press caught up with Alana, in Acapulco, she didn't seem overly concerned either. Because she knew something which nobody outside her own inner circle was yet aware of. She was pregnant.

Somehow, Rod and Alana kept the news – both of Alana's condition and their hastily arranged marriage plans – top secret right up until the last moment. Even the guests at the reception, at Los Angeles' L'Ermitage restaurant, were taken by surprise, while the tabloid newspapers were left gaping in amazement. How had they missed this one? They made up for their tardiness by speculating on exactly what Stewart's motives were.

"There's no reason for any woman to get pregnant today if she doesn't want to," said an unnamed "friend of the bride" after the 6 April, 1979 wedding ceremony. "There's always the possibility that Alana planned it as a surefire way of netting Rod."

Another "confidant" continued, "Rod would have put it off for as long as he could under other circumstances, but being three months pregnant, she wouldn't."

The couple had, in fact, intended waiting another month and tying the knot on Alana's thirty-fourth birthday. Only fears that she might begin to "show" pushed the ceremony forward. Later, an attack of bronchitis flattened Stewart and wiped out the second-choice date, 2 April. In the end, the whole thing was rushed together as swiftly as possible.

"We booked the restaurant less than a day before the ceremony, and only got the licence three hours before getting married," laughed Rod. "The cake was just ordered four hours before." Alana's ring, a black onyx band studded with diamonds, was an equally hasty purchase.

The marriage itself took place at Tina Sinatra's house, in front of just a handful of guests – Ol' Blue Eyes himself, Billy Gaff, little Ashley Hamilton and his governess, and Mr Jackie Eastlund, husband of the renowned psychic and minister who conducted the service itself.

"We wanted it kept secret and private," Stewart continued. "That's the way it should be. Instead of a circus, you should remember the special memories."

Outside, limousine driver Michael Richards waited to chauffeur the happy couple on to the reception. "They were very quiet and withdrawn," he reveals. "Rod sat staring straight ahead. He didn't say a word. He was very nervous. It was almost as if he couldn't believe it was happening. They weren't even sitting close."

"I feel just terrific," Stewart later countered. "I'm glad we've got married. I never thought I'd ever do it, but it's funny how you change your mind as you get older."

There was, however, no time for a honeymoon. Stewart's long-awaited, and massively over-subscribed, American tour was due to kick off just five days later, and while he hoped that Alana would be joining him halfway through the forty-one-concert outing, he admitted that any real chance to celebrate would have to wait until the tour was over, and the couple could fly to England to be with Rod's father.

Despite his lengthy absences from home, Stewart remained very close to his parents. They talked on the telephone every other day, Bob religiously reading off the day's football results to his son. He kept an eye on Rod's Windsor home, and every Saturday he would videotape the weekend's soccer programs and have them air-freighted to his son in LA, or wherever else in the world he was.

Stewart, for his part, liked nothing better than to reminisce about these too-infrequent reunions. "Me and me dad were going to a football match, and me dad came out in his old coat, and it was *rough*. It was an old black coat and he had outgrown it. And me mum says, 'You can't go out in that bloody old coat! Your son's a millionaire! You'll disgrace the street!'

"Then there was this thing about the wine, because no one drinks wine at me house, right? But I brought back a bottle, opened it up and said, 'Mum, we have to decant the wine', and she said 'What?' I said, 'We have to put it into a decanter', and she said, 'Well, what's that?' I said, 'It's like a big vase', and she said, 'We'll take the flowers out of the vase on top of the television and put it in there.'

"I said, 'No, we can't do that', and she said, 'Well, there's an empty milk bottle outside. Why don't you put the wine in the milk bottle?' Little things like that," Rod laughs, "really bring you back to square one."

Stewart tried to return to London every Christmas for a gathering of the clan. Relatives would appear from far and wide, and Rod remembers one particularly spellbinding holiday. "I hired three bagpipers in full regalia for New Year's Eve. Just as the clock struck twelve, they came in and played 'Amazing Grace'. It was so stirring. Me dad cried his eyes out. I'll never forget it. The only thing that could bring a tear to me dad's eye was the sound of pipes and when Scotland scored a goal. Especially against England."

Britt Ekland, too, has happy memories of a Christmas spent with Rod's eldest brother, Don, in his semi-detached house in Cambridge.

"There must have been at least twelve of us who sat down to the traditional turkey and plum pudding. Everyone was so warm and friendly. We had soaked up the luxury of some of the best hotels in the world, but none had ever caught the atmosphere of this simple, ordinary family home at Yuletide."

Now Stewart had his own "ordinary family home" at Carolwood. Baby Kimberley was four months old, a second little Stewart, son Sean, was on the way. And Britt Ekland's memories were not something which they particularly wanted to hear, especially after her kiss and tell memoirs were published almost a year to the day after the couple got married.

Peter Sellers, Ekland's first husband, had already got wind of the book, and threatened legal action if Ekland included his love letters to her in it.

Stewart, however, seems to have been in the dark about the book right up until its appearance on the news-stands. He was passing through Heathrow Airport in London when he finally picked up a copy. "I'm buggered if I'm going to give her any money for this!" was his defense as he stuck it under his coat and sauntered out. He hung on to the book until he next visited Sweden, then threw it out of the window of his limousine. Poor Britt, he sniped. "A born loser and always a bridesmaid."

Alana, however, really let rip at her predecessor. "I honestly don't understand how you can write intimate details about someone you once cared for. It's appalling. I swear to God that if I was starving in the streets and someone offered me a million dollars, I wouldn't write such a book.

"I feel sorry for Britt. She's obviously very bitter because Rod and I are so happy. I know it sounds cruel, but I think he knew he would never marry Britt."

Alana was asked about the rumors that, since the disco incident, she had banned Britt from Rod's concerts. "I'd be happy for her to come if she could conduct herself like a lady," Alana answered. "She used to be quite pretty, but I think it's sad when a woman can't grow up, be her age and can't be graceful."

As for Ekland's continual references to Stewart's much-publicised grip on his money: "If I read any more about how cheap Rod is, I think I'll scream."

Ekland describes how Stewart protested bitterly if she didn't shop at the cheapest grocery stores in town. Alana claims that when it came to food, Stewart didn't know what expensive was. "I saw the grocery bills and told him, 'This has to stop!' And he said, 'Oh, is that expensive?'"

Ekland says she had to pay Rod $100 a month for the upkeep of her two children. Alana claims that she could hardly stop him spoiling hers with expensive treats and presents. Ekland claims Stewart never even bought her a Christmas present, even after she lashed out $2,000 for Dutch artist Guy Peellaert's famous painting of a very drunken Stewart being earholed by a pair of English bobbies. Alana reveals that he had given her an $80,000 Rolls-Royce. "If he was cheap with Britt," she concluded cattily, "maybe it was because he didn't want to spend any money on her."

10

Forever Young

Two years had elapsed since Rod Stewart last ventured into a recording studio, a silence that spoke volumes for the amount of time he was lavishing on his family.

"The kids have been soothing medicine for Rod," Alana said on one of the few occasions the press got close to the couple. "He's crazy about them. He used to think that growing up meant growing old, not having fun. He now realises that fun can be playing with your children. He's grown up a lot."

This new maturity seemed hard for many people to comprehend, but any doubts that lingered were firmly laid to rest by the release of his long-awaited new album, *Foolish Behavior*, in 1980. Rod Stewart must have grown up, they said, because he certainly wasn't much fun any more.

Foolish Behavior was heralded by a single, "Passion", a song widely acclaimed as one of Stewart's finest compositions in years. But Tom Dowd, who was once again producing, says it was also the only "real" song on the album.

"We got into a bind, to the point where all the song concepts were the same, or sounded similar. I have to feel that I can contribute or give some input to the people I'm working with, otherwise I'm not helping them."

The breaking point, he says, came with "Passion" itself. Stewart's humorous version of events simply recalls, "This little bugger took forever to record. Tom Dowd nearly smoked himself into an early grave trying to get it on tape, the trouble being that I couldn't explain to the band the sound that I had in my head."

Dowd remembers the ill-fated sessions. "It's one thing when an artist can sit down at an instrument, play a song and present it to you the way they want it done. But it's quite another when they walk around and sing a song to you and you have to guess at what the underlying chords are."

196

And when he did finally figure it out, "I'd heard it all before." Dowd walked out of the sessions with just one song complete.

Stewart himself described "Passion" as a slice of "inner city blues", and there was no doubting that he had created a masterpiece. But once he had been in the habit of creating several masterpieces at a time; by contrast, too much of *Foolish Behavior* was simply workaday filler, otherwise distinguished only by "Oh God, I Wish I Was Home Tonight", "Sonny", written by Bernie Taupin, and an only marginally more than lukewarm assault on the Motown standard "My Girl".

Stewart himself was well aware of the problem, although he denied that his own situation – cozy, domesticated and happy – had anything to do with it. It wasn't him that was becoming complacent, it was his band.

Throughout the final months of 1980, the Rod Stewart Band toured Europe exhaustively, climaxing with the traditional London Christmas show, spread this year over six nights at the cavernous Wembley Arena.

The performances were massively over-sold; more than 100,000 hopeful fans had their ticket money refunded when the shows sold out within hours. No matter how lackluster his records might have become, Stewart remained the consummate showman.

Offstage, too, Rod knew how to put on a show. The end-of-tour party was to take place at the Embassy Club, New Bond Street, the favored celebrity watering-hole for many a late-night reveler. Also in attendance, perhaps unwisely, was journalist Simon Kinnersley, pop correspondent for the *Daily Mail* and author of a particularly unflattering review of one of Stewart's concerts. He mingled quietly with the other liggers, but slowly word got around that he was there, and that Stewart's entourage was planning revenge.

Suddenly they pounced. In very short order, Kinnersley was wrestled to the ground and his trousers were unceremoniously removed. Then, while one half of Rod's party proudly paraded the trophy around the club, Kinnersley was dumped out of the door in his underpants. Revenge, Stewart was still chuckling later, was very sweet indeed.

As sweet, perhaps, as finding a convenient scapegoat for one's own musical failings. The moment the tour was over, Stewart sacked a full fifty per cent of his band – guitarist Gary Grainger, keyboard player Billy Peek, and bassist Phil Chen, the nucleus of the group.

In their stead, Stewart gathered comparative unknowns Robin Le Mesurier, former guitarist with a band called Limey, keyboard player Kevin Savigar, plus guitarist Danny Johnson and bassist Jay Davis, both from Carmine Appice's brother Vinnie's band, Axis. Ironically, Carmine himself was to be replaced in the line-up shortly afterwards by Tony Brock.

Stewart introduced the new band on a tour of the Far East in the early spring. Satisfied with what he heard, he immediately booked more studio time, and commenced work on a successor to the loathsome *Foolish Behavior*. It was still fresh in many people's minds, and Stewart wanted to exorcise it as swiftly as he could. It may have won him a platinum disc, he said, but it was nevertheless "a disappointment".

Indeed, Stewart found himself suddenly backtracking over the last four years of his career, that period in which he had stopped being a human being and had become a commodity for gossip columnists to bat back and forth.

"I was trying to be something I wasn't," he admits. "It showed on silly album titles like *A Night on the Town*, and when *Atlantic Crossing* came out. You do foolish things when you're in love." Ekland, he now admitted, had tried to turn him into a "Hollywood superstar-about-town. She was putting me up to something I wasn't, like the album cover of *Night on the Town*. I was dressed in a boater, with a glass of champagne. That's not me at all."

With Ekland's memoirs having exposed so much dirty laundry to public scrutiny, the gloves were clearly off. "I shouldn't have listened to her as much as I did. I shouldn't have let her poke her nose into my career. But you do these silly things when you're in love. I was very much in love at the time. I suppose I did leave my class for a year or two. But then we all make mistakes. I think I'm right back where I was in 1971."

The difference was, this time around he had children to think about. "I feel the kids have brought everything into perspective. My brother pointed that out to me at a football match. Scotland was losing, which normally would make me miserable for weeks, but this time I wasn't upset. The Scots football team and rock'n'roll are still up there, but my kids are very important to me. I love them." And from one of the many stops on his next world tour, he continued, "Do you know, they had to push me on a plane because I didn't want to leave my daughter."

Ashley Hamilton does not deny Stewart's affection. He does, however, doubt that even the responsibility of children could truly make Rod "grow up". When Ashley refused to attend Stewart's second marriage to Rachel Hunter, his stepfather simply stopped talking to him. "He's acting like a big kid," Ashley complained. "But that's nothing new. I don't think he's ever grown up.

"Rod is a really moody person. You can walk into a room and say, 'Hi, how are you doing?' and he's a real sweet guy. Then the next day you'll walk into the same room with the same attitude and he'll say, 'What the hell do you want?' You never know where you stand."

Even as Stewart's adoring public was raving over the singer's latest album, *Tonight I'm Yours*, Ashley remembers Stewart's bitter insecurity. "On every tour at every stadium he always wonders if anyone is going to turn up. He would be backstage asking the crew how many people were upfront. He constantly worries about whether his fame and success is over. He got fame so fast, it is something he never wants to be without."

Tonight I'm Yours, his 1981 album, was to be Stewart's return to his roots, a re-affirmation of everything he had once represented, with only age and experience to separate it from the "classics" of his youth – *Every Picture Tells a Story* and *Gasoline Alley*. How was he to know that even as the sessions drew to a close, one of the songs from that so-called golden age, "Jo's Lament", was about to burst back into his life with shattering consequences?

Ever since the first long-ago rumors of an illegitimate Stewart baby, the British press had been tying itself in knots trying to establish whether or not there was any truth behind the stories. They were too persistent, too well detailed, to be wholly without foundation. Even the cum-in-the-tum story, well known as it was, had never been pinned down to a single place and time. Here, though, things seemed considerably more clear-cut. All it would take was a lot of patient digging.

The mystery, however, ended in 1981. Rod *did* have a daughter, her name *was* Sarah, and the youthful Stewart had even been at the hospital when she was born, sitting anxiously in the waiting-room with the expectant mother's best friend Chrissie Shrimpton.

Sarah had been adopted soon after her birth, by Brigadier Gerald Thubron and his wife Eve. She was eighteen before she found out who her father was, and remembers the conversation with her adoptive parents as a stunning revelation which took weeks to truly sink in.

Shortly after, arrangements were made for a London newspaper to fly Sarah and a photographer out to Los Angeles to confront Stewart. Her first contact with the Stewart clan, however, was a meeting with Alana and Rod's lawyer, a terrifying ordeal which was made even harder by Alana's clearly antagonistic attitude.

Fiercely over-protective, Alana plainly thought that the girl was simply after a bite of the family fortune, and had obviously primed the lawyer accordingly. When Sarah did finally get to meet her father in the recording studio, Alana was by his side, her presence only adding to Rod's obvious discomfort. Sarah admits she took an "instant dislike" to the snobbish Alana. "She was off-hand and didn't even look nice. She was too tall.

"When I finally got to see Rod it was all very embarrassing. There were lots of people around. There was no emotion. At one point I

199

walked out in tears. I thought he would be fatherly and hug me like a father should, but I felt more like a fan than a daughter."

"It was all so wrong," Stewart said after she had gone. "It was so awkward . . . this girl came in after all these years. It is a part of my life that has gone now. She can't expect to just step back into my life again. Perhaps she should never have been told. Perhaps that would have been the kindest thing for her."

Sarah returned to England bitterly disappointed, and it was to be another five years before she was to meet her famous father again – once she was certain that Alana was no longer around. "Kelly Emberg was with him and she was really great. She accepted me straight away and was really nice. We all went shopping and he bought some clothes. I suppose he would have bought me something if I had asked, but I didn't bother."

It was with considerable difficulty that Stewart returned to the job in hand – recording and producing his new record. It was the first time he had overseen one of his own albums since *Smiler*, seven years earlier, but even with Jim Cregan helping out, it was hard for Stewart to keep his mind on the album.

Still, he put on a brave face. "The great thing about this business is that you do everything off your own back. We make an album, write the songs, design the cover. No director gets in and chops things out like they do in the movie business. It's all ours, which is great freedom," he enthused, and any critics who may have inwardly groaned at the visions of bloated self-indulgence his remarks brought to mind were regretting their cynicism from the moment "Young Turks" exploded across the airwaves and dragged Stewart back into the Top Five.

The title song was a blatant rocker, one of several on the album, and Stewart admitted that the move back to his roots had been inspired by the kids. "Since Alana had Kimberley and Sean, I've been driven like a madman to work harder than ever. I don't know for sure what the reason is. But I think maybe I have to prove something to the kids so that when they get older, they'll be proud of me."

Sean Roderick Stewart was born in September 1980. It was not an easy birth as he was delivered by Caesarian section, but even before he arrived, he was causing his parents trouble.

Rod and Alana were at their beach house in Malibu when Alana went into labor. Stewart bundled her into the car and set out for the hospital, pushing his foot further toward the floor with every fresh cry of pain from poor Alana.

Stewart was scared, he admitted later. Alana was screaming "I'm going to have it in the car!", and Rod didn't have a clue what he'd do if she did. When he heard a police car wailing immediately behind the speeding Lamborghini, he screeched to a halt and ran toward the two officers.

It was not the smartest thing to do. The policemen immediately dropped to their knees and leveled their service revolvers at Stewart. "Freeze!" they shouted.

It was a terrifying moment, but somehow it was resolved. The police told Stewart to drive as fast as he possibly could and they'd go ahead of him to clear the way. Sean arrived just fifteen minutes after the desperate party reached the hospital.

Stewart's new album arrived with a similar urgency to his youngest son. "Just going out and doing ballads would be a big sign of defeat. I couldn't stand the thought of people saying, 'I remember him when he used to jump all over the place. Look at him now, singing all the slow songs.'"

That, he seemed to be implying, was what Britt Ekland would have reduced him to, and on *Tonight I'm Yours* the only real ballads were the perennial Dylan cover, "Just Like a Woman", together with "Never Give Up on a Dream", a song Rod wrote in honor of Canadian runner Terry Fox, who captured the imagination of the country when, having lost a leg to cancer, he embarked on a cross-Canada jog to raise funds for cancer research.

Almost everything else on the record was a rocker, and as if to emphasise the fact that Alana had very little involvement with his songwriting, Rod laughed, "She hates rock'n'roll, she's into country."

Mrs Stewart especially disliked one of the raunchiest songs on the album, he revealed. "She detests 'Tora Tora Tora (Out with the Boys)'. Alana doesn't understand I get pleasure out of going out with the guys! And that," he added mischievously, "makes me happy!" It was with unquestionable glee that he added that he would be undertaking another world tour and that Alana would be staying at home with the children.

The summer of 1981 was not, perhaps, the ideal time to be touring. The Rolling Stones were also out promoting their recently released *Tattoo You* with a media blitzkrieg that threatened to swamp every other tour of the year. But Stewart was unperturbed. He had finally overcome the bitter sense of rivalry which he and Jagger had once so grimly shared. He knew that now, at long last, he was Jagger's equal.

The night before he was to perform on "Saturday Night Live", Rod ran into Tina Turner at Studio 54. Recently she had taken to wearing a Rod Stewart wig and punctuated her show with his songs. On the spur of the moment, Rod invited her on to the show with him to do "Hot Legs".

"Let's see Jagger top that, then!" Stewart laughed after the show was over. "Mick's a bit more of a showman, and I think I'm a better singer. But rock'n'roll has always been about sex appeal. I'm sure that the Stones wouldn't be drawing 90,000 at a throw if Mick weighed fourteen stone."

"I'm not getting any younger," he once joked. "But I'm not as old as Jagger. Everybody keeps accusing me of trying to outdo him, but I'm not jealous of him. We're two entirely different personalities. I'm boozy, soccer-crazed and one of the boys, and he comes over as the Devil. The last time I saw Jagger he came to my house, drank my booze and then badmouthed me in the music papers. Now it's my turn."

Stewart's four-month Le Grand Tour of North America did not, in the end, out-gross the Stones, but Stewart certainly out-performed them. While the Stones preserved their outing with the sprawling in-concert movie *Let's Spend the Night Together*, shot at so many different locations that the set and costume changes made your head spin, Stewart put all his faith into just one show, in Los Angeles on 20 December, 1981.

Broadcast around the world via satellite, it was the largest televised concert since Presley played Hawaii. An estimated worldwide audience of sixty million people purchased tickets to watch the satellite broadcast in theaters across the world; many millions more listened in on radio or cable television. "I feel like I've never toured before," Stewart enthused as he prepared to go out. "I can't wait to get out on stage and fall about."

For Stewart, keeping his personal and public lives separate was fast becoming second nature. Despite everything, however, many people found it hard to believe that the wild man of rock had been tamed, nor that Alana was the woman who had done it. When the couple visited St Peter's in Rome, they were turned away from the door because of Alana's dress – a skimpy slit mini-skirt and a T-shirt.

Not even the birth of two children in such swift succession could convince the doubters that Rod had finally put his tawdry past behind him. But to insiders within the Stewart camp, there was no doubting either the strength of the wind of change that had roared through their world, or its name. Alana had turned *everything* upside down, distancing even Rod's closest friends. Now when there was a gathering at Carolwood, it was Alana's pals who filled the house. Rod's mates simply made their excuses and stayed away.

Even so, no one ever guessed just how deep into the Stewart entourage Alana would reach in her bid to tear out the dead wood. After more than a decade of faithfully serving Rod, Billy Gaff was unceremoniously fired shortly after the tour ended – at Alana's say-so, Gaff alleged.

Alana denies it, but when the ever-faithful Tony Toon also found himself looking for a new job, Mrs Stewart quickly confessed, "He blames me for losing his job, probably with good reason."

Toon was just one of a growing number of disaffected friends, employees and all-purpose hangers-on who had dubbed Mrs Stewart "Alana the Piranha". He may even have been responsible for spraying those words in fat, high letters across the Carolwood walls. Everybody was sick and tired of this domineering, demanding woman, whose sole mission in life seemed to be to keep her man on the straight and narrow, and bugger the consequences. Alana herself admitted, "Rod has had all these people around him all his life, telling him he's wonderful." That, she decided, had to stop. Because sometimes, maybe, he wasn't quite so wonderful.

Neither, say Stewart's old associates, was Alana. Jimmy Horowitz, Billy Gaff's longtime partner, admits, "I never got on very well with Alana. She was a very odd choice for Rod. She thought she was the Queen of Beverly Hills or something. I think she liked Rod because he was one of the top ten big rock'n'roll stars in the world, but she really wasn't very comfortable with musicians."

Prone to tantrums if she didn't get her own way, Horowitz remembers one incident when Alana exploded because she couldn't get four connecting seats in the exact part of an aircraft she wanted. Mrs Stewart was even responsible for Rod earning a new title amongst the world's airlines. Horowitz was booking tickets for them one day some time later, "and I saw the airline computer come up with Rod and Alana's name followed by the initials DP . . . Difficult Passenger."

May Pang, John Lennon's sometime mistress, and Jimmy Horowitz's secretary at Riva's busy New York office, remembers the "hoops" which Alana seemingly delighted in forcing the staff to jump through.

"Jimmy was a very nice, sweet person, but Alana didn't like him," says Pang. "I personally stayed out of that kind of thing. I was more on the business side of it, although I do know that Jimmy and Alana used to have battles." They did not like one another, she says, and Alana would often go to great lengths to let him know how she felt. "If he found something, a flight, a hotel room or whatever, she'd say the stars weren't right, that kind of thing.

"They did not get along – why, I can't say, but Alana was a very strong-willed person. If somebody says something and she doesn't like it, that's the end of them. If Jimmy did something and Alana didn't like it, she'd call up and scream bloody murder."

Billy Gaff, too, was similarly determined – "he knew what he wanted for his artists", as Pang remembers – and for Stewart it sometimes felt as though he were being torn apart by wild horses, Gaff pulling him in one direction, Alana in the other.

"Rod wants me to tell him the truth," she announced, "but then he gets angry when I do. He's torn between wanting to be told he's wonderful and wanting the truth. Well, he's just got to get used to honesty. Rod is a very talented, brilliant, creative man. But the time comes when the public looks and thinks, 'Oh, grow up.' You can't be stupid at nearly forty years of age."

Stewart was, in fact, removed from Gaff's orbit at a very propitious time. Shortly afterwards, the tabloid the *Sun* went to press with a story about Elton John and Gaff which, although there was no merit in it, became one of the most sensational showbiz scandals in years.

At first, Stewart was spared any part in these sordid revelations, although he had once been a more than regular visitor to Gaff's home in Finchampstead, Berkshire. But even as Elton and a battery of lawyers destroyed the newspaper's stories word by word, "fact" by reckless "fact", and they did indeed apologise and pay substantial damages, the old rumors began to creep out again.

Dee's revelation about his alleged fetish for ladies' undergarments, similar tales from Britt Ekland, the old cum-in-the-tum tale, every last scrap of "evidence" was hauled out for public scrutiny and debate, and Stewart once again found himself forced to defend his own sexuality. This time, however, he was able to laugh it off. "I do enjoy men's company," he laughed. "But I am not homosexual."

In April 1982, Stewart made headlines of a quite different kind when he was held up at gunpoint and relieved of his car keys, followed by his car, a 1977 black Porsche Turbo Carrera with the license plates RIVA III. Shortly afterwards, his friend Maggie Abbott was robbed, again at gunpoint, outside her Los Angeles home. His voice heavy with irony, Stewart said, "I have the feeling that violence in America is getting worse." Then he dropped a bombshell – he was returning home to England. "I'm not having my kids grow up in an environment like that," he declared. "I don't want them brought up where they can never go out and play on the streets." And besides, he continued, "I really do want the kids to grow up with English accents."

Stewart promised that he would be returning home as soon as he finished recording his next album. In the event, another two years were to pass before even that simple task was accomplished. His only recorded offerings in 1982 were one track on the soundtrack of the movie *Nightshift*, and *Absolutely Live*, a barnstorming in-concert album, taped on both the 1980 and 1981 tours, and featuring almost all of Rod's greatest hits, plus several new songs, including "Guess I'll Always Love You", co-written by Stewart and Bernie Taupin. An added bonus was the appearance of Tina Turner and Kim Carnes for the final song, the Faces' "Stay with Me".

"Unlike most live albums," Stewart said at the time, "this recording is absolutely live. The few errors and mistakes that occurred on the night were left in to bring about an air of authenticity . . . listen to the saxophone solo on 'Tear It Up'.

"The audience has not been tampered with – if you will pardon the expression – to create a false sense of merriment and/or excitement. Listen to the last few bars of 'Do Ya Think I'm Sexy', whence from within the gathering two likely females did hitherto make their presence known by clambering upon the stage to show their appreciation in topless fashion. This was not banished from the listener's earhole."

Strangely, *Absolutely Live* sold poorly. In the US, it failed to make the Top Forty, the first such disappointment since Stewart's last live album, *Coast to Coast*, climbed no higher than number 35 in Britain. Stunned, Stewart returned to the studio and asked Tom Dowd to come back into the fold, to begin work on a new album.

"For the first time in my career I'm really scared," Rod confessed. "I'm absolutely terrified of failure – that one day I'll make a mess of things and the fans will turn nasty." Alana continued to support him, of course, and publicly he continued to sing her praises – "on the road, temptation is never far away, but knowing Alana is at home waiting stops me dead in my tracks."

Lawyers, too, apparently had a similar effect on him. Billy Gaff, still fuming over his surprise dismissal, had filed a suit against his old boss with the Los Angeles Superior Court.

When his 1983 album, *Body Wishes*, proved to be another tread-water turkey, Stewart was quick to excuse himself. "Going down to the courthouse at eight every morning, then staying in the studio until midnight, was not conducive to doing my best work," he complained, adding both in and out of court, that Gaff "used to show me my projected earnings on a cocktail napkin, then halfway through the tour he'd say, 'Well, you're not doing as good as I thought. I miscalculated.'"

Gaff claimed that his dismissal was invalid, and that it was he, and not Stewart's new manager, Arnold Stiefel, who controlled the singer's career. It took a hefty out-of-court settlement, not to mention the bloody sacrifice of yet another album, to end both the wrangling and Gaff's claims.

Neither were things particularly rosy at home. Rod and Alana were arguing constantly, not only about Stewart's predilection for going out with the guys, but about other, more serious things as well. Rod was back playing the field; had been, Alana accused, since the couple first met. The latest was Danish model Christina Meyer, a stunning brunette Stewart met in London, who hit the headlines in New York when the couple were locked out of the Mayfair Regent Hotel in the early hours

205

of the morning. It later transpired that Stewart's London office had paid her airfare over.

Three times the Stewarts took their troubled marriage to a counsellor; three times they returned from the meetings in despair and disgust. Finally, Alana announced she was leaving. "If he wants to go out with a whole series of mindless, moronic young models rather than being with me and the children," Alana spat, "I don't really think I'm losing anything. I still love Rod, and I know he cares for me. But I don't want to be anything but friends with him."

Although Stewart had begun turning up once again in the gossip columns in the company of a succession of little-known but strikingly similar-looking blonde nubiles, there appeared to be no single woman at whom Alana could vent her spleen. Rather, it was Stewart himself who caught the full fury. Although apparently Alana did leave a notice pinned to one of the wardrobes at Stewart's Malibu hideaway saying "Attention all sluts. Hands off my clothes". It was signed "the soon-to-be-ex-mistress of this house".

"Rod's thirty-nine years old and turning forty and he is very worried about his age. You can be Jack-the-lad when you're twenty-five or twenty-six. But when you're forty, it looks pathetic if you're still chasing after young blondes and always out drinking with the boys."

Stewart tried denying that he had done anything to merit this kind of treatment, but he had never been a particularly good liar, or at least, not accomplished enough to fool his demanding wife. "Alana can be very volatile," he has said. "I've had a few things thrown at me, I can tell you, but I never really fought back. I don't like hitting a woman."

It was, perhaps, the sudden return of Stewart to the unsavory headlines of old which further damaged his new album's prospects. The photograph of the plainly aging and, in truth, somewhat disreputable-looking Stewart on the cover of *Body Wishes* was surely one of the most unpleasant sleeve designs of the year, and while the first single from the album, the rocking "Baby Jane", made number one in Britain, the album's performance left a lot to be desired.

The United States was even crueller. *Body Wishes* peaked at number 30; even "Baby Jane" could only scrape to 14. If people were sick of reading about Rod Stewart, they could not have voiced their displeasure any louder.

But Stewart appeared not to hear them, or maybe he simply preferred not to listen. In August 1983, he flew to South Africa, for an appearance at the Sun City leisure complex in Bophuthatswana. It was an incredibly stupid thing to do. South Africa was a pariah in the international artistic community, embargoed by most nations, banned even from maintaining sporting links with the rest of the world. The entertainment industry spurned it, and both the British Musicians Union and its US equivalent counselled its members not to accept invitations to play there, whatever the financial rewards might be. The potential for violent repercussions, both personal and professional, simply outweighed any profits which might accrue from such a venture.

Stewart, however, ignored their warnings. So, surprisingly, did Elton John, in later years one of the anti-apartheid movement's staunchest allies. John, who was appearing as Stewart's "special guest", immediately made plans to return there for his own show the following year. Only the vehemence of the furious mobs of anti-apartheid protesters who marred even his honeymoon – he had recently married West German Renate Blauel – finally dissuaded him from going ahead with his scheme.

Stewart, too, returned home to a reception of almost staggering hostility. Anti-apartheid groups added his name to their list of blacklisted performers. His new record stiffed and his fatally wounded marriage was still making headlines. But perhaps the hardest pill to swallow was learning that he was losing the respect of his peers.

Several years earlier, Faces' bassist Ronnie Lane had been officially diagnosed as suffering from multiple sclerosis. It was, ironically, the same illness that had stricken Stewart's sister Peggy during her youth, and which eventually took her life during those first months after Rod and Dee parted. Harrington remembers how, in happier times, she and Rod used to go and visit her, "Rod always being very jolly, trying to cheer everybody up."

Later, Stewart's mother too had fallen prey to the disease, and while Ronnie's illness, thankfully, was considerably less advanced than hers, still Stewart was under no misapprehension as to just what suffering from MS meant.

As word of Ronnie's plight got around, a group of musicians, led by Jeff Beck, Bill Wyman, Charlie Watts and Eric Clapton, banded together for a series of benefit concerts, under the overall banner of ARMS – Action for Research into Multiple Sclerosis. The shows were to take place in September 1983, and when Beck mentioned the scheme to Stewart that spring, the singer's response seemed positive.

Nobody heard another word out of him.

Suddenly, the man whom Pete Townshend had once described as "so good it makes you wanna throw up" was an outcast. If he shows up and tries to get on stage, vowed Clapton, "I'm going home." Behind him, other participants nodded their agreement.

Arnold Stiefel, not surprisingly, flew to Stewart's defense. The only invitation Rod had heard, he insisted, was Beck's vague "would you *like* to?" There had been no official confirmation of the shows, no attempt to follow up with Rod's office, nothing whatsoever to suggest that the ARMS shows were anything more than another well-meaning pipe-dream. The fact that the shows had actually gotten off the ground, Stiefel inferred, was, under those circumstances, a miracle.

His pleas, however, fell on deaf ears. Within a matter of days, word got around that Rod Stewart had just dumped on Ronnie Lane . . . again! Once more Stiefel tried to dampen the flames of outrage and again he picked totally the wrong words with which to do it. Arrogantly, he accused the other performers of being afraid that his client would steal the show from under them. "I guess they thought Rod would have tipped the scales, because he is an international superstar. Those other people are great musicians, but you can't make an equation between an Eric Clapton and a Rod Stewart. It's just not the same thing."

And where was Stewart on the night of the show? "Rod left England a week earlier than intended. He just couldn't do the concert." What Stiefel didn't say, but what more than a few people suspected, was that the whole subject was simply too painful for the singer to deal with. He had seen his sister die of multiple sclerosis and his mother crippled by it. Better he be called heartless by his peers than that he should have to see someone else who had once been so dear to him suffering in the same way they had.

Stewart was in London for only a few weeks that September, although it was long enough for the gossip columnists to link him with yet another mystery blonde. He was also sighted at a football match with Elton John, but rejected every reporter's question with a terse "Go away". It was left to his mother, Elsie, to paint the picture of domestic horror which awaited Rod when he did finally return to Los Angeles.

"I could never understand why he married her," Mrs Stewart told the Daily Express. "After all the lovely girls he had seen and been with. Oh, blast!" She revealed that "there was always an atmosphere while Alana was around. She is not a sociable sort of girl who will sit down and chat with you. In fact she doesn't say anything much at all." And her influence, apparently, rubbed off on Rod, to the extent that only when Alana was absent would he relax, "and we can all get together properly like we used to." Old Robert, she revealed, still wished Rod had married a Scottish girl. "He'd have been a lot better off."

Almost as soon as Stewart returned to Los Angeles, Hurricane Alana struck. Moving herself and the children down to Malibu, she declared that the marriage was finally and forever over.

The only thing Stewart could salvage from this disastrous summer was financial. Before he and Alana married, Stewart had drawn up a pre-nuptial agreement that demanded that should the marriage not work out – and now he was claiming that he had known all along that it wouldn't – she would not be able to drag him through the same mill as Britt Ekland. And surprisingly Alana seemed to be accepting that. "I don't think I deserve a large portion of Rod's earnings, because I didn't write his songs and I don't sing them," she told the world. "One thing I will take, however, is the children."

"We were always miles apart," Stewart was now claiming. "I think nine out of ten men had to be pushed into marriage, and I was no different. I tried to worm my way out of it, but we got married in a haze of euphoria. We never really sat down and worked out what we expected of each other. It was like – bang! Suddenly we were married."

Stewart denied that adultery played any part in their break-up. "The idea that I was always cheating on my wife is rubbish. That Romeo Rod image has been greatly exaggerated. I'd love to have had all the girls I'm supposed to!" Rather, the problem was "she has an unfortunate knack of upsetting people. That was the biggest breakdown in our marriage. I accepted all of her wealthy and famous Beverly Hills friends, and welcomed them into my house with open arms. But she would never do the same for the ordinary people among my friends, who do not happen to be rich and famous." Stewart resented the way she treated the expatriate Brits he was playing soccer with three times a week – "just ordinary guys, a few names in soccer circles, but hardly the sort of person she was used to." She wasn't rude to them, he was at pains to explain, she just appeared that way.

There were other things, too. Stewart had sold off most of his car collection to please her, simply because he'd once scared the life out of her when he slammed one of his sports cars into a tennis court fence. Alana had changed his eating habits, stopped him drinking . . . everything he enjoyed in life, it seemed, he had shrugged to one side to please his demanding wife.

Back in South Africa, Rod and Elton had re-activated their plans to make a movie together. They would assume the roles of a modern Crosby and Hope in an update on the old "Road" movies with Liza Minnelli playing the Dorothy Lamour character.

They also announced they would be undertaking a world tour together, beginning in Sydney, Australia early the following year. John was already scheduled to tour there, so it would be no trouble to add Rod's name to the billing. But with Stewart's life seemingly falling apart, there was no way the tour could go ahead. Appearing on English television shortly after the Stewarts' separation was announced, John confirmed that the joint tour was now off.

By now, the tabloid press was in perpetual overdrive. Stewart was apparently consoling himself by falling into whichever arms were the most welcoming at the end of every evening. What really put the icing on the cake, however, was that Alana didn't seem much more discriminating. She too was seen out on the town with quite a number of male friends, and she admitted, "I'm enjoying my freedom right now. I'm starting to go out again, see friends I haven't seen in a long time, and I'm starting to become a person in my own right."

In a last, desperate attempt to get their marriage back on track, Rod and Alana agreed to spend Christmas 1983 together in London. It was, Alana later admitted, "a disaster". They returned separately to the United States, and set about putting their own lives back together again.

Stewart knew, and openly admits, that much of the blame for this breakdown, and those which had preceded it, should be laid at his door. "I can never face them and make a clean break," he said of his women. "I'm a bit lily-livered when it comes to that. I just wait until I'm found out, which always happens in the end.

"I'd like to change the way I handled some personal relationships. I wish I wasn't so cowardly when it comes to dealing with people, but it comes from shyness and not wanting to hurt anyone. I have been rotten to women, but not intentionally. I never wanted to hurt anybody. From the outside it may look as if I hate women, but I don't. I need a woman by my side. I need a woman to bounce off. They give me so many things."

At the same time, though, he was taking great pleasure in being on his own again. "Now that I'm separated, I live very simply in a small place. It's great. I've had servants around me for ten years and it was really starting to get on my nerves."

Remembering how much he had liked doing the housework during his years with Dee, Rod threw himself into "keeping house", and admitted he was enjoying himself more than he had "in quite a while. I used to live up there with the rich and famous when I was married. Now I live with regular people. I guess I've got back to the streets – or as near as I'm ever going to. Because when you literally come from the streets, you're not in too much bloody hurry to get back!"

For Stewart, that meant getting to work on a new album – "something to take me mind off all this other shit" – and putting himself back into public circulation. He had recently been spending more and more time with the same two girls – both blondes, both models, and both, as the press never tired of reminding its readers, named Kelly. One, actress Kelly LeBrock, was American, the beautiful star of *The Woman in Red*; the other, Kelly Emberg, was Swedish, and had first been sighted alongside Stewart when he turned up at a beauty contest she was judging in Acapulco.

As soon as they were introduced, Emberg co-opted Stewart to sit on the judging panel with her, and the tabloid press simply took it from there. While Alana was working on her own new movie, *Swing Shift*, Stewart and Emberg were being photographed in Dallas . . . New York . . . Los Angeles. It was not long before the reporters, whose sole duty, they believed, was to follow Stewart everywhere, had the revealing shots they had been hunting, and even Arnold Stiefel was admitting his bewilderment. "God, this is confusing – like something out of *As the World Turns*."

Before that awful Christmas reunion, Stewart had been unable – or unwilling – to make a commitment to any one woman. Now, with everything over between Alana and himself, Rod's domestic side again came into play. By the end of January, it was Emberg, and Emberg alone, whose name was being linked with his. The next time a journalist asked him how he reacted to Alana's accusation that he was sleeping around like a teenager, he accused. "As it happens, it is Alana who is going out with every guy she wants to, and me who is sticking to one girl, Kelly."

From the outset, *Camouflage* – the thirteenth all-new Rod Stewart album, recorded in 1984 – looked like a monster. Both "Infatuation" and "Some Guys Have All the Luck" made the US Top Ten, and even "All Right Now", the old Free song which ranked among the most uninspired cover versions Stewart ever recorded, made the Hot 100.

Yet overall, *Camouflage* was perhaps Stewart's worst album, not, as with *Foolish Behaviour*, because of poor songs, nor, as with *Body Wishes*, because so much of it seemed rushed and impatient. *Camouflage* bombed because, just as he had done in 1978, Rod had spotted a fast-moving bandwagon and thrown himself directly into its path.

The early–mid 1980s were the age of synthesised pop, where the style of one's hair seemed considerably more important than the nature of one's music. Groups like the Thompson Twins, Tears for Fears and, worst of all, the hatefully bloated Simple Minds, were introducing a new sense of pomposity to music, combining the last dregs of post-Punk dance music with a growing preoccupation with electronic gimmickry. *Camouflage*, which paired Stewart with Michael Omartian (best known for his work with the loathsome Donna Summer), was the epitome of this most moronic of musical fashions.

The worst thing was, parts of it could have been genuinely great. Certainly not "All Right Now". Fed through Omartian's disco beatbox, it emerged neatly sanitised and thoroughly flat. But "Some Guys Have All the Luck", in later years a mega-hit for Robert Palmer, was at least a great song, while "Infatuation" not only blazed a similar trail to the immortal "Passion", but also returned Stewart to perhaps the most legendary of all his past partners, one Jeff Beck.

Stewart repaid Beck's guest appearance by furthering their collaboration on the guitarist's own new album, *Flash*. "People Get Ready" followed "Infatuation" into the charts on both sides of the Atlantic. The riveting single melded Beck's piercing guitar work with Stewart's equally powerful vocal, perhaps his finest on record. Rod recalls the song's inauspicious genesis: "Jeff had come over to the States on holiday and he'd done the track as a demo. He played it for me and I said, 'Let me do a vocal just to see how it turns out.' So I went round to someone's house to do it. The entire track was made in people's houses and garages; it was never a professional studio job. It took me three takes for my vocal and I never thought anything would happen with it. All of a sudden, I hear it on the radio! I was caught off guard that it would be liked at all, let alone highly thought of."

Beck in particular had defected far from the course he had once seemed destined to follow, moving deeper and deeper into territory normally associated only with jazzmen. *Flash*, which went on to earn Beck his first ever Grammy award, was his return to basics, and when it was announced that he would be joining Stewart on the singer's next American tour, the response to one of the most eagerly awaited reunions of all time was staggering.

"After the record was done," says Stewart, "we talked and I said, 'Why don't we work together?' And he said, 'Fine.' So I told him he could open the show, close the show, play on every track – any way he wanted it. So he said, 'Fine.'"

Seven nights into the tour, Beck unceremoniously jacked it in.

"Stewart just wasn't forthcoming with any ideas which involved me," Beck laments. "I was slotted to about fifteen minutes and I just couldn't see the sense of touring the US in that context. When my fans turned up they'd be thinking I'd gone mad . . . or moody!"

The canny Stewart was no kinder in his summary of Beck's contribution. "Jeff is an amazing guitar player alright," he related, "but self-destructive." He described his solos as "taking the show to a low point", and laughed, "The rest of the band were actually laying bets on how long Jeff would stay around!

"The man has got a touch of genius in him, but he is his own worst enemy. I mean, a couple of years later, he backed out of Mick Jagger's tour and caused him a lot of problems! At least I got him for seven dates."

Beck later confided to Stewart, "I'm so fed up with singers!"

Despite a slew of gloomy predictions, Beck's defection did nothing to dampen ticket sales as the tour, scheduled to run for a staggering eight months, continued. In Brazil, Stewart performed in front of audiences of 200,000 people, but the greatest thrill came when he was invited to appear at the Harlem Apollo, still a musical mecca more than fifteen years after he and Woody had dropped by there on their first free evening in America.

"You sing with so much soul!" Little Richard told him after the show. "You sing more like a black man than I do!"

In many ways, Stewart was now saying, this tour was to be the last of his Great Rock'n'Roll Freak-Outs. "My really wild and crazy days are over. I am going to try and change my image. I have done my share of smashing up hotel rooms and getting drunk on planes.

"I am not giving up my career completely, just cutting down on the lunacy that has been a major part of my life for more than twenty years." The reason for the change, he explained, was Kimberley and Sean. "I am turning over a new leaf," he said, not for the first time! "If I don't, I won't see my kids grow up at all; before I know it they'll be teenagers and I'll have missed all those good years when I could have been a proper dad", and not, as Alana had once remarked, a "rented" one.

"I have already missed some of their formative years," mourned Stewart. "I wasn't around when they needed to be fed or washed or have their diapers changed. But their mother is picking up her career as an actress again, so that means I can see them more often if she is going to be away working."

But he admitted that he would have to keep a closer eye on them when they were together. Sean, on an ocean cruise with his dad, had thrown Rod's $10,000 Cartier wristwatch overboard.

Unfortunately, Stewart's declaration of intent was not enough for Alana. Furiously she blasted, "They see Rod when he has time to see them, and then he can go off on his merry way. He can pack up and go wherever and with whomever he wants. He gets to pick them up and take them to the park or out to dinner. The kids think it's great because when they see Dad they have candy and ice-cream. They've suffered. It's been difficult for them, and the hardest part is for me to see the pain the children are going through. It's hard not to be angry or resentful when you see what it does to little kids who really don't understand why their lives have suddenly been turned upside down."

What increased the pain, both for Alana and Rod, was the divorce settlement. Alana filed papers on 1 February, 1984, but signing that pre-nuptial agreement, she admitted in her least guarded moments, was a big mistake. Her lawyer announced "she was eight and a half months pregnant and was suffering from both Yuppie flu and mono" when she signed it. "Besides that, for the agreement to be valid there has to be a full disclosure of all assets, and there are millions of dollars from his recording that were not set forth."

Mrs Stewart, for her part, denied that she intended fleecing her celebrated husband, "vacuuming his leopardskin pockets", as one observer

213

put it. But it would have been nice to have arrived at some sort of amicable arrangement. When she split up with George Hamilton, she revealed, "we sat down over a hamburger and worked out something comfortable." This time, it was to take close to seven long years before Rod and Alana settled their differences. Until then, Stewart paid her an interim allowance of $25,000 a month.

Why so much? "If you go to the grocery store these days," Alana shrieked, "the prices are just outrageous."

Stewart had not, for once, been mean with his money. Besides the monthly payments, he also agreed to continue paying Alana's servants' wages, and even handed over two cars – a Porsche and a Rolls-Royce Corniche. Ironically, a few months after they separated, Rod called Alana to ask if he could borrow the Rolls while she was on holiday. Alana agreed, only to get another call from a friend a few days later, asking what Kelly Emberg was doing driving her car around?

Furious, Alana got back on the phone with Rod. "Return the car this instant!" she demanded. He did.

Cars seemed to be giving Stewart as much trouble as women back then. On 12 May, 1984 he was arrested on drink-driving charges after California Highway Patrol officers spotted him weaving erratically down Sunset Boulevard in his Porsche. Before the law hauled him down to the station, Rod spent half an hour signing autographs for the cops and the ever-growing crowd of onlookers. Only later did the lucky recipients realise that he had signed Elton John's name to most of them!

A urine test later revealed that Stewart had not, in fact, been intoxicated, but the Highway Patrol were not about to let him off the hook. Instead he was charged with following too closely behind another vehicle.

The news that Stewart had been elected to the National Academy of Video Arts and Sciences Hall of Fame in April came as a welcome respite from the near non-stop tabloid angst which had held him in a media maelstrom since before Christmas. "Rod Stewart's unique talent has helped shape the music video industry," Academy Director Jennifer Libbee said as she announced the award.

The prestigious honor stood out as the lone highlight in an otherwise turbulent, forgettable year. However, as 1985 rolled around, Stewart was to experience the single most demoralising blow of his career. In one of the all-time colossal snubs, one of pop music's premiere superstars was left out of the single greatest event in rock history: Live Aid.

11

One More Time

Stewart looked on in horrified outrage at the television pictures of mass starvation in Africa. Why wasn't somebody doing something about this obscene tragedy? he wondered in frustration.

As it turned out, somebody was. At the end of 1984, Bob Geldof, the charismatic former singer with Ireland's Boomtown Rats, and Midge Ure of Ultravox, came together at the helm of Band Aid, a high-profile project aimed at raising funds for the famine and civil war then sweeping the African nation of Ethiopia.

Together with Europe's top music luminaries, including George Michael, Elton John and Boy George, Geldof composed and produced the number-one single "Feed the World" which not only raised money for the plight but drew the world's attention to this urgent crisis.

Six months later, in July 1985, with both the British-based Band Aid and the American counterpart USA for Africa having generated an unprecedented response from both within and without the music industry, Geldof organised Live Aid, a transcontinental pop festival televised globally from stages as far apart as London, Philadelphia, Tokyo and Moscow.

The list of contributing artists was phenomenal, so great that at first a certain, very conspicuous absentee was allowed to pass without comment: Rod Stewart.

Stewart himself was desperate to play. The mounting "Sexy" royalties were proof of his concern – up to that point, he was almost certainly UNICEF's greatest rock'n'roll contributor. But his public requests for consideration went unheeded by Geldof. It was, perhaps, a sign of Stewart's bitter disappointment that he was to make just one more live performance during 1985, appearing alongside Cyndi Lauper for a rousing rendition of "I Heard It Through the Grapevine" at an AIDS benefit at the LA Forum on 19 September.

Unfortunately Stewart was completely overshadowed by the solemnity of the event. The actor Rock Hudson, at that time the disease's best-known victim, was the "star", sending a heartfelt message of thanks from his deathbed at the UCLA Medical Center.

Strangely, though, this sudden loss of exposure may have done Stewart more good than harm. Live Aid, for all its noble intentions, was less the sumptuous banquet of rock'n'roll which most observers had expected than a bloated spectacle of self-glorification and mutual back-slapping. Too many acts played it safe, running through their greatest hits, and it was a bitter irony that those who did go out on a limb and tried something different – Adam Ant, who courageously introduced a collection of brand-new songs, and Bob Dylan, who brought on Keith Richard and Ronnie Wood for a shambolic, near-discordant performance of "Masters of War" and "Blowing in the Wind" – suffered from something of a *falling off* in their record sales.

Stewart may have deeply regretted missing the opportunity to contribute publicly to such a high-profile charity, but in terms of maintaining the public's respect, it may have been the shrewdest move he had made in years. For eight years now, ever since Britt Ekland first sashayed into view, Stewart had lived his life in the full glare of the media spotlight, to the point where many people could be forgiven for wondering just what he was these days – a rock'n'roll artist or a raucous tabloid star?

"The way the public looks at me, I'm probably a bit of each," he reasons. "But in my own heart, not many work much harder than I do. The music counts more than anything. More so than image. I dearly like to think that it will be the music that survives, above the flashy clothes, funny haircuts, whatever. It should always be the music before the fashion." When Princess Stephanie of Monaco launched her short-lived journalistic career with an interview with Rod, the only answer he could give to her most probing question – "Do you think you're sexy?" – was a heartfelt "Hmmmm."

All of these thoughts were with him as he began work on his 1985 record. On the cover, he would appear in the most casual attire he could muster: no satin, no flash, no tat. Even the title would reflect his current state of mind – no allusive jokes, no more nights on the town or tarty blondes having fun. The record would be called simply *Rod Stewart*.

The only taste of Hollywood glitz, Stewart vowed, would be "Love Touch", recorded for the theme of the new Robert Redford movie, *Legal Eagles*. And that, he promised, would be the weakest tune on the record. "What a silly pop song," he smirks dismissively. "How on earth could I sing a lyric that went 'Ooooh you're gonna getta, oooh you're gonna getta love touch!'?"

But even Stewart's disdain could not stop "Love Touch" from earning a unique distinction among the singer's classic recordings. It was his first single ever to achieve what *Billboard* magazine called Triple Format Status – rotation play on Hard Rock, Adult Contemporary and Top Forty radio.

Rod Stewart was produced by Bob Ezrin, a man best known for the "everything but the kitchen sink" ethic he had used to such devastating effect on albums by Kiss, Alice Cooper and Lou Reed. Ezrin harnessed a side of Stewart which had not been in evidence, *Tonight I'm Yours* excepted, in years – a tender, emotionally resonant sound which had even Stewart's harshest detractors looking back toward *Every Picture Tells a Story*.

It was this apparently sudden awareness of his roots that prompted Stewart to concentrate his energies on Europe. His longest tour of the continent yet, five full months, attracted ecstatic reviews everywhere it touched down. No longer the tinseltown glamor-puss or the working-class yobbo made good with the jet set, when Rod Stewart took the stage, it was as the rough'n'ready Rodders who had fronted the Faces all those years ago.

Of course, there were still glimpses of the more recent incarnation: the mournful "Another Heartache", with its very obvious references to Stewart's failed marriage; "In My Own Crazy Way" and "Ten Days of Rain" – further tales of love sadly lost; and "Red Hot in Black", the story of a one-night stand with a woman with legs "like a young giraffe".

But just as often a younger, reflective Stewart would emerge, and nowhere so obviously as on "A Night Like This", which returned him to his mid-teens and his first, fumbling taste of sex. How hard it must have been for him to sing the line "One thing I'm lacking is sexual experience"! It wasn't quite a new "Maggie May" – that honor was reserved for the yearning "Every Beat of My Heart" – but even the critics admitted it was certainly a step in the right direction.

The most important song on the album, at least in terms of lyrical content, was "Who's Gonna Take Me Home", subtitled "The Rise and Fall of a Budding Gigolo". Uproariously funny, it completely destroyed the image of Randy Rod falling into bed with every girl he set his eye on, portraying instead a pitiful buffoon whose attempts to be the life and soul of the party fall very flat indeed. Here it's the boys he's asking to take him home, incidentally, not the girls.

Throughout the spring of 1986, the tour wound its way across Europe, prompting some of the most appreciative reviews of Stewart's career. Maybe it was that, as the final British dates approached, which inspired in Stewart an idea even more sensational than his reunion with Jeff Beck. He was going to reform the Faces!

Stewart was still in regular touch with Ronnie Wood. For the past fifteen years they'd been working on a book of song lyrics and poems together, and while no one knew whether *A Collection of Annoyances* would ever be ready for publication, it had served to keep them close.

Mac and Kenney Jones – the one a top-notch session man, the other on perpetual stand-by for whenever the Who decided to get back on the road – were ready and willing as well. The only question mark hung over Ronnie Lane, stricken with multiple sclerosis and forced, against every instinct, to give up even the handful of small club gigs he'd been playing as the illness took its toll.

Stewart hadn't actually seen Lane in years, and his first sight of his old drinking partner making his painful way around with the aid of a stick brought tears to his eyes. Suddenly the bitter recriminations that had marred Ronnie's last years with the Faces seemed so stupid and unnecessary.

For a moment, Stewart wondered if the reunion could go ahead. Certainly he wanted it to, but who could possibly replace Ronnie? He had been thinking of inviting Andy Taylor, bassist with teenybop fops Duran Duran, but somehow that didn't seem right. This was the Faces' show, not Rod's, and certainly not Duran's. In the end, says Ronnie Wood, "Bill Wyman volunteered to play bass", and Stewart agreed. "But it was still the only thing that stood out as being different," Wood continues, "although Ronnie was still singing great" – Lane was to appear on stage to contribute his familiar backing vocals.

As the big day approached, nerves began to fray. "What are we going to play?" "What are we going to do?" "How long are we going to do it for?"

Stewart suggested the Faces go on for thirty minutes, right at the end of the show. And as for rehearsals – "We'll wing it. Instead of rehearsing, let's go down the pub, just like the old days."

The others roared their approval. "After all the shit we'd been through individually," says Woody, "and after eleven years since we'd played as a group, we still had that carefree attitude. Who are we to fuck with tradition?"

Word of the reunion spread like wildfire. MTV even arranged to film the event, "poking their cameras in our faces backstage", as Woody puts it, but keeping a discreet distance during the show itself. There could be no intrusions tonight.

Stewart went on first with his regular band, togged out in the leather trousers, baggy striped soccer shirt and battered hat which had become *de rigueur* for his live performances. He ran through his programmed set, as exuberant as always, conducting the audience as they sang along with his hits. And then, just as the crowd was wondering if all the promises and fuss had been naught but a rumor, instead of an encore the Faces trouped out.

The show was a triumph, the closing, racing "Stay with Me" searing itself into the memory of everybody present that beautiful July afternoon. When the band closed in on one another at the end of the show, brothers in arms and raised glasses in hand, it seemed as though the applause would never die. A week later, people were still talking about that brief, fleeting thirty minutes when the Faces got back together.

Stewart took two months off after the tour. Emotionally and physically drained, he had to get back to the sanctity of Carolwood and Kelly. But he was already making plans for the future – first a new album, then a new family. In September 1986, Emberg fell pregnant.

It was, as Arnold Stiefel admitted when the news finally reached the press, a delicate situation. Although Alana had filed divorce papers three years ago, neither she nor Rod seemed in any hurry to make their break-up final. "They're getting along better than ever," Stiefel laughed enigmatically. And when the inevitable question of Stewart tying the knot with Kelly came up, his reply was guaranteed to baffle his interrogators. "Rod's already married to one of the most beautiful women in the world. Why would he want another wife?"

Emberg, whom Stewart kept in high heels and short skirts until she was eight months pregnant, merely let it be known that she was "looking forward to the baby with glee." She had considerably more to say, however, a couple of months later. In one of those newspaper stories that rely almost exclusively upon unnamed observers to fill in the details, it was revealed that Stewart had been seen out on the town once again.

"Rod was all over a new girl at the Wall Street nightclub just a couple of nights ago," the anonymous watcher reported. "They were hugging, kissing and snuggling."

The mystery girl was model Regan Newman, twenty years Stewart's junior. While Rod's co-manager Randy Phillips tried to make light of the situation – "There will always be women hanging on his arm. Rod is a rock star – it just comes with the territory!" – when Rod and Kelly met for lunch at Butterfield's on Sunset Strip, the alleged infidelity was all they could talk of, according to the press at least.

"I did not go out on the town," said Stewart loudly.

"Well, your black Porsche certainly was," said Kelly. "I saw it."

"To go off with another woman while I was pregnant was the lowest thing he could have done," Kelly swore later. "I wonder what'll happen if one day he sleeps around with a woman who has AIDS. I could be subjecting myself to that. It's a terrifying prospect.

"The trouble is, he wants me to be faithful, but then he expects me to accept him being unfaithful." It was a savage breach of trust, made

219

all the worse by its proximity to the birth of Rod and Kelly's first child, Ruby, on 17 June, 1987.

Ruefully, Stewart admitted that he wouldn't have blamed Kelly if she had walked out on him right there and then. She remained by his side, however, and only when Ruby was born did she make it clear just what she expected from him – stop screwing around with Alana and the divorce settlement, and get it sorted out now so the couple could marry. Stewart promised he would do his best.

But first there was a new album to record, followed by all the many details that accompany the birth of a new baby. As 1987 dribbled away, Stewart didn't even have time to make any concert appearances, let alone drop everything and get married. It was to be the first year in a quarter-of-a-century-long career when he had not taken to the boards in some form or another.

Instead, Stewart's fans were offered nothing more than a re-recording of "Twisting the Night Away", on the soundtrack of the movie *Inner Space*; the long-awaited compact disc repackaging of *Atlantic Crossing*; and a reissue of "Sailing", released to raise funds for the victims of the terrible ferry disaster in the North Sea off Zeebrugge the previous autumn. It reached number 41 on the British charts, easily outselling "Twisting the Night Away" in the process.

The new album, however, continued to dominate Stewart's thoughts. "I want everything about it to be just right," Rod told friends. "And if that means spending the next year recording it, I will." He talked of calling it *Pardon My Past*, and both on and off the record he raved about the band he had put together for the sessions – Andy Taylor on guitar, Bernie Edwards on bass, and drummer Tony Thompson.

The trio had, until recently, been working under the guise of Power Station, a band that scored several massive hits in its own right. "Andy and I started producing the album," Stewart said, but then he discovered that Taylor was very much like "a young Ronnie Wood. We both like a drink or two after hours . . . I have too much fun with him, like I did with Woody. Some nights we just disappeared up our own asses."

One too many nights, it seemed, and realising that it was difficult to produce even a half-decent album from that position, Taylor finally suggested bringing in Bernie Edwards. He in turn recruited Thompson, and the sessions got under way once again.

"Andy is probably the closest collaborator I've had since Ronnie Wood," Stewart enthused. "Andy'll just start strumming along. He doesn't believe in rehearsals, just going into the studio, laying it straight down as it comes off the top of his head, recording it." After years of working to such strict regimens as he had, it was a refreshing, and nostalgic, change. "I'm more or less inclined that way my-self."

One of the future hits off the album-in-progress was written in just that loose style. Stewart relates how he and Andy had been toiling away in the studio all day, getting nowhere. He had a football match that evening and told the guitarist, "Look, I'm gonna leave you here with the guys. Just try and work something out to save the day." Stewart returned three hours later to discover Andy had been penning a love ballad he had titled "Lost in You". Rod picks up the story: "I sat down and wrote the melody and the hook. It was just a question of slotting the title somewhere in the song. We didn't finish that day but came back fresh the next morning and nailed it. I'm not a very swift lyricist so it took me a couple of weeks to complete the words."

Interestingly, the female voice cooing "I miss you too" on the song is none other than Kelly Emberg. "It took about four months to get her to do that," Rod reveals. "It was so nerve-wracking to her, so I applied tons of wine down her throat and once she was nicely drunk she couldn't stop laughing. Then it took another four hours to stop her giggling!

"Doing that live I kept trying to get one of the guys to sing it and none of them wanted to. You know: 'I miss you baby.' 'I miss you toooo!'"

The result, Stewart promised, would be "the best album I've done for some time. I haven't made silly commercial mistakes like I did on the last album with 'Love Touch'."

Pardon My Past eventually emerged as the energetic 1988 album, *Out of Order* – a title, Rod stressed, that had nothing to do with faulty work-manship or mechanical breakdown. "'Out of order' is an English expression – it means misbehaving like ''ere, Guv, your behavior's right out of order.' I think it's fairly appropriate."

But was the man himself still out of order? He swore not; not any more, anyway. "I don't want to be a sex symbol any more. I've proved all that and it's so silly really. If George Michael wants to take over the sex symbol crown he can – I've given up all that, I want to make mature rock'n'roll. I want to write and sing from experience and share it with people."

But would he be sharing it with Kelly Emberg? Rod and Alana's divorce had *still* to be settled, and in her darker moments Emberg could almost imagine that the delay was deliberate. Stewart constantly expressed his urge to remarry, but trying to pin him down to a date, or even a year, was impossible.

Instead, she could do no more than sit on the sidelines while Stewart pronounced, "I've been promising it to her for so long, and unlike

Mick Jagger I'm going to go through with it." Of the wedding itself, he commented, "We'll do it real quiet . . . or we'll do it real noisy. It won't be in between."

Yet the only real sign that Stewart had any intention of actually going ahead with the ceremony came when he drew up another of his infamous pre-nuptial agreements, then permitted a story to circulate that June 1988 was the most likely month.

Behind the scenes, however, the divorce wranglings continued. And now Stewart had a new distraction. The wedding month (he had still to settle on a precise day) was just weeks away when Rod announced, "I've got a new band I've got to rehearse. If you want to plan a wedding in a church, it takes time and we want to do it right. The tour's starting earlier than we thought. We have a break in London in August; we might do it then."

Or they might not. Rehearsals for the tour took an early set-back when first guitarist Eddie Martinez, then drummer Tony Thompson bowed out of the picture. With time ticking away, Stewart recalled Tony Brock, who had replaced Carmine Appice in 1981 and was now becoming accustomed to being Stewart's last-minute substitute, then contacted guitarist Jeff Golub, best known for his stellar work with the likes of Peter Wolf and Billy Squier.

For Golub, the chance to work with Rod Stewart was a dream come true. "I was influenced heavily by Stewart when I was a kid," he admitted. "Especially the records he made with Jeff Beck. I was a big fan of his and had always thought of playing with him." His audition, he says, was classic Rod Stewart. "I flew out to Los Angeles and played a couple of songs. Stewart said 'All right, I've heard enough. You got the job – now let's go to the pool.'"

Although he was ostensibly promoting Out of Order, Stewart had no intention of letting the new record dominate the concerts. It was already well on its way to earning him a platinum disc for sales of one million. Both "Lost in You" and "Forever Young" were hit singles – Out of Order, he joked, could take care of itself. Just three songs from the record were included in the live show; the rest of the set, he insisted, would be a résumé of his entire career, all the way back to the days with Jeff Beck.

"We do 'Ain't Superstitious'," Golub enthused, "just like the Jeff Beck Group did it at the Boston Tea Party." Other oldies – including "Mandolin Wind" and "Reason to Believe", neither of which Stewart had ever performed in concert before – were revived, and when the concert reviews came in, they were unanimous.

"We're here to please," Stewart announced as the band kicked off at Madison Square Gardens on 26 September, and proved it by starting, and swiftly discarding, the hated "Love Touch". "We've got better songs than that!" he said, half to the band, half to the audience.

Less than three months into the tour, however, disaster struck. Stewart's voice – often a delicate commodity, as he well knew – had started giving him real problems. At times, his throat was so sore that he could barely talk, let alone sing.

Doctors were not encouraging. Although tests eventually turned out negative, for a time there were fears that he had developed the strength-sapping Epstein-Barr virus. The only thing he could do was stop performing.

Stewart, however, defied them. A tour insider reported that at one point he was walking around with an antibiotic drip strapped to his body, "because he was so desperate to carry on the tour at any cost. He spent hours and hours with doctors, trying to get his voice better."

Finally, however, Stewart had no choice but to surrender to the inevitable. A string of shows was canceled, including a benefit gala for Terry Fox, the courageous cancer victim who had inspired "Never Give Up on a Dream", and Rod, Kelly and Stewart's three children headed off for a week's vacation in Hawaii.

The break did the trick, and returning to the road, Stewart thanked God that he had looked after his voice so well. "I've never smoked, so my voice is in pretty good condition. I don't drink nearly as much as I used to. Different alcohol can kill you – white wine takes all the lining off the throat, red wine just the opposite. A glass of red can help you."

Stewart continued to heed his doctors' advice, however – one scare was enough. He hadn't cried off alcohol completely, but he had drastically lowered his consumption in favor of more healthy beverages. Where once he had insisted upon a dressing-room swimming in alcohol, now all he required was fresh fruit, twelve bottles of Evian water (four, he stipulated, at room temperature), three quarts of fresh orange juice, and two each of fresh grapefruit and apple juice. For the band, there were also two bottles of Mateus Rosé and a bottle each of hot sake, Remy Martin VSOP, Kahlua, Bailey's Irish Cream and frozen Stolichnaya vodka. And to get Rod himself around town a late-model, white, air-conditioned Rolls-Royce.

But who, the press was asking, was he getting around with? In December, Stewart was spotted nightclubbing in New York with a six-foot stripper named Jeanie. And while it was Kelly who accompanied him back to England for Christmas, the amply proportioned Jeanie had obviously made a big impression on Rod as he celebrated his fortieth birthday in London with a cake in the shape of a 44D-cup bra.

Then there was the unknown beauty who accompanied him to the New York nightspot MKs, the evening Stewart ran up a $350 champagne bill and reportedly left a $4 tip. The waiter supposedly threw the desultory offering to the floor in disgust.

Next in the spotlight, accompanying Stewart to a cancer research benefit in Boston, was model Tami Koaller, although she admitted that any relationship with Stewart wasn't likely to last long. "I'm twenty-six," she confessed. "He thought I was nineteen."

Once again, Stewart's office poured out the usual string of denials and excuses. Dating beautiful young strangers was all part of being a rock'n'roll star, they said. Kelly was at home with baby Ruby, and their client was simply enjoying these bright young things for their charming company. Stewart had a lot of important functions to attend. No one could expect him to attend on his own.

To emphasise further Stewart's innocence, they leaked a story about his recent lunch at the Sherry Netherlands Quaglino's restaurant. He took a window seat, ordered a Bellini, then asked bartender Harry Mendiburo to round up some ladies for him. "He told me he wanted only beautiful girls to come join him," Mendiburo revealed. "He got about five girls to come, in off the street, but all he did was smile at them."

Such innocence in the face of temptation! When Stewart said he had turned over a new leaf, even his harshest critics were beginning to believe him, beginning to believe that behind the glitz and glamor, behind the raucous living and rock'n'roll lifestyle, there really did beat a true heart.

"I think people expect me to be a little flamboyant," Stewart mused. "I can't close down shop altogether and just be humble little Rod. But these days when I do shake my butt, people realise I'm just doing it for a laugh. Even Bruce Springsteen shakes his butt."

Arnold Stiefel continued, "Rod had a terrible image problem. His image became this glitzy guy with Britt Ekland and beautiful blonde girls who wore fabulous things and drove fabulous cars. It was nothing inside of life. It was outside of life."

In a long heart-to-heart, shortly after he replaced Billy Gaff as Stewart's manager, Stiefel revealed that he had told Rod it would take "four to six years to sort of rebuild himself, without ever admitting to the world that there was any rebuilding to be done." By 1989, that process had been completed. "Lost in You", the first single from *Out of Order*, was the final piece of the jigsaw, as Stiefel explains.

"There was never any question that 'Forever Young' and 'My Heart Can't Tell You No' would be giant hits, but it was important that the first single be a song that could be played on Adult Oriented Rock radio." "Lost in You" perfectly fit those requirements.

Manager Randy Phillips continues, "I think people are rediscovering what they liked about Rod in the old days – things that were obscured with some of the disco and more Top Forty stuff he did."

Finally, in 1989, Kelly decided she'd had enough. Eight years of Stewart's dalliances, the rollercoaster separation and reunions, plus the painful reality that he would never marry her, took their painful, frustrating toll. She packed her bags and moved out, reportedly into the arms of a more attentive lover.

According to Stewart, this marked the first time he hadn't been the one to break off an affair. "I've always been the one who leaves in every relationship," he once boasted. "I've never been hurt in love, I've been the one to push and shove and say 'Sorry, that's it, darlin', it's all over, goodbye.' I've been very lucky, but I know that one day I'm going to get fucking stung something terrible."

That day, it appeared, had finally arrived. However, with a track record like his, Stewart didn't pine for long. By the summer of 1990, he once again plucked another long, leggy blonde off the top shelf of the world's great beauties. Of New Zealand model Rachel Hunter he boldly declared, "This bird has given me a deep and meaningful relationship. For the first time in my life I would see my cock cut off before being unfaithful to this woman."

The twenty-one-year-old Hunter, perhaps too young to know better, nonetheless seemed unfazed by the parade of kiss-and-tell tabloid stories regarding her husband's infidelities. "I don't really care what's happened in his past," she shrugged. "Those girls can all say what they like, but I don't give a damn. There's a quote I really like which goes, 'The past is the past, the future is what we've got together', and that sums up the way I feel."

Following eighteen months of wedded bliss, Rachel presented Rod with his third child whom they named Renee on 1 June, 1992. While the delivery was a brief and easy one, the expectant father, present for the entire labor, was a tumbleweed of nervous energy, dashing from one side of the bed to the other, dressed in a medical gown and surgical mask.

"He kept kissing me as well," smiles Rachel, "all over, anywhere, everywhere, telling me not to worry and that everything was going to be fine. Which was hilarious because that's what I kept saying to him!"

Stewart alerted the entire maternity ward at London's Portland Hospital to the new arrival by singing lustily even as his child was being born. As he explained, "Rachel and I travel everywhere together so Renee has actually been to every one of my gigs for the past nine months. She's been listening to me singing from *inside* Rachel's tummy so singing to her the minute she came into the world seemed the most sensible way to help her get her bearings."

Settling the newborn into the couple's country retreat in Epping gave Stewart the opportunity to demonstrate his new vow of family commitment. He promptly became the very picture of a devoted husband and father, cuddling the infant in bed, taking her on long walks in the park, even changing the occasional nappy.

"I'm besotted with my wife and daughter," he sighed. "All I do is follow them around. I haven't even thought about football lately, which gives you an idea how wrapped up in them I am."

For Stewart, it was vital that Renee be born on English soil so she could have a British passport and grow up with a proper London accent, as well as get to know her family heritage. Within twenty-four hours, the entire Stewart and Hunter clans had gathered, including Rachel's mom Janine who made the day-long journey from New Zealand despite recovering from a serious stomach operation.

The only note of sadness was the absence of Rod's beloved father Bob, who passed away while he and Rachel were first dating. "I wish he was around to see her," says Stewart wistfully. "He'd have gone crazy over her."

London ties notwithstanding, early in 1993 the couple moved into their newly built Beverly Hills estate which Rachel helped decorate. "It's big and private, behind huge gates and a wall," she says. "It's got its own four-acre park so I'll be able to say to Renee, 'Okay, you can go out and play in the park without worrying about the dangers that go on in the streets of LA.'"

To the envy of women everywhere, Rachel sprang back to her hourglass model's figure within three months of the birth, just in time to shoot her own pin-up calendar as well as headlining an MTV fitness video. For the international supermodel – who commands upwards of $10,000 per hour – bristles at being perceived as a mere window-dressing draped on the arm of a famous man. "Models have been shunned for so many years as being dumb and stupid. Real models don't spend their nights partying in nightclubs, hanging out with playboys or taking drugs. We are hard-working girls who usually start work at 6.00 a.m. and have to be fit and alert because of all the traveling that's involved."

Casting a giant shadow over this idyllic domestic bliss came a rash of troubles over the stormy winter of 1992/93. Stewart's recurrent throat ailments erupted again. On a visit to the UK the effects of steroid therapy caused his throat to swell. "Steroids took my voice down," he revealed. "It made me fat around the face and took seven or eight months to get it out of my body. It didn't make me sing better, but it made me able to sing."

However, the effects were clearly evident on Stewart's 1993 release, ironically entitled *Lead Vocalist*. Despite the herculean efforts of producer

Trevor Horn, who made Holly Johnson of Frankie Goes to Hollywood sound downright macho, Stewart's vocals came across as lackluster and even frail. Nevertheless, Rod scored a Top Ten hit in the British charts with his version of Tom Waits' "Tom Traubert's Blues".

His weakened voice was so evident that critics universally panned the twelve-track album of less than sterling cover versions of the Stones' "Ruby Tuesday" and Rod's own "I Ain't Superstitious" as well as a shaky remake of the Faces' "Stay with Me".

There were no plans for Stewart to go out on the road in 1993, lending credence to the rumors that the plagued vocalist could no longer secure insurance for his tours. Faced with the prospect of having to cover costs himself, failure to turn up for a show would cause enormous pain to those famously sensitive pockets.

Throat problems weren't the only worries plaguing the reluctant rock star. Back into the picture stormed Kelly Emberg, a scorned woman out to exercise California's generous palimony settlements. Eventually, the Los Angeles court ordered Stewart to pay ten million pounds to his former live-in. This exorbitant sum, on top of the £7,400 in monthly child-support payments and $15,000 a month to Alana and their two children, had Rod fuming. "I don't mind supporting Ruby," he cried, "but I'll be damned if I'm going to keep Kelly in luxury!"

Although Stewart's fortune is estimated at over one hundred million pounds, Rod-watchers couldn't help but wonder if he was scrambling to drum up ready cash by auctioning off his Lamborghini Countach QV. Stewart purchased the supercar in 1989 at the height of the booming prestige-car market. He paid a whopping £135,000, nearly three times its worth, and a devastated Rod took a shattering £90,000 loss on his investment.

In December, while participating in a soccer charity match in Glasgow, Stewart suffered severe cartilage damage to his knee. Doctors in Britain pronounced it so devastating that not only would he never play football again, but they blatantly told the performer to forget about doing any more live shows. "They made it sound like it was what Paul Gascoigne had," charged an outraged Rod. "They wanted to take me in and fucking tear me open."

Fortunately, Stewart returned to the States for a second opinion. He underwent a less extensive operation in January and was back on the football field, albeit gingerly, by March.

If the winter of 1992 was one of discontent to Rod, then spring found the rocker emerging stronger than ever, marching back to back milestones. The first occurred on 16 February with the Lifetime Achievement Award at the annual Brit Awards, a £500,000 bash held at London's Alexandra Palace. Accepting the prestigious honor from Long John

Baldry, Stewart addressed the crowd. "When I started out at nineteen I made myself three promises: to stay in a job for more than six months, to save three hundred pounds to buy a sports car, and to pull as many birds as I could. All those dreams have come wonderfully true!"

Following an emotional performance of his latest single, "Ruby Tuesday", Rod had a surprise in store for the star-studded audience. Announcing, "I'd like to thank the Faces for doing their best to ruin my liver!", he then proceeded to bring on his old mates Ian MacLagan, Ronnie Wood and Kenney Jones, plus Bill Wyman to fill in for the wheelchair-bound Ronnie Lane. As the stunned and delighted audience applauded, the reunited band launched into a raw, throbbing rendition of their first mega-hit, "Stay with Me", easily the show-stealer of the night.

On the heels of that heady festivity, Stewart headed back to LA to become the latest in line of rock's élite, including Paul McCartney and Eric Clapton, to headline MTV's acclaimed "Unplugged". The ninety-minute all-acoustic special featured the added attraction of accompanying guitarist Ron Wood.

Taking the stage in an electric-blue suit and backed by an eleven-piece band – steel guitar, mandolins and violins plus a Hammond organ – Stewart proceeded to tackle a generation's worth of music, drawing heavily on Faces' material as well as his own early solo hits from *Every Picture Tells a Story* and *Gasoline Alley*.

Almost as entertaining as the songs themselves was the amusing, unforced dialogue between two heel-worn friends. Both joked about becoming rock relics donning glasses simultaneously to peruse the set list and reminisced about the old days. "Remember," Stewart quipped, "when Mickey Waller would turn up at the recording studio with his dog!"

"But never his drum kit," Woody grinned.

This was Rod, grabbing the reins of the elder statesman, finally all grown up. Any doubt as to his sincerity was quickly put to rest when he paid touching tribute to Ronnie Lane, now badly deteriorated from his long haul with MS. It was a moment so poignant and candid it seemed to hang over the hushed audience, becoming a lasting memory in the thickly emotional evening.

In the immediate afterglow of the MTV triumph, Stewart himself was caught up in the nostalgia. "The love people have for my early work, those records definitely meant a lot more to me than some of the more recent stuff like *Camouflage*. That's the magical connection between Woody and me. We would just go in and hum something and it would turn into a song. I've tried writing with other people like that, but it just doesn't work.

"The Faces were just a poor man's Rolling Stones when we started out. We never admitted it, of course, just as the Black Crowes would never admit they copy us. The Crowes' singer the other night had an identical jacket Woody had in 1970, with big feathers on it. I like them, though, they're a loose band, always on the edge, just like we were. The singer's a little arsehole, but he'll grow out of that.

"Just like us, Woody and me. We've changed a bit in the twenty-two years but our humor's still intact. We've been very successful, of course, made lots of money, got married, had kids, all those things change you."

Ever the optimist, Stewart points to three albums due for release in 1993 and excitedly talks about spending a month in Ireland to record his next project. Despite his recurrent throat ailments, claims a buoyant Rod, "My voice has never sounded better. I know I'm a better singer today. Most people don't realise I've had to work at what they call my so-called gravelly voice. It's amazing how high I sing. In fact, some of the things I was singing in the seventies are a bit too low for me now, like 'Maggie May'. I've still got a long way to go, I haven't yet made the definitive Rod Stewart record. I think I've got better albums to come."

Stewart looks back on his first two decades with reflective stoicism. "I don't get sentimental over the old days. The past is the past. I'm not one to look back. I'm just so pleased I've come through all this. How can I complain about life? It's been far too good to me."

Some of the women . . . some of the records. "There was a falling off for a while – after *Footloose and Fancy Free*. The records still sold well, but they were fairly shallow. I still haven't made what I consider the classic album, for me anyway. The nearest would be perhaps *Every Picture Tells a Story*. That came close. And *Out of Order* pretty close, but there's still some flaws on it. It's possible to make an album that totally satisfies you ten years down the line.

"This whole business of 'He's not what he used to be' they say about a lot of artists. They don't realise that everything can't be 'Maggie May' because it's twenty years later. I'm not sure I could even write another 'Maggie May'." He was, he says, twenty-four or twenty-five then. Now he's pushing fifty. "It's like asking why Dylan doesn't do 'Blonde on Blonde' again. Because he's not the same person, that's why. And I'm not the same person."

Who is he, then? When Rod Stewart runs into the people his career has driven him to leave far behind, what do they find?

"Rod's turned into everything I thought he would," laughs Brian Auger, today working in a new group with Animal Eric Burdon. "The last time I saw him was around 1976. My band, Oblivion Express, was opening for him at the University of Maryland. I brought a copy of my current album with me, signed it 'God bless you Rod', and left it in the band room. He never even bothered to come over and say anything to me. I thought that was about par for the course."

Pete Bardens, who invited Stewart into Shotgun Express and later went on to notoriety with Camel, continues, "I don't think any of us stayed that close to Rod. I met him at the Speakeasy during the seventies, and he was very off-ish, very off-hand. I felt he was looking down his nose at me."

Dave Ambrose, bassist in that band, recollects that he got the same treatment when he bumped into Rod.

Wizz Jones, the arch-busker who is still fending off reporters demanding to know about his early days with Rod the Mod, insists that the last time he saw the singer it was to ask him to stop mentioning him in interviews. "Stop giving me all this publicity! I don't want to become famous!"

Of the Faces, only Woody is still in regular contact with Stewart. There is, in fact, just one person from his now distant past with whom Rod retains a constant relationship – and that is the man who arguably started it all for him, Long John Baldry.

Now living in Canada, still making records but branching out into television work as well, Baldry says, simply, "I still see Rod quite constantly. I was down at his wedding and various other functions in Los Angeles. He's still great fun to be around."

"You have to admire what he's done," Dee Harrington says. "Sometimes it seems as though half of his career has been based on changing his women, but the other half on his music, and that is what Rod should be judged upon; and judged very highly."

But does he have any dreams left? Is there any one thing Rod Stewart hasn't done that he desperately wishes he had? Strangely enough, there is. After all the women and the awards, all the records and all the tours, there is just one thing which Stewart still dreams about.

In this dream, he is no longer Rod the father, Rod the rocker, Rod the superpop tart, or even Rod the Mod. He is a middle-aged man taking the field with the all-star Goaldiggers, a charity soccer team he has played for throughout much of his career. He is that teenaged apprentice at Brentford FC, chipping the mud off the professionals' boots, and dreaming of the day when he too will be out on the field, making passes, scoring goals, and collecting the honors. He is the skinny, grinning schoolboy cutting pictures of footballers out of the newspapers and fixing them on his bedroom wall.

Leaving his seat, Rod picks up the tartan tammy he was given after representing a Scottish Select team in a veterans' charity match in 1975 ("The Day Superscot Rod Got His First Cap!" bellowed the *Daily Mail* the following morning). He turns it over in his hands, and standing there surrounded by a quarter of a century's worth of rock'n'roll memorabilia, his smile will tell you that this, a simple, single cap, means more to him than anything.

England are playing Scotland at Hampden Park in Glasgow. There are thirty seconds left to play, and the scores are tied, 1–1. The English are playing it safe and tight, kicking the ball back and forth in the center of the field, just waiting for the whistle.

Suddenly Johnny White, dead thirty years (but this is Rod's dream after all), tears down the right wing and crosses the ball into the England goal area.

There is a sudden melee of blue Scottish shirts. Denis Law is there, rising to meet the ball with his head. And then from nowhere, another blue shirt, topped by a wild shag of mousy-blond hair, rockets into view.

Throwing himself forward, his head connects perfectly with the ball – and bang! The ball smashes into the back of the England net. The game ends, Scotland have won.

"That's me up there scoring that goal," Stewart says wistfully. "I tell you, I'd give up everything I've got for just that one moment."

He pauses, and takes stock of all he is throwing to the winds. Then he smiles, and shakes his head. The dream is over.

"Well, almost everything."

Rod Stewart Discography

Compiled by Geoffrey Giuliano, Brenda Giuliano, Dave Thompson and Joanne Thompson

SINGLES

With Long John Baldry
Up Above My Head/You'll Be Mine (UK) UP 1056 (1964)

With Shotgun Express
* denotes no Stewart involvement
I Could Feel the Whole World Turn Round/Curtains (UK) Columbia DB 8025 (10/66)
I Could Feel the Whole World Turn Round/Curtains (US) Uptown 747 (10/66)
I Could Feel the Whole World Turn Round/Curtains/Funny Cos Neither Could I*/Indian Thing* (UK) See for Miles CYM 2 (6/83)

With the Jeff Beck Group
* denotes no Stewart involvement
Tallyman*/Rock My Plimsoul (UK) Columbia DB 8227 (8/67)
Tallyman*/Rock My Plimsoul (US) Epic 10218 (8/67)
Love Is Blue*/I've Been Drinking (UK) Columbia DB 8359 (3/68)
Jailhouse Rock/Plynth (US) Epic 10484 (3/69)
Hi Ho Silver Lining*/Beck's Bolero*/Rock My Plimsoul (UK) RAK RR3 (11/72)
I've Been Drinking/Morning Dew/Greensleeves* (UK) RAK RR4 (4/73)

With Python Lee Jackson
* denotes no Stewart involvement
In a Broken Dream/Doing Fine* (UK) Youngblood YB 1002 (1970)
In a Broken Dream/Doin' Fine* (US) GNP/Crescendo 449 (1972)
Cloud Nine*/Stewart's Blues (US) GNP/Crescendo 462 (1973)
In a Broken Dream/The Blues 12" single + Cloud 9* (UK) Youngblood 1289 (7/80)
In a Broken Dream/The Blues 12" single + Cloud 9* (UK) Bold Reprieve 004 (8/87)

With Ted Wood
Am I Blue? (UK) Penny Farthing (1973)

233

With the Faces
* Rod Stewart solo
** credited to Rod Stewart only
*** recorded live
**** credited to Rod Stewart and the Faces
Around the Plynth/? (US) WB 7393 (1970)
Flying/Three Button Hand Me Down (UK) WB 8005 (1970)
Had Me a Real Good Time/Rear Wheel Skid (US) WB 7442 (1970)
Had Me a Real Good Time/Rear Wheel Skid (UK) WB 8018 (1970)
Maybe I'm Amazed/Oh Lord I'm Browned Off (US) WB 7483 (1971)
I Know I'm Losing You/Mandolin Wind* (US) Mercury 83244** (11/71)
Stay with Me/Debris (UK) WB K16136 (1/72)
Stay with Me/You're So Rude (US) WB 7545 (1/72)
Cindy Incidentally/Skewiff (UK) WB K16247 (3/73)
Cindy Incidentally/Skewiff (US) WB 7681 (3/73)
Dishevelment Blues (UK) NME flexidisc (11/73)
Ooh La La/Borstal Boys (US) WB 7711 (2/74)
Poolhall Richard/I Wish It Would Rain*** (UK) WB K16341 (11/74)
Cindy Incidentally/Memphis/Stay with Me/Poolhall Richard (UK) WB K16406 (1974)
Dance, Sing or Anything/As Long as You Tell Him (UK) WB K16494*** (11/74)
Dance, Sing or Anything/As Long as You Tell Him (US) WB 8102*** (11/74)
Cindy Incidentally/Memphis/Stay with Me/Poolhall Richard (UK) Riva 8 (7/77)

As the Atlantic Crossing Drum and Pipe Band
Skye Boat Song/Instrumental (UK) Riva 2 (1/76)

With the Scotland World Cup Squad
Ole Ola/I'd Walk a Million Miles (UK) Riva 15 (5/78)
Ole Ola/My Mammy/Que Sera (US) WB 17181 (5/78)

With Jeff Beck
* denotes no Stewart involvement
People Get Ready/Back on the Street* 12" single + You Know We Know* (UK) Epic A 6387 (6/85)
People Get Ready/Back on the Street* (US) Epic 05416 (6/85)

Rod Stewart
* denotes reissue
** denotes withdrawn from release
*** denotes live recording
Good Morning Little Schoolgirl/I'm Gonna Move to the Outskirts of Town (UK) Decca F11996 (10/64)
Good Morning Little Schoolgirl/I'm Gonna Move to the Outskirts of Town (US) Press 9722 (10/64)
The Day Will Come/Why Does It Go On? (UK) Columbia DB 7766 (11/65)
Shake/I Just Got Some (UK) Columbia DB 7892 (4/66)
Little Miss Understood/So Much to Say (UK) Immediate IM 060 (4/66)
An Old Raincoat Won't Ever Let You Down/Handbags and Gladrags (US) Mercury 73009 (1970)
Handbags and Gladrags/Man of Constant Sorrow (US) Mercury 73031 (1970)
It's All Over Now/Jo's Lament (UK) Vertigo 6086 002 (9/70)
Only a Hobo/? (US) Mercury 73115 (1970)

Gasoline Alley/Cut Across Shorty (US) Mercury 73156 (1970)
My Way of Giving/Dirty Old Town (US) Mercury 73175 (1971)
Country Comfort/Gasoline Alley (US) Mercury 73196 (7/71)
Reason to Believe/Maggie May (UK) Mercury 6052 097 (7/71)
Maggie May/Reason to Believe (UK) Mercury 6052 097 (8/71)
Maggie May/Reason to Believe (US) Mercury 73224 (7/71)
Pinball Wizard (US) Ode EP-10 (3/72)
You Wear It Well/Los Paraguayos (UK) Mercury 6052 171 (8/72)
You Wear It Well/True Blue (US) Mercury 73330 (8/72)
Maggie May/I Know I'm Losing You (US) Mercury 30157 (1972)
Angel/What Made Milwaukee Famous (UK) Mercury 6052 198 (11/72)
Angel/Los Paraguayos (US) Mercury 73344 (11/72)
Shake/Runaway (US) Pride 1006* (1972)
Twisting the Night Away/True Blue/Lady Day (US) Mercury 73412 (1973)
Oh No Not My Baby/Jodie (UK) Mercury 6052 371 (8/73)
Oh No Not My Baby/Jodie (US) Mercury 73426 (8/73)
Farewell/Bring It On Home to Me/You Send Me (UK) Mercury 61667 033 (9/74)
Farewell/Mine for Me (US) Mercury 73636 (1974)
Sailor/Let Me Be Your Car (US) Mercury 73660 (1974)
Sailing/Stone Cold Sober (UK) WB K16600 (8/75)
Sailing/All in the Name of Rock'n'Roll (US) WB 8146 (8/75)
This Old Heart of Mine/All in the Name of Rock'n'Roll (UK) Riva 1 (11/75)
This Old Heart of Mine/Still Love You (US) WB 8170 (1/76)
It's All Over Now/Handbags and Gladrags (UK) Mercury 6167 327* (2/76)
Tonight's the Night/First Cut Is the Deepest (UK) Riva 3** (5/76)
Tonight's the Night/The Ball Trap (UK) Riva 3 (5/76)
Tonight's the Night/Fool for You (US) WB 8262 (5/76)
Killing of Georgie/Fool for You (UK) Riva 4 (8/76)
Get Back/Trade Winds (UK) Riva 6 (11/76)
Maggie May/You Wear It Well/Twisting the Night Away (UK) Mercury 6160 006* (11/76)
What Made Milwaukee Famous (US) Mercury 73802* (11/76)
First Cut Is the Deepest/Rosie (US) WB 8321 (2/77)
First Cut Is the Deepest/The Ball Trap (US) WB 8321 (2/77)
First Cut Is the Deepest/I Don't Want to Talk about It (UK) Riva 7 (4/77)
Killing of Georgie/Rosie (US) WB 8396 (6/77)
Mandolin Wind/Girl from the North Country/Sweet Little Rock'n'Roller (UK) Mercury 6160 007* (6/77)
Sailing/Stone Cold Sober (UK) Riva 9* (6/77)
You're in My Heart/You Got a Nerve (US) WB 8475 (10/77)
You're in My Heart/You Got a Nerve (UK) Riva 11 (10/77)
First Cut Is the Deepest/Tonight's the Night (US) WB 349* (1977)
Hot Legs/I Was Only Joking (UK) Riva 10 (1/78)
Hot Legs/You're Insane (US) WB 8535 (2/78)
I Was Only Joking/Born Loose (US) WB 8568 (4/78)
Do Ya Think I'm Sexy?/Dirty Weekend (UK) Riva 17 (11/78)
Do Ya Think I'm Sexy?/Scarred and Scared (US) WB 8724 (11/78)
Ain't Love a Bitch/Scarred and Scared (UK) Riva 18 (1/79)
Ain't Love a Bitch/Last Summer (US) WB 8810 (3/79)
Best Days of My Life/Blondes Have More Fun (UK) Riva 19 (4/79)
I Don't Walk to Talk About It/Best Days of My Life (US) WB 49138* (11/79)

Maggie May/You Wear It Well (UK) Mercury 6160 006* (11/79)
Ain't Love a Bitch/Do Ya Think I'm Sexy? (US) WB 382* (1979)
If Loving You Is Wrong/Last Summer (UK) Riva 23 (5/80)
Little Miss Understood/So Much to Say (UK) Virgin VS 366* (9/80)
Passion/Better Off Dead (UK) Riva 26 (11/80)
Passion/Better Off Dead (US) WB 49617 (11/80)
My Girl/She Won't Dance with Me (UK) Riva 28 (12/80)
Oh God I Wish I Was Home Tonight/Somebody Special (UK) Riva 29 (3/81)
Somebody Special (US) WB 49686 (3/81)
Tonight I'm Yours/Sonny (UK) Riva 33 (10/81)
Young Turks/Sonny (US) WB 49843 (10/81)
Young Turks/Tora Tora Tora (UK) Riva 34 (12/81)
Passion/Somebody Special (US) WB 404* (1981)
Tonight I'm Yours (US) WB 49886 (12/81)
Tonight I'm Yours/Young Turks (US) WB 427* (1982)
How Long/Jealous (UK) Riva 35 (2/82)
How Long/Jealous (US) WB 50051 (4/82)
Good Morning Little Schoolgirl/I'm Gonna Move to the Outskirts of Town
(UK) Decca F11996* (3/82)
Guess I'll Always Love You (US) WB 7-29874 (10/82)
Little Miss Understood/So Much to Say (UK) Immediate IM 060* (2/83)
Baby Jane/Ready Now (UK) WB W9608 (5/83)
Baby Jane/Ready Now (US) WB 29608 (5/83)
What Am I Gonna Do?/Dancin' Alone 12" single + Sailing*** (UK) WB W9564
(8/83)
What Am I Gonna Do? (US) WB 29564 (8/83)
Sweet Surrender/Ghetto Blaster 12" single + Oh God I Wish . . . (UK)
WB W9440 (11/83)
Sailing/Stone Cold Sober (UK) WB K16600* (1/84)
Infatuation/Tonight's the Night 12" single + 3 Time Loser (UK) WB W9256
(5/84)
Infatuation/She Won't Dance (US) WB 29526 (5/84)
Infatuation (one-sided picture disc) (UK) WB SAM 194 (6/84)
Some Guys Have All the Luck/I Was Only Joking 12" single + Killing of Georgie
(UK) WB W9204 (7/84)
Some Guys Have All The Luck (US) WB 29215 (7/84)
Maggie May/Reason to Believe (UK) Mercury CUT 201* (10/84)
Trouble/Tora Tora Tora 12" single + This Old Heart of Mine (UK) WB W9115
(11/84)
Alright Now (US) WB 29122 (11/84)
Love Touch/Heart Is on the Line 12" single + Hard Lesson to Learn (UK)
WB W8668 (5/86)
Love Touch/Heart Is on the Line (US) WB 28668 (5/86)
Every Beat of my Heart/Trouble 12" single + Some Guys Get All The Luck***
(UK) WB W8625 (8/86)
Another Heartache (US) WB 28631 (8/86)
Another Heartache/You're in My Heart 12" single + You're in My Heart***
(UK) WB W8631 (9/86)
Every Beat of My Heart (US) WB 28625 (11/86)
Sailing/Stone Cold Sober (UK) WB K16600 (3/87)
Twistin' the Night Away (US) Geffen 28303 (7/87)

Twistin' the Night Away/Let's Get Small (UK) Geffen RODS 1 (10/87)
Maggie May/You Wear It Well (UK) Old Gold 9765* (4/88)
Lost in You/Almost Illegal CD + Baby Jane/Every Beat of My Heart (UK) WB W152 (5/88)
Lost in You/Almost Illegal (US) WB 27927 (4/88)
Forever Young/Days of Rage/Forever Young (remix) CD + Every Beat of my Heart (UK) WB W7796 (7/88)
Forever Young/Days of Rage (US) WB 27796 (7/88)
My Heart Can't Tell You No/Wild Horses (US) WB 27729 (11/88)
My Heart Can't Tell You No/Wild Horses (UK) WB W7729 (11/88)
Lost in You/Forever Young (US) WB 21884* (1/89)
Crazy about Her (remix)/Dynamite (US) WB 27657 (4/89)
Crazy about Her (remix)/Dynamite (UK) WB W7657 (4/89)
Crazy about Her (four remixes)/Dynamite (US) WB 22268 (6/89)
Downtown Train/Killing of Georgie (US) WB 22685 (11/89)
Downtown Train/Killing of Georgie (UK) WB W2685 (11/89)
This Old Heart of Mine/You're in My Heart (US) WB 19983 (2/90)
It Takes Two/? (UK) WB (3/90)
My Heart Can't Tell You No/Crazy about Her (US) WB 21865* (4/90)
Rhythm of My Heart/Moment of Glory (US) WB 19366 (3/91)
Rhythm of My Heart (UK) WB W9366 (3/91)
The Motown Song/Sweet Soul Music*** (US) WB 19322 (6/90)
The Motown Song/Sweet Soul Music*** (UK) WB W9322 (6/90)
Broken Arrow/The Wild Horse (US) WB 19274 (9/90)
Broken Arrow/I Was Only Joking 12" + Killing of Georgie (UK) WB W9274 (9/90)
Tom Traubert's Blues/No Holding Back (UK) WB 18643 (92)
Shotgun Wedding/Sweet Soul Music (UK) WB 18508 (93)
Ruby Tuesday/Stay With Me (Faces) (UK) WB 18559 (93)

ALBUMS

With Steampacket
(all Steampacket releases are compilations)

ROCK GENERATION VOLUME SIX: includes Can I Get a Witness?
(France) BYG 529 706 (1971)

ROD STEWART AND STEAMPACKET: Can I Get a Witness?/The In Crowd/ Baby Take Me/Baby Baby/Back at the Chicken Shack/Cry Me a River/Oh Baby/ Don't You Do It/Holy Smoke/Lord Remember Me
(US) Springboard SPB 4063 (1973)

FIRST OF THE SUPERGROUPS: reissue of above.
(UK) Charley 30020 (1977)

With Jeff Beck
* denotes no Stewart involvement
** credited to Jeff Beck Group
*** compilation
**** credited to Jeff Beck and Rod Stewart

TRUTH: Shapes of Things/Let Me Love You/Morning Dew/You Shook Me/Ol' Man River/Greensleeves*/Rock My Plimsoul/Beck's Bolero*/Blues DeLuxe/Ain't Superstitious

(US) Epic PE26413 (8/67)/(UK) Columbia SCX 6293 (10/67)

COSA NOSTRA BECK-OLA**: All Shook Up/Spanish Boots/Girl from Mill
Valley*/Jailhouse Rock/Plynth/The Hangman's Knee/Rice Pudding*
(US) Epic 26478 (3/69)/(UK) Columbia SCX 6351 (3/69)

THE MOST OF JEFF BECK: reissue of Cosa Nostra Beck-Ola
(UK) Music For Pleasure MFP 5219 (1971)

FLASH: includes People Get Ready****
(US) Epic (1985)/(UK) Epic (1985)

THE LATE 60s WITH ROD STEWART***: Hi Ho Silver Lining*/Tallyman*/Love
Is Blue*/Beck's Bolero*/Rock My Plimsoul/I've Been Drinking/Shape of Things/
Let Me Love You/Morning Dew/You Shook Me/All Shook Up/Spanish Boots/
Jailhouse Rock/Plynth/Hangman's Knee/Rice Pudding*/Ol' Man River/
Greensleeves*/Ain't Superstitious
(UK) EMI CDP 7467102 (1988)

BECKOLOGY***: includes Shape of Things/Ain't Superstitious/Rock My
Plimsoul/Jailhouse Rock/Plynth/I've Been Drinking (all **)/People Get Ready****
(US) Epic E3K 48661 (1991)

With Aynsley Dunbar's Retaliation

THE STORY OF BRITISH BLUES: includes Stone Crazy
(US) Sire SAS 3701 (1973)

With the GTOs

PERMANENT DAMAGE: includes Shock Treatment
(US) Straight RS 6390 (11/69)/(UK) Straight STS 1059 (4/70)

With Long John Baldry

EVERYTHING STOPS FOR TEA: includes Mother Ain't Dead
(UK) WB K46160 (3/72)

With Python Lee Jackson

IN A BROKEN DREAM: includes In A Broken Dream/Stewart's Blues
(US) GNP/Crescendo 2066 (1974)/(UK) Youngblood 3001 (1973)

With Ronnie Wood

I'VE GOT MY OWN ALBUM TO DO: includes Mystifies Me/Take a Look at
the Guy/If You Gotta Make a Fool of Somebody
(US) WB 2819 (10/74)/(UK) WB K56065 (10/74)

The Faces
* compilation
** recorded live
*** credited to Rod Stewart and the Faces

FIRST STEP: Wicked Messenger/Devotion/Shake Shudder Shiver/Stone/
Around the Plynth/Flying/Pineapple and the Monkey/Nobody Knows/Looking
out the Window/Three Button Hand Me Down
(US) WB 1851 (1970)/(UK) WB 3000 (1970)

LONG PLAYER: Bad'n'Ruin/Tell Everyone/Sweet Lady Mary/Richmond/
Maybe I'm Amazed/Had Me a Real Good Time/On the Beach/I Feel So Good/
Jerusalem
(US) WB 1892 (1971)/(UK) WB 3011 (1971)

A NOD'S AS GOOD AS A WINK: Miss Judy's Farm/You're So Rude/Love Lived Here/Last Orders Please/Stay with Me/Debris/Memphis/Too Bad/That's All You Need
(US) WB 2574 (1972)/(UK) WB K56006 (1972)

OOH LA LA: Silicone Growth/Cindy Incidentally/Flags and Banners/My Fault/Borstal Boys/Fly in the Ointment/If I'm on the Late Side/Glad and Sorry/Just Another Honky/Ooh La La
(US) WB 2665 (1973)/(UK) WB K56011 (1973)

COAST TO COAST – OVERTURE AND BEGINNERS**/***: It's All Over Now/Cut Across Shorty/Too Bad/Every Picture Tells a Story/Angel/Stay with Me/I Wish It Would Rain/I'd Rather Go Blind/Borstal Boys/Amazing Grace
(US) Mercury SRM-1 697 (1/74)/(UK) Mercury 9100 011 (1/74)

READING FESTIVAL 1973: includes (I Know) I'm Losing You**
(UK) GM GML 1008 (1974)

ROD STEWART AND THE FACES*: includes no Faces' material (see under Rod Stewart for further details)
(US) Springboard SPB 4030 (1975)

TWO ORIGINALS OF THE FACES: reissue of FIRST STEP/LONG PLAYER
(UK) WB K66027 (1/76)

SNAKES & LADDERS*: Around the Plynth/Pineapple and the Monkey/Sweet Lady Mary/Stay with Me/Cindy Incidentally/Had Me a Real Good Time/Miss Judy's Farm/Silicone Growth/Poolhall Richard/You Can Make Me Dance
(US) WB 2897 (1976)/(UK) WB K56172 (1976)

THE BEST OF THE FACES*: Around the Plynth/Flying/Nobody Knows/Three Button Hand Me Down/Sweet Lady Mary/Maybe I'm Amazed/Stay with Me/Cindy Incidentally/Had Me a Real Good Time/Miss Judy's Farm/Memphis/Too Bad/That's All You Need/Flags and Banners/Borstal Boys/I Wish It Would Rain**/Poolhall Richard/You Can Make Me Dance Sing or Anything
(UK) Riva RVLP 3

FIRST STEP/LONG PLAYER: reissue of TWO ORIGINALS OF THE FACES
(UK) WB K66027

FACES FEATURING ROD STEWART*: Cindy Incidentally/On the Beach/Glad and Sorry/Maybe I'm Amazed/Shake Shudder Shiver/I Feel So Good/I'm on the Late Side/Three Button Hand Me Down/Ooh La La/Looking out the Window/Devotion/Had Me a Real Good Time
(UK) Pickwick SSP 3074 (9/80)

Rod Stewart
* compilation
** recorded live
*** duet with Denis Law
**** with Tina Turner/Kim Carnes
***** with Tina Turner
****** with Ronnie Isley

THE ROD STEWART ALBUM – THIN: Street Fighting Man/Man of Constant Sorrow/Blind Prayer/Handbags and Gladrags/An Old Raincoat/I Wouldn't Ever Change a Thing/Cindy's Lament/Dirty Old Town
(US) Mercury SR6 1237 (10/69)

AN OLD RAINCOAT WON'T EVER LET YOU DOWN: as above

239

(UK) Vertigo VO4 (2/70)

GASOLINE ALLEY: Gasoline Alley/It's All Over Now/Only a Hobo/My Way of Giving/Country Comfort/Cut Across Shorty/Lady Day/Jo's Lament/I Don't Want to Discuss It
(US) Mercury SR61264 (9/70)/(UK) Vertigo 6360 500 (9/70)

EVERY PICTURE TELLS A STORY: Every Picture Tells a Story/Seems Like a Long Time/That's All Right/Tomorrow Is a Long Time/Maggie May/Mandolin Wind/(I Know) I'm Losing You/Reason to Believe
(US) Mercury SRM-1 609 (7/71)/(UK) Mercury 6338 063 (7/71)

NEVER A DULL MOMENT: True Blue/Los Paraguayos/Mama You Been on My Mind/Italian Girls/Angel/Interludings/You Wear It Well/I'd Rather Go Blind/ Twisting the Night Away
(US) Mercury SRM1 646 (7/72)/(UK) Mercury 6499 153 (7/72)

TOMMY – A ROCK OPERA: includes Pinball Wizard
(UK) Ode SP9901 (1972)

SING IT AGAIN ROD*: Reason to Believe/You Wear It Well/Mandolin Wind/ Country Comfort/Maggie May/Handbags and Gladrags/Street Fighting Man/ Twistin' the Night Away/Los Paraguayos/(I Know) I'm Losing You/Pinball Wizard/Gasoline Alley
(US) Mercury SRMI 680 (8/73)/(UK) Mercury 6499 484 (8/73)

SCOTLAND SCOTLAND: includes Angel***
(UK) Polydor 2383 282 (7/74)

SMILER: Sweet Little Rock'n'Roller/Lochinvar/Farewell/Sailor/Bring It On Home to Me/You Send Me/Let Me Be Your Car/A Natural Man/Dixie Toot/Hard Road/I've Grown Accustomed to Her Face/Girl from the North Country/Mine for Me
(US) Mercury SRM1 1017 (10/74)/(UK) Mercury 9104 001 (10/74)

ROD STEWART AND THE FACES*: includes Come Home Baby (remaining cuts by Small Faces)
(US) Springboard SPB 4030 (1975)

ATLANTIC CROSSING: Three Time Loser/Alright for an Hour/All in the Name of Rock'n'Roll/Drift Away/Stone Cold Sober/I Don't Want to Talk About It/It's Not the Spotlight/This Old Heart of Mine/Still Love You/Sailing
(US) WB 2875 (8/75)/(UK) WB K56151 (8/75)

THE VINTAGE YEARS 1969–70: reissue of AN OLD RAINCOAT/GASOLINE ALLEY
(UK) Mercury 6672 013 (2/76)

A NIGHT ON THE TOWN: The Ball Trap/Pretty Flamingo/Big Bayou/Wild Side of Life/Trade Winds/Tonight's the Night/First Cut Is the Deepest/Fool for You/Killing of Georgie Parts One and Two
(US) WB 3116 (6/76)/(UK) Riva RVLP 1 (6/76)

RECORDED HIGHLIGHTS AND ACTION REPLAYS*
(UK) Philips SON 001 (7/76)

A SHOT OF RHYTHM & BLUES*: Work Song/Ain't That Loving You Baby/ Mopper's Blues/Don't You Tell Nobody/She's a Heavy Heavy Momma/Just Like I Treat You/Bright Lights Big City
(US) Private Stock 2021 (1976)/(UK) Crystal 98198 (1976)

ALL OF THIS AND WORLD WAR TWO: includes Get Back

(UK) Riva RVLP 2 (11/76)

THE BEST OF ROD STEWART*: Angel/Cut Across Shorty/Every Picture Tells a Story/Gasoline Alley/Handbags and Gladrags/(I Know) I'm Losing You/It's All Over Now/Jodie/Let Me Be Your Car/Maggie May/Mine for Me/Oh No Not My Baby/An Old Raincoat/Pinball Wizard/Sailor/Street Fighting Man/What Made Milwaukee Famous
(US) Mercury SRM27507 (6/77)/(UK) Mercury 6643 030 (6/77)

ATLANTIC CROSSING: reissue
(UK) Riva RVLP 4 (7/77)

THE MUSIC OF ROD STEWART 1970–71*: Blind Prayer/Country Comfort/Cut Across Shorty/Every Picture Tells a Story/Gasoline Alley/Handbags and Gladrags/(I Know) I'm Losing You/Man of Constant Sorrow/Mandolin Wind/An Old Raincoat/Reason to Believe/Street Fighting Man
(UK) Mercury 7145 069 (7/77)

THE BEST OF ROD STEWART VOL. 2*
(US) Mercury SRM27509 (8/77)/(UK) Mercury 6619 031 (8/77)

FOOTLOOSE AND FANCY FREE: Hot Legs/You're Insane/You're in My Heart/Born Loose/You Keep Me Hanging On/(If Loving You Is Wrong) I Don't Want to Be Right/You Gotta Nerve/I Was Only Joking
(US) WB 3092 (11/77)/(UK) Riva RVLP 5 (11/77)

BLONDES HAVE MORE FUN: Do Ya Think I'm Sexy?/Dirty Weekend/Ain't Love a Bitch/The Best Days of my Life/Is That the Thanks I Get/Attractive Female Wanted/Blondes Have More Fun/Last Summer/Standing in the Shadows of Love/Scarred and Scared
(US) WB 3261 (11/78)/(UK) Riva RVLP 8 (11/78)

THE MUSIC FOR UNICEF CONCERT: includes Do Ya Think I'm Sexy?**
(UK) Polydor 2335 214 (1979)

GREATEST HITS VOLUME ONE*: First Cut Is the Deepest/I Was Only Joking/You're in My Heart/Tonight's the Night/Hot Legs/Killing of Georgie/Maggie May/Do Ya Think I'm Sexy?/Sailing/I Don't Want to Talk about It
(US) WB 3373 (11/79)/(UK) Riva StewartTV 1 (11/79)

HOT RODS*
(UK) Mercury 6463 061 (9/80)

FOOLISH BEHAVIOUR: Better Off Dead/Passion/Foolish Behaviour/So Soon We Change/Oh God I Wish I Was Home Tonight/Gimme Wings/My Girl/She Won't Dance with Me/Somebody Special/Say It Ain't True
(US) WB 3485 (11/80)/(UK) Riva RVLP 11 (11/80)

MAGGIE MAY*: Maggie May/Sailing/Oh No Not My Baby/Street Fighting Man/It's All Over Now/Mandolin Wind/Man of Constant Sorrow/Reason to Believe/Twisting the Night Away/Angel/Girl of the North Country/Sweet Little Rock'n'Roller
(UK) Pickwick CN 2045 (9/81)

TONIGHT I'M YOURS: Tonight I'm Yours/How Long/Tora Tora Tora/Tear It Up/Only a Boy/Just Like a Woman/Jealous/Sonny/Young Turks/Never Give Up on a Dream
(US) WB 3602 (11/81)/(UK) Riva RVLP 14 (11/81)

ROD STEWART*: You Wear It Well/Gasoline Alley/(I Know) I'm Losing You/Pinball Wizard/Every Picture Tells a Story/Amazing Grace/I'd Rather Go Blind/

241

I Don't Want to Discuss It/That's Alright/An Old Raincoat/What Made Milwaukee Famous/Handbags and Gladrags
(UK) Pickwick CN 2059 (10/82)

ABSOLUTELY LIVE**: The Stripper/Tonight I'm Yours/Sweet Little Rock'n'Roller/Hot Legs/Tonight's the Night/The Great Pretender/Passion/She Won't Dance with Me/Little Queenie/You're in My Heart/Rock My Plimsoul/ Young Turks/Guess I'll Always Love You/Gasoline Alley/Maggie May/Tear It Up/Do Ya Think I'm Sexy?/Sailing/I Don't Want to Talk about It/Stay with Me****
(US) WB 23743 (11/82)/(UK) Riva RVLP 17 (11/82)

NIGHTSHIFT: includes That's What Friends Are For
(UK) WB K57024 (12/82)

BACK ON THE STREET AGAIN*: Just Like I Treat You/Don't You Tell Nobody/ Mopper's Blues (remaining cuts by Small Faces)
(US) Quicksilver QS 5054 (1982)

BODY WISHES: Dancin' Alone/Baby Jane/Move Me/Body Wishes/Sweet Surrender/What Am I Gonna Do/Ghetto Blaster/Ready Now/Strangers Again/ Satisfied
(US) WB 23877 (6/83)/(UK) WB 9238 771 (6/83)

ROD STEWART*: Maggie May/Pinball Wizard/Every Picture Tells a Story/ Gasoline Alley/Bring It On Home to Me/You Send Me/Angel/Street Fighting Man/Mandolin Wind/An Old Raincoat/Farewell/Sweet Little Rock'n'Roller/ What Made Milwaukee Famous/Country Comfort/Handbags and Gladrags/It's All Over Now/You Wear It Well/Reason to Believe/Mine for Me/That's All Right/Oh No Not My Baby/Twisting the Night Away
(UK) CAMBRA CRT 026 (7/83)

CAMOUFLAGE: Bad for You/Heart Is on the Line/Camouflage/Trouble/ Infatuation/All Right Now/Some Guys Have All the Luck/Can We Still Be Friends?
(US) WB 25095 (6/84)/(UK) WB 9250 951 (6/84)

ROD STEWART: Here to Eternity/Another Heartache/A Night Like This/Who's Gonna Take Me Home/Red Hot in Black/Love Touch/In My Own Crazy Way/ Every Beat of My Heart/Ten Days of Rain/In My Life
(US) WB 25446 (6/86)

EVERY BEAT OF MY HEART: as above
(UK) WB 25446 (6/86)

JUKE BOX HEAVEN*
(UK) Pickwick CN 2082 (1/87)

INNERSPACE: includes Twisting the Night Away
(UK) Geffen 4602 231

OUT OF ORDER: Lost in You/The Wild Horse/Lethal Dose of Love/Dynamite/ My Heart Can't Tell You No/Nobody Loves You When You're Down and Out/ Crazy About Her/Try a Little Tenderness/When I Was Your Man/Almost Illegal/ Moment of Glory/If Only
(US) WB 25684 (5/88)/(UK) WB WX 152 (5/88)

NIGHTRIDIN'*
(UK) Knight 10002 (7/88)

STORYTELLER*: Good Morning Little Schoolgirl/Can I Get a Witness?

(Steampacket)/Shake/So Much to Say/Little Miss Understood/I've Been Drinking (with Jeff Beck)/Ain't Superstitious (with Jeff Beck)/Shape of Things (with Jeff Beck)/In a Broken Dream (with Python Lee Jackson)/Street Fighting Man/ Handbags and Gladrags/Gasoline Alley/Cut Across Shorty/Country Comforts/ It's All Over Now/Sweet Lady Mary (with the Faces)/Had Me a Real Good Time (with the Faces)/Maggie May/Mandolin Wind/(I Know) I'm Losing You (with the Faces)/Reason to Believe/Every Picture Tells a Story/Stay with Me (with the Faces)/True Blue/Angel/You Wear It Well/I'd Rather Go Blind/Twisting the Night Away/What Made Milwaukee Famous/Oh No Not My Baby/Pinball Wizard/Sweet Little Rock'n'Roller/Let Me Be Your Car/Dance Sing or Anything (with the Faces)/Sailing/I Don't Want to Talk About It/Stone Cold Sober/To Love Somebody/Tonight's the Night/First Cut Is the Deepest/Killing of Georgie/Get Back/Hot Legs/I Was Only Joking/You're in My Heart/Do Ya Think I'm Sexy?/ Passion/Oh God I Wish I Was Home Tonight/Tonight I'm Yours/Young Turks/ Baby Jane/What Am I Gonna Do/People Get Ready (with Jeff Beck)/Some Guys Have All the Luck/Infatuation/Love Touch/Every Beat of my Heart/Lost in You/ My Heart Can't Tell You No/Dynamite/Crazy About Her/Forever Young/I Don't Want to Talk About It/This Old Heart of Mine******/Downtown Train
(US) WB 25987 (11/89)/(UK) WB 25987 (11/89)

DOWNTOWN TRAIN – SELECTIONS FROM 'STORYTELLER'*
(US) WB 26158 (1990)/(UK) WB 26158 (1990)

THE ORIGINAL FACES*: Ain't That Loving You Baby/Mopper's Blues/Don't You Tell Nobody/Just Like I Treat You/Bright Lights Big City/Shake/Little Miss Understood/Why Does It Go On/The Day Will Come/I Just Got Some/Keep Your Hands Off Her/Baby Come Home/Sparky Rides/Can I Get a Witness/Baby Take Me
(UK) Thunderbolt CDTB 085 (1990)

VAGABOND HEART: Rhythm of my Heart/Rebel Heart/Broken Arrow/It Takes Two*****/When a Man's in Love/You Are Everything/The Motown Song/ Go Out Dancing/No Holding Back
(US) WB 26300 (1991)/(UK) WB 26300 (1991)

BRING IT ON HOME*
(UK) Pickwick (12/91)

UNPLUGGED: Hot Legs/Tonight's the Night/Handbags and Gladrags/Cut Across Shorty/Every Picture Tells a Story/Maggie May/Reason to Believe/People Get Ready/Have I Told You Lately/Mandolin Wind/Stay With Me/Having a Party
(UK) WB 45289 (1993)

LEAD VOCALIST: I Ain't Superstitious (the Jeff Beck Group)/Handbags and Gladrags/Cindy Incidentally (Faces)/Stay With Me/True Blue/Sweet Lady Mary (Faces)/Hot Legs/Stand Back/Ruby Tuesday/Shotgun Wedding/First I Look at the Purse/Tom Traubert's Blues
(UK) WB 45258 (1993)

NOTE: In June 1983 Mercury (UK) and WB (UK) launched major reissue programs on vinyl and, later, CD.

VIDEOS

The Faces

LIVE AT KILBURN, DECEMBER 1974: It's All Over Now/Take a Look at the Guy/Bring It On Home/You Send Me/Sweet Little Rock'n'Roller/ I'd Rather Go Blind/Angel/I Can Feel the Fire/You Can Make Me Dance/ Twisting the Night Away/You Wear It Well/Maggie May/We'll Meet Again
(UK) Media Home Entertainment

VIDEO BIOGRAPHY 1969–74: Three Button Hand Me Down/It's All Over Now/Gasoline Alley/Maggie May/I'm Losing You/I Feel So Good/ Memphis/Stay with Me/Miss Judy's Farm/That's All You Need/I'd Rather Go Blind/True Blue/You Wear It Well/Angel/Cindy Incidentally/ Poolhall Richard/Sweet Little Rock'n'Roller/Dance Sing or Anything
(UK) Virgin VC 4053

Rod Stewart

LIVE AT THE LA FORUM – JUNE 1979: Hot Legs/Tonight's the Night/ Do Ya Think I'm Sexy?/I Just Wanna Make Love to You/Blondes Have More Fun/Maggie May/(If Loving You Is Wrong) I Don't Want to Be Right/The Wild Side of Life/You're in My Heart/Sweet Little Rock'n'Roller/Stay with Me/Twisting the Night Away
(UK) Warner Home Video IN 4007 (1980)

TONIGHT HE'S YOURS – DECEMBER 1981: Gimme Wings/Sweet Little Rock'n'Roller/Tear It Up/Passion/She Won't Dance with Me/You're in My Heart/Rock My Plimsoul/Get Back/Hot Legs/Young Turks/Tora Tora Tora/Maggie May/Do Ya Think I'm Sexy?/I Was Only Joking/You Wear It Well/Wild Side of Life/(If Loving You Is Wrong) I Don't Want to Be Right
(UK) Embassy Home Entertainment VHS 1211 (1982)

TONIGHT HE'S YOURS (video single): Do Ya Think I'm Sexy?/Young Turks/Passion
(UK) Embassy Home Entertainment VHS 1211-45 (1982)

THE ROD STEWART CONCERT VIDEO – NOVEMBER 1984
Infatuation/Bad for You/Tonight's the Night/I Don't Want to Talk About It/Dance with Me/Hot Legs/You're in My Heart/Baby Jane/Dock of the Bay/Young Turks/Passion/Do Ya Think I'm Sexy?/Maggie May/Some Guys Have All the Luck/Stay with Me/We'll Meet Again
(UK) Karl-Lorimar Home Video VHS 099 (1986)

STORYTELLER 1984–91: Infatuation/Some Guys Have All the Luck/ People Get Ready (with Jeff Beck)/Every Beat of My Heart/Lost in You/ Forever Young/My Heart Can't Tell You No/Downtown Train/This Old

Heart of Mine/Rhythm of My Heart/Motown Song/Broken Arrow
(US) Warner/Reprise Video 38255

PROMOTIONAL VIDEOS

The Faces
You Can Make Me Dance Sing or Anything (1974)

With Jeff Beck
People Get Ready (1985)

Rod Stewart
Oh No, Not My Baby (1973)
Farewell (1974)
Bring It On Home to Me/You Send Me (1974)
Sailing (1975)
Tonight's the Night (1976)
Wild Side of Life (1976)
First Cut Is the Deepest (1976)
Killing of Georgie (1976)
Hot Legs (1977)
You're in My Heart (1977)
I Was Only Joking (1977)
Do Ya Think I'm Sexy (1978)
Ain't Love a Bitch (1978)
Blondes Have More Fun (1978)
Passion (1980)
Dance with Me (1980)
Oh God I Wish I Was Home Tonight (1980)
Tonight I'm Yours (1981)
Young Turks (1981)
Jealous (1981)
How Long (1981)
Baby Jane (1983)
What Am I Gonna Do (1983)
Infatuation (1984)
Some Guys Have All the Luck (1984)
All Right Now (1984)
Love Touch (1986)
Every Beat of My Heart (1986)
Another Heartache (1986)
Twisting the Night Away (1987)
Lost in You (1988)
Forever Young (1988)
My Heart Can't Tell Me No (1988)
Crazy about Her (1989)
Downtown Train (1989)
This Old Heart of Mine (with Ron Isley) (1990)
Rhythm of My Heart (1991)
The Motown Song (1991)
Broken Arrow (1991)

Acknowledgments

Assisting Mr Giuliano with this project was Dave Thompson, the British-born author of a number of popular rock biographies, including the best-selling *U2 – Stories for Boys, Moonage Daydream – the Life of David Bowie*, and *From a Spark to a Flame*, the authorised biography of singer-songwriter Christ DeBurgh. A former contributor to *Melody Maker*, Thompson has written regularly for *Goldmine, Record Collector, Alternative Press*, and the *Seattle Times*. He lives in Burien, Washington. Many thanks are due to Mr Thompson for his superlative work and unflagging commitment to the actualisation of the book.

Researcher Deborah Lynn Black is a frequent contributor to many leading national periodicals such as *Woman's World, Modern Maturity, American Way, Lady's Circle* and *Country*. Her photographs have appeared in numerous prominent outdoor and children's magazines. Ms Black has assisted Geoffrey Giuliano on several past projects including, *Dark Horse/The Private Life of George Harrison*. She lives in Western New York.

SOURCES

For brief quotations excerpted from the published works of other authors and journalists, I should like the acknowledge the following:

Books

Bangs, Lester and Nelson, Paul: Rod Stewart (1981)
Ekland, Britt: True Britt (Sphere Books, 1980)
Norman, Philip: Elton (Harmony Books, 1992)
Tremlett, George: The Rod Stewart Story (Futura Books, 1976)
Wood, Ron and German, Bill: The Works (1987)

Original Interviews

Former lovers Jo Jo Laine and Dee Harrington.

Musical collaborators Long John Baldry and Brian Auger.

Friends and contemporaries Ginger Baker, Tony Secunda, May Pang, Chris Townson and Tim Renwick, guitarist on the original version of "Sailing".

ACKNOWLEDGEMENTS

Also immensely helpful in the production of this work were: Avalon and India, Ginger Baker, Mirza Beg, His Divine Grace A. C. Bhaktivedanta Swami Prabhupada, Deborah Lynn Black, Carol Bonnett, Dr H. Braden-Fitzgerald, Larry Brown, Eric Clapton, Paul Conew, Matt Conley, Rachel Connolly, Brant and Maria Cowie, Frederic and Kathy Doldan, Michael Downey, Michael Dunn, Enzo of Valentino, Jim Fitzgerald, Devin Giuliano, Robin Scott Giuliano, Robert Giuliano, Sesa Giuliano, Dee Harrington, Ritchie Havens, Roger Hitts, Steve Holly, M. S. Irani, ISKCON, Jagannatha Dasa, Suneel Jaitly, Joan and Wendell, Joseph Juliana, Myrna Juliana, Stan Kittrick, Dr Michael Klapper, Leif Leavesley, Marcus Lecky, Donald Lehr, William Linehan, Andrew Lownie, George Lucas, His Divine Grace Mangalalniloy Goswami Maharaja, Judy McGuire, David L. McIntyre, Linda McKnight, Wilder Penfield III, PETA, Phyllis Phipps, Anna Powell, Satyaraja Dasa, Marty Schiffert, Skyboot Productions Ltd, Sean Smith, Something Fishy Productions Ltd, SRI America, Roy Stockdill, Vrinda Rani Devi Dasi, Robert Wallace, Wendell and Gina, Ronald Zuker.

PHOTO RESEARCH

Sesa Giuliano.

PHOTO CREDITS

Photo section one

page 1 Robert Ellis, courtesy Square Circle Archives

page 2 Top: Barry Plummer, courtesy Square Circle Archives
Bottom: Courtesy Square Circle Archives

page 3 Top left: Courtesy Square Circle Archives
Top right: Gary Merrin, courtesy Square Circle Archives
Middle: Joseph Stevens, courtesy Square Circle Archives
Bottom: Joseph Stevens, courtesy Square Circle Archives

page 4 Top left: Courtesy Square Circle Archives
Top right: Gary Merrin, courtesy Square Circle Archives
Bottom: Courtesy Square Circle Archives

page 5 Top: Joseph Stevens, courtesy Square Circle Archives
Middle: Courtesy Square Circle Archives
Bottom: Courtesy Square Circle Archives

page 6 Top left: Kate Simon, courtesy Square Circle Archives
Top right: T Ross, courtesy Square Circle Archives
Bottom left: Courtesy Square Circle Archives
Bottom right: Joseph Stevens, courtesy Square Circle Archives

page 7 Top left: David Gerrard, courtesy Rex Features Ltd
Top right: Robin Platzer, courtesy Square Circle Archives
Middle: Jeff Slocomb, courtesy Square Circle Archives
Bottom: Courtesy Square Circle Archives

247

page 8   Courtesy Square Circle Archives

Photo section two

page 1   Pennie Smith, Courtesy Square Circle Archives

page 2   Top: Courtesy Square Circle Archives
Bottom: Phil Ranley, courtesy Square Circle Archives

page 3   Top: Courtesy Square Circle Archives
Bottom: Brad Elterman, courtesy Square Circle Archives

page 4   Top: Joseph Stevens, courtesy Square Circle Archives
Bottom: Courtesy Square Circle Archives

page 5   Left: Courtesy Square Circle Archives
Top right: Walter McBride, courtesy Square Circle Archives
Bottom right: courtesy Square Circle Archives

page 6   Top left: courtesy Square Circle Archives
Top right: Dennis Stone, courtesy Rex Features Ltd
Bottom: Courtesy Square Circle Archives

page 7   Top: Brian Cooke, courtesy Square Circle Archives
Bottom left: Steve Granitz, courtesy Square Circle Archives
Bottom right: David Fisher, courtesy London Features International Ltd

page 8   David McGough, courtesy Square Circle Archives

Index

747076